Bethlehem, Pennsylvania

Renee Browning

Contents

Articles

Overview of Pennsylvania   **1**

Pennsylvania   1

Harrisburg, Pennsylvania   32

Geography of Pennsylvania   57

List of counties in Pennsylvania   60

Climate of Pennsylvania   69

History of Pennsylvania   72

List of towns and boroughs in Pennsylvania   81

List of cities in Pennsylvania   111

Education in Pennsylvania   115

Philadelphia Zoo   123

List of airports in Pennsylvania   128

Sports in Pennsylvania   138

Overview of Bethlehem   **147**

Bethlehem, Pennsylvania   147

Lehigh County, Pennsylvania   162

Northampton County, Pennsylvania   176

Center Valley, Pennsylvania   186

Hanover Township, Pennsylvania   187

Things to Do and See   **188**

Musikfest   188

Zoellner Arts Center   198

Sands Casino Resort Bethlehem   200

NEARfest   203

SouthSide Film Festival   206

Attractions   **208**

Lehigh Canal   208

Lehigh River   211

Bethlehem Steel F.C.   214

John Andretti   217

Michael Andretti   226

Dwayne Johnson   235

Transport   **253**

Transportation in the Lehigh Valley   253

Lehigh Valley International Airport   257

Trans-Bridge Lines   262

Interstate 78   264

Allentown Queen City Municipal Airport   270

Lehigh and Northampton Transportation Authority   273

References

Article Sources and Contributors   279

Image Sources, Licenses and Contributors   280

Overview of Pennsylvania

Pennsylvania

Commonwealth of Pennsylvania	
 Flag	 Seal
Nickname(s): Keystone State; Quaker State; Coal State; Oil State; State of Independence	
Motto(s): Virtue, Liberty and Independence	
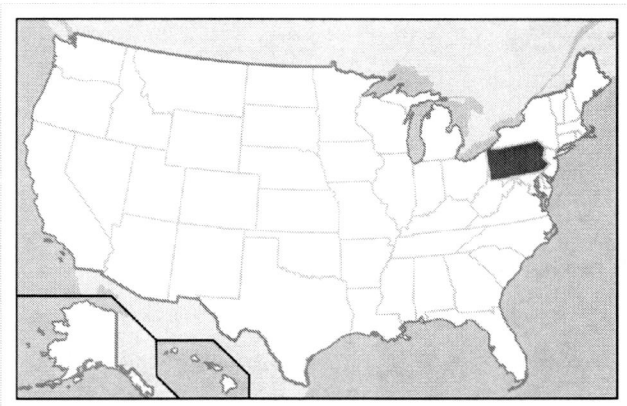	
Official language(s)	None (English, *de facto*)
Spoken language(s)	English 90.7% Spanish 3.1% Pennsylvania Dutch
Demonym	Pennsylvanian
Capital	Harrisburg

Largest city	Philadelphia
Largest metro area	Delaware Valley
Area	Ranked 33rd in the US
- Total	46,055 sq mi (119,283 km^2)
- Width	280 miles (455 km)
- Length	160 miles (255 km)
- % water	2.7
- Latitude	39°43' N to 42°16' N
- Longitude	74°41' W to 80°31' W
Population	Ranked 6th in the US
- Total	12,604,767 (2009 est.)
- Density	274.02/sq mi (105.80/km^2) Ranked 10th in the US
- Median income	US$48,562 (26th)
Elevation	
- Highest point	Mount Davis 3,213 ft (979 m)
- Mean	1,099 ft (335 m)
- Lowest point	Delaware River 0 ft (0 m)
Admission to Union	December 12, 1787 (2nd)
Governor	Edward G. Rendell (D)
Lieutenant Governor	Joseph B. Scarnati III (R)
Legislature	General Assembly
- Upper house	State Senate
- Lower house	House of Representatives
U.S. Senators	Arlen Specter (D) Bob Casey, Jr. (D)
U.S. House delegation	12 Democrats, 7 Republicans (list)
Time zone	Eastern: UTC-5/-4
Abbreviations	PA Penn. or Penna. US-PA

Website	http://www.pa.gov

The **Commonwealth of Pennsylvania** ([i] /ˌpɛnsɪlˈveɪnjə/) is a U.S. state and Commonwealth located in the Northeastern and Middle Atlantic regions of the United States. The state borders Delaware and Maryland to the south, West Virginia to the southwest, Ohio to the west, New York and Ontario, Canada, to the north, and New Jersey to the east. The state's four most populous cities are Philadelphia, Pittsburgh, Allentown and Erie. The state capital is Harrisburg.

Pennsylvania has 51 miles (82 km) of coastline along Lake Erie and 57 miles (92 km) of shoreline along the Delaware Estuary.

Geography

Further information: Geography of Pennsylvania and List of Pennsylvania counties

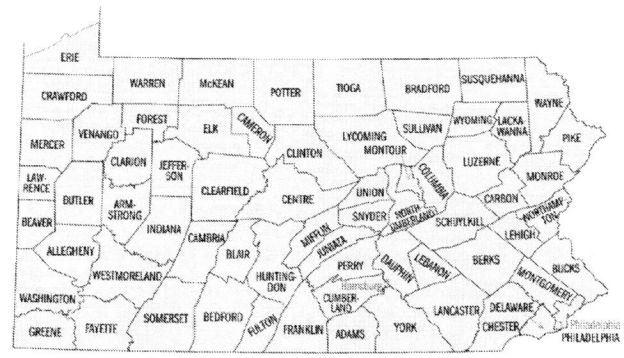

Counties of Pennsylvania

Pennsylvania is 170 miles (274 km) north to south and 283 miles (455 km) east to west. Of a total 46055 square miles (119282 km^2), 44817 square miles (116075 km^2) are land, 490 square miles (1269 km^2) are inland waters and 749 square miles (1940 km^2) are waters in Lake Erie. It is the 33rd largest state in the United States.

The bounds of the state are the Mason-Dixon Line (39° 43' N) to the south, the Delaware River to the east, 80° 31' W to the west, and the 42° N to the north, with the exception of a short segment on the western end, where a triangle extends north to Lake Erie. Pennsylvania borders six other states: New York to the north; New Jersey to the east; Delaware and Maryland to the southeast; West Virginia to the southwest, and Ohio to the west. Pennsylvania also shares a water border with Canada.

It has the cities of Philadelphia, York, Reading and Lancaster in the southeast, Pittsburgh in the southwest, the tri-cities of Allentown, Bethlehem, and Easton in the central east (known as the Lehigh Valley), the tri-cities of Scranton, Wilkes-Barre, and Hazleton in the northeast, and Erie in the northwest, Williamsport serves as the "hub" of the commonwealth's north-central region, with state capital Harrisburg on the Susquehanna River in the central region of the commonwealth.

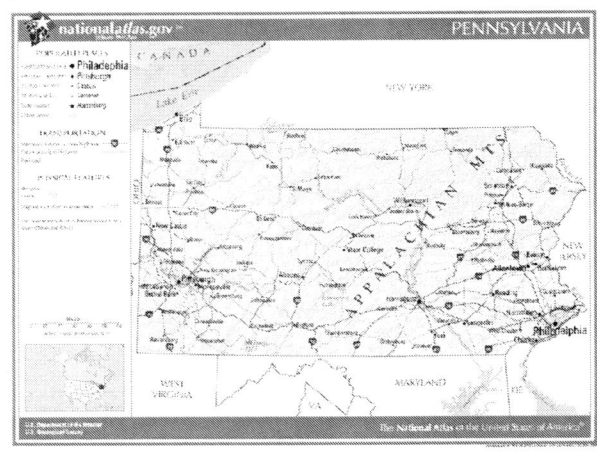

Map of Pennsylvania, showing major cities and roads

Climate

Main article: Climate of Pennsylvania

Pennsylvania's diverse topography also produces a variety of climates. Straddling two major zones, the majority of the state, with the exception of the southeastern corner, has a humid continental climate. Greater Philadelphia has some characteristics of the humid subtropical climate that covers much of Delaware and Maryland to the south. Moving toward the mountainous interior of the state, the climate becomes markedly colder, the number of cloudy days increases, and winter snowfall amounts are greater. Western areas of the state, particularly cities near Lake Erie, can receive over 100 inches (254 cm) of snowfall annually, and the entire state receives plentiful precipitation throughout the year. The state may be subject to severe weather from spring through summer into fall, as an average of 10 tornadoes touch down each year in the state.

City	Jan	Feb	Mar	Apr	May	Jun	Jul	Aug	Sep	Oct	Nov	Dec
Monthly Normal High and Low Temperatures For Various Pennsylvania Cities in Fahrenheit												
Scranton	34/18	37/20	47/28	59/38	71/48	78/57	83/61	81/60	72/53	61/42	49/34	39/24
Erie	33/20	36/21	45/28	56/38	67/49	76/59	80/64	79/63	72/56	61/46	49/36	39/27
Pittsburgh	37/20	39/21	50/29	62/38	71/48	80/56	85/62	83/60	76/53	64/41	53/33	42/25
Harrisburg	38/23	41/25	51/33	63/42	73/51	81/61	86/66	84/64	76/57	64/45	53/36	42/28
Philadelphia	39/25	42/28	51/35	62/44	72/55	81/64	86/70	84/69	77/61	66/49	55/40	44/31
Allentown	35/19	39/21	49/29	60/38	71/48	79/58	84/63	82/61	74/53	63/41	51/33	40/24

East Stroudsburg	35/16	39/17	49/26	61/36	72/46	80/55	85/59	83/58	75/50	64/38	51/30	40/22
Philadelphia [1], Brooklyn,New York [2], Harrisburg [3], Pittsburgh [4], Erie [5], Allentown [6], East Stroudsburg [7]												

See also: Climate change in Pennsylvania

History

Main article: History of Pennsylvania

See also: Province of Pennsylvania

Before the Commonwealth was settled by Europeans, the area was home to the Delaware (also known as Lenni Lenape), Susquehannock, Iroquois, Eriez, Shawnee, and other American Indian Nations. Both the Dutch and the English claimed both sides of the Delaware River as part of their colonial lands in America. The Dutch were the first to take possession, and this has impact on the history of Pennsylvania. By June 3, 1631, the Dutch had started up the DelMarVa Peninsula by establishing the Zwaanendael Colony on the site of present day Lewes, Delaware. In 1638, Sweden heated up the issue by establishing the New Sweden Colony, centered on Fort Christina, on the site of present day Wilmington, Delaware. New Sweden claimed and, for the most part, controlled the lower Delaware River region (Parts of present Delaware, New Jersey and Pennsylvania), but settled few colonists there.

On March 12, 1664, King Charles II of England gave James, Duke of York a Grant that included all of the lands included in the original Virginia Company of Plymouth Grant as well as other lands. This grant was – again – in conflict with the Dutch claim for New Netherland, which included parts of today's Pennsylvania.

On June 24, 1664, The Duke of York sold the portion of his large grant that included present day New Jersey to John Berkeley and George Carteret for a proprietary colony. As of yet, the land was not in English possession, but the sale boxed in the portion of New Netherland on the West side of the Delaware River. The English conquest of New Netherland was commenced on August 29, 1664, when New Amsterdam was coerced to surrender facing the cannons on English ships in New York Harbor. This conquest continued, and was completed in October of 1664, when the English captured Fort Casimir in what today is New Castle, Delaware.

The Peace of Breda between England, France and the Netherlands confirmed the English conquest on July 21, 1667, although there were temporary reversions.

On September 12, 1672, as part of the Third Anglo—Dutch War, the Dutch re-conquered New York Colony/New Amsterdam, the Dutch established three County Courts which went on to become original Counties in present day Delaware and Pennsylvania. The one that later transferred to Pennsylvania was Upland. This was partially reversed on February 9, 1674, when the Treaty of Westminster ended the

Third Anglo-Dutch War, and reverted all political situations to the ***Status Quo Ante Bellum***. The English retained the Dutch Counties with their Dutch names. By June 11, 1674, New York reasserted control over the outlying colonies, including Upland, but the names started to be changed to English names by November 11, 1674. Upland was partitioned on November 12, 1674, producing the general outline of the current border between Pennsylvania and Delaware.

On February 28, 1681, Charles II granted a land charter to William Penn to repay a debt of £16,000 (around £2,100,000 in 2008, adjusting for retail inflation) owed to William's father, Admiral Penn. This was one of the largest land grants to an individual in history. It was called Pennsylvania, meaning "Penn's Woods", in honor of Admiral Penn. William Penn, who had wanted his province to be named "Sylvania", was embarrassed at the change, fearing that people would think he had named it after himself, but King Charles would not rename the grant. Penn established a government with two innovations that were much copied in the New World: the county commission and freedom of religious conviction.

What had been Upland on what became the Pennsylvania side of the Pennsylvania-Delaware Border was renamed as Chester County when Pennsylvania instituted their colonial governments on March 4, 1681.

Between 1730 and when it was shut down by Parliament with the Currency Act of 1764, the Pennsylvania Colony made its own paper money to account for the shortage of actual gold and silver. The paper money was called Colonial Scrip. The Colony issued "bills of credit", which were as good as gold or silver coins because of their legal tender status. Since they were issued by the government and not a banking institution, it was an interest-free proposition, largely defraying the expense of the government and therefore taxation of the people. It also promoted general employment and prosperity, since the Government used discretion and did not issue too much to inflate the currency. Benjamin Franklin had a hand in creating this currency, of which he said its utility was never to be disputed, and it also met with the "cautious approval" of Adam Smith.

President's House, Philadelphia. The Masters-Penn mansion housed Pennsylvania's governor in the early 1770s. It later served as the presidential mansion of George Washington and John Adams, 1790-1800, while Philadelphia was the temporary national capital.

After the Stamp Act Congress of 1765, Delegate John Dickinson of Philadelphia, Pennsylvania, wrote the *Declaration of Rights and Grievances*. The Congress was the first meeting of the thirteen colonies, called at the request of the Massachusetts Assembly, but only nine colonies sent delegates. Dickinson then wrote *Letters from a Farmer in Pennsylvania, To the Inhabitants of the British Colonies*, which were published in the Pennsylvania Chronicle between December 2, 1767, and February 15, 1768.

When the Founding Fathers of the United States convened in Philadelphia in 1774, 12 colonies sent representatives to the First Continental Congress. The Second Continental Congress, which also met in Philadelphia (in May, 1775), drew up and signed the Declaration of Independence in Philadelphia, but when that city was captured by the British, the Continental Congress escaped westward, meeting at the Lancaster courthouse on Saturday, September 27, 1777, and then to York. There they drew up the Articles of Confederation that formed 13 independent colonies into a new nation. Later, the Constitution was written, and Philadelphia was once again chosen to be cradle to the new American Nation.

Pennsylvania became the second state to ratify the U.S. Constitution on December 12, 1787, five days after Delaware became the first.

Dickinson College of Carlisle was the first college founded in the United States. Established in 1773, the college was ratified five days after the Treaty of Paris on September 9, 1783. The school was founded by Benjamin Rush and named after John Dickinson.

For half a century, the Commonwealth's legislature met at various places in the general Philadelphia area before starting to meet regularly in Independence Hall in Philadelphia for 63 years. But it needed a more central location, as for example the Paxton Boys massacres of 1763 had made the legislature aware. So, in 1799 the legislature moved to the Lancaster Courthouse, and finally in 1812 to Harrisburg. The legislature met in the old Dauphin County Court House until December 1821, when the *Redbrick Capitol* was finished. It burned down in 1897, presumably because of a faulty flue. The legislature met at Grace Methodist Church on State Street (still standing) until the present capitol was finished in 1907.

The "Redbrick Capitol", used from 1821 until it burned down in 1897

The new state Capitol drew rave reviews. Its dome was inspired by the domes of St. Peter's Basilica in Rome and the United States Capitol. President Theodore Roosevelt called it "the most beautiful state Capitol in the nation" and said, "It's the handsomest building I ever saw" at the dedication. In 1989, the *New York Times* praised it as "grand, even awesome at moments, but it is also a working building, accessible to citizens ... a building that connects with the reality of daily life".

Pennsylvania accounts for nine percent of all wooded areas in the United States. In 1923 President Calvin Coolidge established the Allegheny National Forest under the authority of the Weeks Act of 1911 in the northwest part of the state in Elk, Forest, McKean, and Warren Counties for the purposes of timber production and watershed protection in the Allegheny River basin. The Allegheny is the state's only national forest.

James Buchanan, of Franklin County, was the only bachelor President of the United States and the only one to be born in Pennsylvania. The Battle of Gettysburg—the major turning point of the Civil War—took place near Gettysburg. An estimated 350,000 Pennsylvanians served in the Union Army forces along with 8,600 African American military volunteers.

Pennsylvania was also the home of the first commercially drilled oil well. In 1859, near Titusville, Pennsylvania, Edwin L. Drake successfully drilled the well, which led to the first major oil boom in United States history.

See also: List of Pennsylvania firsts and List of people from Pennsylvania

Demographics

Further information: List of people from Pennsylvania

By race	White	Black	AIAN*	Asian	NHPI*
					Demographics of Pennsylvania (csv) [8]
2000 (total population)	87.60%	10.71%	0.43%	2.04%	0.07%
2000 (Hispanic only)	2.74%	0.44%	0.06%	0.03%	0.02%
2005 (total population)	86.83%	11.20%	0.45%	2.46%	0.09%
2005 (Hispanic only)	3.52%	0.53%	0.07%	0.05%	0.02%
Growth 2000–05 (total population)	0.32%	5.83%	5.64%	22.23%	18.99%
Growth 2000–05 (non-Hispanic only)	-0.64%	5.21%	2.77%	21.86%	14.13%
Growth 2000–05 (Hispanic only)	29.86%	20.24%	23.61%	45.64%	35.44%

* AIAN is American Indian or Alaskan Native; NHPI is Native Hawaiian or Pacific Islander

The center of population of Pennsylvania is located in Perry County, in the borough of Duncannon.

As of 2006, Pennsylvania has an estimated population of 12,440,621, which is an increase of 35,273 from the previous year, and an increase of 159,567 since the year 2000. Net migration from other states resulted in a decrease of 27,718, and immigration from other countries resulted in an increase of 126,007. Net migration to the Commonwealth was 98,289. Migration of native Pennsylvanians resulted in a decrease of 100,000 people. In 2006, 5.00% of Pennsylvanians were foreign born (621,480 people). The state has an

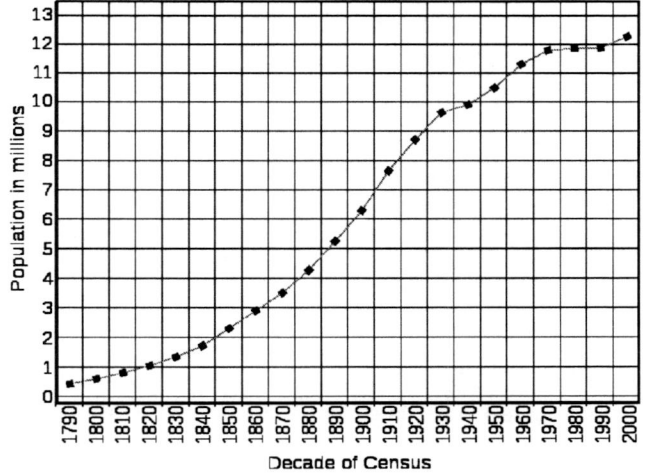

Decade of Census
Populations from 1790 to 2000

estimated 2005 poverty rate of 11.9%. The state also has the 3rd highest proportion of elderly (65+) citizens in 2005.

Foreign-born Pennsylvanians are largely from Asia (36.0%), Europe (35.9%), Latin America (30.6%), Africa (5%), North America (3.1%), and Oceania (0.4%).

Pennsylvania's reported population of Hispanics, especially among the Asian, Hawaiian and White races, has markedly increased in recent years. The Hispanic population is greatest in Allentown, Lancaster, Reading, Hazleton, and around Philadelphia, with over 20% being Hispanic. It is not clear how much of this change reflects a changing population and how much reflects increased willingness to self-identify minority status. As of 2010, it is estimated that about 85% of all Hispanics in Pennsylvania live within a 150 miles radius of Philadelphia, and about 20% within the city itself.

Pennsylvania's population was reported as 5.9% under 5 and 23.8% under 18, with 15.6% aged 65 or older. Females made up 51.7% of the population. The largest ancestry groups are listed below, expressed as a percentage of total people who responded with a particular ancestry for the 2006-2008 census:

- 28.5% German
- 18.2% Irish
- 12.8% Italian
- 10.3% African American
- 8.5% English
- 7.2% Polish
- 1.9% French
- 4.3% United States or American
- 4.2% French Canadian
- 2.5% Puerto Rican
- 2.2% Dutch
- 2.0% Slovak
- 2.0% Scotch Irish
- 1.7% Scottish
- 1.6% Russian
- 1.5% Welsh
- 1.2% Hungarian
- 1.0% Ukrainian

The five largest estimated ancestry groups in Pennsylvania are: German (28.5%), Irish (18.2%), Italian (12.8%), English (8.5%) and Polish (7.2%).

Historical populations

Census	Pop.	%±
1790	434373	—
1800	602365	38.7%
1810	810091	34.5%
1820	1049458	29.5%
1830	1348233	28.5%
1840	1724033	27.9%
1850	2311786	34.1%
1860	2906215	25.7%
1870	3521951	21.2%
1880	4282891	21.6%
1890	5258113	22.8%
1900	6302115	19.9%
1910	7665111	21.6%
1920	8720017	13.8%
1930	9631350	10.5%
1940	9900180	2.8%
1950	10498012	6.0%
1960	11319366	7.8%
1970	11793909	4.2%
1980	11863895	0.6%
1990	11881643	0.1%
2000	12281054	3.4%
Est. 2009	12604767	2.6%

Religion

❝ The new sovereign also enacted several wise and wholesome laws for his colony, which have remained invariably the same to this day. The chief is, to ill–treat no person on account of religion, and to consider as brethren all those who believe in one God. ❞
- Voltaire, speaking of William Penn

Of all the colonies, only in Rhode Island had religious freedom as secure as in Pennsylvania, and one result was an incredible religious diversity, one which continues to this day.

Pennsylvania's population in 2000 was 12,281,054. Of these, 8,448,193 were estimated to belong to some sort of organized religion. According to the Association of religion data archives at Pennsylvania State University, reliable data exists for 7,116,348 religious adherents in Pennsylvania in 2000 following 115 different faiths. Their affiliations, including percentage of all adherents, were:

- Roman Catholic: 3,802,524 (53.43%)
- Orthodox: 75,354 (1.06%)
- Mainline Protestant: 2,140,682 (30%)

    - United Methodist Church: 659,350 (9.27%)
    - Evangelical Lutheran Church in America: 611,913 (8.60%)
    - Presbyterian Church: 324,714 (4.56%)
    - United Church of Christ: 241,844 (3.40%)
    - American Baptist Churches in the USA: 132,858 (1.87%)
    - Episcopal Church: 116,511 (1.64%)
- Evangelical Protestant: 704,204 (10%)

    - Assemblies of God: 84,153 (1.18%)
    - Church of the Brethren: 52,684 (0.74%)
    - Mennonite Church USA: 48,215 (0.68%)
    - Christian and Missionary Alliance: 45,926 (0.65%)
    - Southern Baptist Convention: 44,432 (0.62%)
    - Independent Non-charismatic churches: 42,992 (0.60%)
- Other theology: 393,584 (5.53%)

    - Jewish estimate: 283,000 (3.98%)(4th largest in the United States) (Could be as high as 350,000)
    - Muslim estimate: 71,190 (1.00%) (Could be as high as 150,000)
    - The Church of Jesus Christ of Latter-day Saints: 31,032 (0.44%)
    - Unitarian Universalist Association of Congregations: 6,778 (0.10%)

While Pennsylvania has a very numerous Amish population, Holmes County, Ohio has the largest Amish population in the world. While Pennsylvania owes its existence to Quakers and many of the older trappings of the Commonwealth are rooted in the teachings of the Religious Society of Friends (as they are officially known), practicing Quakers are a small minority today.

Pennsylvania Dutch

The term "Dutch," when referring to the Pennsylvania Dutch, means "German" or "Teutonic" rather than "Netherlander." Germans, in their own language, call themselves "Deutsch," which in English became, misleadingly, "Dutch." The Pennsylvania Dutch language is a descendant of German, in the West Central German dialect family. Although it is still spoken as a first language among some Old Order Amish and Mennonites (principally in the Lancaster County area), the language is almost extinct as an everyday language among the non-religious, though a few words have passed into English usage.

Economy

Pennsylvania's 2008 total gross state product (GSP) of $553.3 billion ranks the state 6th in the nation. If Pennsylvania were an independent country, its economy would rank as the 18th largest in the world. On a per-capita basis, Pennsylvania's per-capita GSP of $35,641 ranks 26th among the 50 states.

Philadelphia in the southeast corner, Pittsburgh in the southwest corner, Erie in the northwest corner, Scranton-Wilkes-Barre in the northeast corner, and Allentown-Bethlehem-Easton in the east central region are urban manufacturing centers. Much of the Commonwealth is rural; this dichotomy affects state politics as well as the state economy. Philadelphia is home to six Fortune 500 companies, with more located in suburbs like King of Prussia; it's a leader in the financial and insurance industry.

Bethlehem Steel's closed manufacturing facility in Bethlehem, Pennsylvania. This site became the site of the new multi-million dollar Sands Casino Resort in 2009.

Pittsburgh is home to eight Fortune 500 companies, including U.S. Steel, PPG Industries, and H.J. Heinz. In all, Pennsylvania is home to fifty Fortune 500 companies. Erie is also home to GE Transportation Systems, which is the largest producer of train locomotives in the United States.

As in the US as a whole and in most states, the largest private employer in the Commonwealth is Wal-Mart, followed by the University of Pennsylvania.

As of January 2010, the state's unemployment rate is 8.8%.

Banking

The first nationally chartered bank in the United States, the Bank of North America, was founded in 1781 in Philadelphia. After a series of mergers, the Bank of North America is part of Wachovia, which uses national charter 1. It is not known if the Bank of North America's charter will be retained after March 2010 when Wells Fargo, which acquired Wachovia in 2008, consolidates its own charter and Wachovia's under the name Wells Fargo, N.A.

Pennsylvania is also the home to the first nationally-chartered bank under the 1863 National Banking Act. That year, the Pittsburgh Savings & Trust Company received a national charter and renamed itself the First National Bank of Pittsburgh as part of the National Banking Act. That bank is still in existence today as PNC Financial Services, and remains based in Pittsburgh. PNC is the state's largest bank, and the fifth-largest in the United States.

Agriculture

Pennsylvania ranks 19th overall in agricultural production, but 1st in mushrooms, 3rd in Christmas trees and layer chickens, 4th in nursery and sod, milk, corn for silage, grapes grown (including juice grapes), and horses production. It also ranks 8th in the nation in Winemaking.

Gambling

Casino gambling was legalized in Pennsylvania in 2004. Currently, there are nine casinos across the state with three under construction or in planning. Only horse racing, slot machines, and electronic table games were legal in Pennsylvania, although a bill to legalize table games was being negotiated in the fall of 2009. Tables games such as poker, roulette, black jack and dice were finally approved by the state legislature in January 2010, being signed into law by the Governor on January 7. Sports betting is illegal.

Governor Ed Rendell has considered legalizing video poker machines in bars and private clubs, since an estimated 17,000 operate illegally across the state. Under this plan, any establishment with a liquor license would be allowed up to 5 machines. All machines would be connected to the state's computer system, like commercial casinos. The state would impose a 50% tax on net gambling revenues, after winning players have been paid, with the remaining 50% going to the establishment owners.

Politics

Presidential elections results

Year	Republican	Democratic
2008	44.15% 2,655,885	**54.47%** *3,276,363*
2004	48.42% 2,793,847	**50.92%** *2,938,095*
2000	46.43% 2,281,127	**50.60%** *2,485,967*
1996	39.97% 1,801,169	**49.17%** *2,215,819*
1992	36.13% 1,791,841	**45.15%** *2,239,164*
1988	**50.70%** 2,300,087	48.39% *2,194,944*
1984	**53.34%** 2,584,323	45.99% *2,228,131*
1980	**49.59%** 2,261,872	42.48% *1,937,540*
1976	47.73% 2,205,604	**50.40%** *2,328,677*
1972	**59.11%** 2,714,521	39.13% *1,796,951*
1968	44.02% 2,090,017	**47.59%** *2,259,405*
1964	34.70% 1,673,657	**64.92%** *3,130,954*
1960	48.74% 2,439,956	**51.06%** *2,556,282*

Voter Registration and Party Enrollment as of June 28, 2010			
Party		Number of Voters	Percentage
	Democratic	4,309,604	51.00%
	Republican	3,122,036	36.95%
	Unaffiliated	492,077	5.82%
	Minor Parties	525,962	6.22%
Total		**8,449,679**	**100%**

Government

Main article: Government of Pennsylvania

See also: Commonwealth (U.S. state)

Pennsylvania has had five constitutions during its statehood: 1776, 1790, 1838, 1874, and 1968 [9]. Prior to that, the province of Pennsylvania was governed for a century by a Frame of Government, of which there were four versions: 1682, 1683, 1696, and 1701. The capital of Pennsylvania is Harrisburg. The legislature meets in the State Capitol there.

In recent elections, Pennsylvania has leaned Democratic; however, the defeat of Incumbent Senator Arlen Specter in the Pennsylvania Primary in 2010 is seen as a possible first step of a Republican takeover—but this is only speculation. In the fall, Joe Sestak will run against Pat Toomey for Specter's senate seat.

Governor

Main article: Governor of Pennsylvania

The current Governor is Ed Rendell, a former head of the Democratic National Committee who began as a District Attorney and mayor in Philadelphia. The other elected officials composing the executive branch are the Lieutenant Governor Joseph Scarnati, Attorney General Tom Corbett, Auditor General Jack Wagner, and State Treasurer Robert McCord.

See also: List of Pennsylvania state agencies

General Assembly

Main article: Pennsylvania General Assembly

Pennsylvania has a bicameral legislature set up by Commonwealth's constitution in 1790. The original Frame of Government of William Penn had a unicameral legislature. The General Assembly includes 50 Senators and 203 Representatives. Joseph B. Scarnati III is currently President Pro Tempore of the State Senate, Dominic Pileggi the Majority Leader, and Robert J. Mellow the Minority Leader. Keith R. McCall is Speaker of the House of Representatives, with Todd A. Eachus as Majority Leader and Samuel Smith as Minority Leader. As of the 2008 elections, the Democrats have a narrow majority in the state house and the Republicans retain their lead in the state senate.

Judiciary

Main article: Unified Judicial System of Pennsylvania

Pennsylvania is divided into 60 judicial districts, most of which (except Philadelphia) have magisterial district judges (formerly called district justices and justices of the peace), who preside mainly over preliminary hearings in felony and misdemeanor offenses, all minor (summary) criminal offenses, and small civil claims. Most criminal and civil cases originate in the Courts of Common Pleas, which also serve as appellate courts to the district judges and for local agency decisions. The Superior Court hears all appeals from the Courts of Common Pleas not expressly designated to the Commonwealth Court or Supreme Court. It also has original jurisdiction to review warrants for wiretap surveillance. The Commonwealth Court is limited to appeals from final orders of certain state agencies and certain designated cases from the Courts of Common Pleas. The Supreme Court of Pennsylvania is the final appellate court. All judges in Pennsylvania are elected; the chief justice is determined by seniority.

Taxation

Sales tax provides 39% of Commonwealth's revenue; personal income tax 34%; motor vehicle taxes about 12%, and taxes on cigarettes and alcohol beverage 5%.

Personal income tax is a flat 3.07%. An individual's taxable income is based on the following eight types of income: compensation (salary); interest; dividends; net profits from the operation of a business, profession or farm; net gains or income from the dispositions of property; net gains or income from rents, royalties, patents and copyrights; income derived through estates or trusts; and gambling and lottery winnings (other than Pennsylvania Lottery winnings).

Counties, municipalities, and school districts levy taxes on real estate. In addition, some local bodies assess a wage tax on personal income. Generally, the total wage tax rate is capped at 1% of income but some municipalities with home rule charters may charge more than 1%. Thirty-two of the Commonwealth's sixty-seven counties levy a personal property tax on stocks, bonds, and similar holdings.

Representation in the 111th Congress

Pennsylvania's two U.S. Senators in the 111th Congress are Arlen Specter and Bob Casey, Jr.

Pennsylvania's U.S. Representatives for the term beginning January 2009 are Robert Brady (1st), Chaka Fattah (2nd), Kathy Dahlkemper (3rd), Jason Altmire (4th), Glenn "G.T." Thompson (5th), Jim Gerlach (6th), Joe Sestak (7th), Patrick Murphy (8th), Bill Shuster (9th), Chris Carney (10th), Paul E. Kanjorski (11th), Mark Critz (12th), Allyson Schwartz (13th), Michael F. Doyle (14th), Charlie Dent (15th), Joe Pitts (16th), Tim Holden (17th), Tim Murphy (18th), and Todd Russell Platts (19th).

See map of congressional districts

Regional strength

In the past decade, no political party has been clearly dominant in Pennsylvania. This, combined with Pennsylvania's rank of 6th in the country in population, has made it one of the most important swing states. Democrats are strong in Philadelphia County, Delaware County, Erie County, Allegheny County, Lehigh County, Northampton County, Luzerne County, and Lackawanna County. Republicans are strong in Lancaster County, York County, Franklin County, Westmoreland County, Butler County, Blair County, Lycoming County, and Cumberland County. Swing counties in the state include Bucks

County, Chester County, Berks County, Dauphin County, Cambria County, Beaver County, and Mercer County. In general, the Democrats are strongest in the large metro areas, particularly Philadelphia, Pittsburgh, Erie, and Allentown, while Republican support is widespread in rural areas in the central Allegheny Mountains and in the northern counties.

Since 1992, Pennsylvania has been trending Democratic in Presidential elections (though the Pittsburgh metropolitan area trended more Republican in the 2008 Presidential election), voting for Bill Clinton twice by large margins, and slightly closer in 2000 for Al Gore. In the 2004 Presidential Election, Senator John F. Kerry beat President George W. Bush in Pennsylvania 2,938,095 (50.92%) to 2,793,847 (48.42%). Most recently, in the 2008 Presidential Election, Democrat Barack Obama defeated Republican John McCain in Pennsylvania, 3,184,778 (54%) to 2,584,088 (44%). The state holds 21 electoral votes.

Further information: Political party strength in Pennsylvania

Municipalities

See also: List of counties in Pennsylvania, List of townships in Pennsylvania, List of towns and boroughs in Pennsylvania, and List of cities in Pennsylvania

The skyline of Philadelphia, the largest city and county in Pennsylvania

Pennsylvania is divided into 67 counties. Counties are further subdivided into municipalites that are either incorporated as cities, boroughs, or townships. One county, Philadelphia County, is coterminus with the city of Philadelphia after it was consolidated in 1854.

There are a total of 56 cities in Pennsylvania, which are classified, by population, as either first, second, or third class cities. Philadelphia, Pennsylvania's largest city, has a population of 1,547,297 and is the state's only first class city. Pittsburgh (311,647) and Scranton (71,944) are second class and second class 'A' cities, respectively. The rest of the cities, like the third and fourth largest—Allentown (107,815) and Erie (103,571)—to the smallest—Parker with a population of only 738—are third class cities. First and second class cities are governed by a "strong mayor" form of mayor–council government, whereas third class cities are governed by either a "weak mayor" form of government or a council–manager government.

Boroughs are generally smaller than cities, with most Pennsylvania cities having been incorporated as a borough before being incorporated as a city. There are 958 boroughs in Pennsylvania, all of which governed by the "weak mayor" form of mayor–council government.

The skyline of Pittsburgh, the second largest city in Pennsylvania

Townships are the third type of municipality in Pennsylvania and are classified as either first class or second class townships. There are 1,454 second class townships and 93 first class townships. Second class township can become first class townships if it has a population density greater than 300 inhabitants per square mile (120 /km^2) and a referendum is passed supporting the change.

There is one exception to the types of municipalities in Pennsylvania: Bloomsburg was incorporated as a town in 1870 and is, officially, the only town in the state. In 1975, McCandless Township adopted a home-rule charter under the name of "Town of McCandless", but is, legally, still a first class township.

Education

Main article: Education in Pennsylvania

Pennsylvania has 500 public school districts, thousands of private schools, publicly funded colleges and universities, and over 100 private institutions of higher education.

Primary and secondary education

In general, under state law, school attendance in Pennsylvania is mandatory for a child from the age of 8 until the age of 17, or until graduation from an accredited high school, whichever is earlier. As of 2005, 83.8% of Pennsylvania residents age 18 to 24 have completed high school. Among residents age 25 and over, 86.7% have graduated from high school. Additionally, 25.7% have gone on to obtain a bachelor's degree or higher. State students consistently do well in standardized testing. In 2007, Pennsylvania ranked 14th in mathematics, 12th in reading, and 10th in writing for 8th grade students.

In 1988, the Pennsylvania General Assembly passed Act 169, which allows parents or guardians to homeschool their children as an option for compulsory school attendance. This law specifies the requirements and responsibilities of the parents and the school district where the family lives.

Higher education

See also: List of colleges and universities in Pennsylvania

There are dozens of colleges and universities throughout the state. Four are members of the Association of American Universities, an invitation only organization of leading research universities: Carnegie Mellon University, Pennsylvania State University, the University of Pennsylvania, and the University of Pittsburgh.

The University of Pennsylvania quadrangle in autumn.

Recreation

Pennsylvania is home to the nation's first zoo, the Philadelphia Zoo. Other long-accredited AZA zoos include the Erie Zoo and the Pittsburgh Zoo & PPG Aquarium. The Lehigh Valley Zoo and ZOOAMERICA are other notable zoos. The Commonwealth boasts some of the finest museums in the country, including the Carnegie Museums in Pittsburgh, the Philadelphia Museum of Art, and several others. One unique museum is the Houdini Museum in Scranton, the only building in the world devoted to the legendary magician. Pennsylvania is also home to the National Aviary, located in Pittsburgh.

All 121 state parks in Pennsylvania feature free admission.

Pennsylvania offers a number of notable amusement parks, including Camel Beach, Conneaut Lake Park, Dorney Park & Wildwater Kingdom, Dutch Wonderland, DelGrosso Amusement Park, Hersheypark, Idlewild Park, Kennywood, Knoebels, Lakemont Park, Sandcastle Waterpark, Sesame Place, Great Wolf Lodge and Waldameer Park. Pennsylvania also is home to the largest indoor waterpark resort on the East Coast, Splash Lagoon in Erie.

There are also notable music festivals that take place in Pennsylvania. These include Musikfest and NEARfest in Bethlehem, the Philadelphia Folk Festival, Creation Festival, the Great Allentown Fair, and Purple Door.

There are nearly one million licensed hunters in Pennsylvania. Whitetail deer, cottontail rabbits, squirrel, turkey, and grouse are common game species. Pennsylvania is considered one of the finest wild turkey hunting states in the Union, alongside Texas and Alabama. Sport hunting in Pennsylvania provides a massive boost for the Commonwealth's economy. A report from The Center for Rural Pennsylvania (a Legislative Agency of the Pennsylvania General Assembly) reported that hunting, fishing, and furtaking generated a total of $9.6 billion statewide.

The Boone and Crockett Club shows that five of the ten largest (skull size) black bear entries came from the state. The state also has a tied record for the largest hunter shot black bear in the Boone &

Crockett books at 733 lb (332 kg) and a skull of 23 3/16 tied with a bear shot in California in 1993. The largest bear ever found dead was in Utah in 1975, and the second largest was shot by a poacher in the state in 1987. Pennsylvania holds the second highest number of Boone & Crockett-recorded record black bears at 183, second only to Wisconsin's 299.

Transportation

See also: List of airports in Pennsylvania

Exterior

Interior

The Allegheny Mountain Tunnel is the longest of the five tunnels on the Pennsylvania Turnpike.

The Pennsylvania Department of Transportation, abbreviated as PennDOT, owns 39861 miles (64150 km) of the 121770 miles (195970 km) of roadway in the state, making it the fifth largest state highway system in the United States. The Pennsylvania Turnpike system is 535 miles (861 km) long, with the mainline portion stretching from Ohio to Philadelphia and New Jersey. It is overseen by the Pennsylvania Turnpike Commission. Another major east–west route is Interstate 80, whichs runs primarily in the northern tier of the state from Ohio to New Jersey at the Delaware Water Gap. Interstate 90 travels the relatively short distance between Ohio and New York through Erie County, in the extreme northwestern part of the state.

Primary north–south highways are Interstate 79 from its terminus in Erie through Pittsburgh to West Virginia, Interstate 81 from New York through Scranton, Lackawanna County and Harrisburg to Maryland and Interstate 476, which begins 7 miles (11 km) north of the Delaware border, in Chester, Delaware County and travels 132 miles (212 km) to Clarks Summit, Lackawanna County, where it joins I-81. All but 20 miles (32 km) of I-476 is the Northeast Extension of the Pennsylvania Turnpike, while the highway south of the main line of the Pennsylvania Turnpike is officially called the "Veterans Memorial Highway", but is commonly referred to by locals as the "Blue Route".

The Southeastern Pennsylvania Transportation Authority (SEPTA) is the sixth largest transit agency in the United States and operates the commuter, heavy and light rail transit, and transit bus service in the Philadelphia metropolitan area. The Port Authority of Allegheny County is the 25th largest transit agency and provides transit bus and light rail service in and around Pittsburgh.

Intercity passenger rail transit is provided by Amtrak, with the majority of traffic occurring on the *Keystone Service* in the high-speed Keystone Corridor between Harrisburg and Philadelphia's 30th Street Station before heading north to New York City; the *Pennsylvanian* follows the same route from New York City to Harrisburg, but extends out to Pittsburgh. The *Capitol Limited* also passes through Pittsburgh, as well as Connellsville, on its way from Chicago to Washington, D.C. Traveling between Chicago and New York City, the *Lake Shore Limited* passes through Erie once in each direction. There are 67 short-line, freight railroads operating in Pennsylvania, the highest number in any U.S. state.

Pennsylvania has six major airports: Philadelphia International, Pittsburgh International, Lehigh Valley International, Harrisburg International, Erie International, and Wilkes-Barre/Scranton International. A total of 134 public-use airport are located in the state. The port of Pittsburgh is the second largest inland port in the United States and the 18th largest port overall; the Port of Philadelphia is the 24th largest port in the United States. Pennsylvania's only port on the Great Lakes is located in Erie.

The Allegheny River Lock and Dam Two is the most-used lock operated by the United States Army Corps of Engineers of its 255 nationwide. The dam impounds the Allegheny River near Downtown Pittsburgh.

Sports

Main article: Sports in Pennsylvania

Further information: List of people from Pennsylvania

Pennsylvania is home to many professional sports teams, including the Philadelphia Phillies and Pittsburgh Pirates of Major League Baseball, the Philadelphia Eagles and Pittsburgh Steelers of the National Football League, the Philadelphia 76ers of the National Basketball Association, the Philadelphia Flyers and Pittsburgh Penguins of the National Hockey League, the Philadelphia Union of Major League Soccer, the Erie Bayhawks of the National Basketball Association Development League, the Wilkes-Barre/Scranton Penguins and Hershey Bears of the American Hockey League, and the Philadelphia Soul of the Arena Football League. Among them, these teams have accumulated 7 World Series Championships (Pirates 5, Phillies 2), 16 National League Pennants, 3 pre-Super Bowl era NFL Championships (Eagles), 6 Super Bowl Championships (Steelers), 1 Arena Bowl Championship (Soul), 2 NBA Championships (76ers), 5 Stanley Cups (Flyers 2, Penguins 3), and 11 Calder Cups (Bears).

There are many minor league baseball teams located throughout the state; several of these teams are associated with either the Phillies or the Pirates. In 2008, the Phillies moved their AAA-level team, the Lehigh Valley IronPigs, from Ottawa, Ontario, in Canada, to a newly-constructed stadium, Coca-Cola

Park in Allentown. The Lehigh Valley is a core fan base for both the Phillies and the Philadelphia Eagles, who conduct their pre-season training camp on the practice fields of Lehigh University. Therefore, expectations are that the Lehigh Valley IronPigs (named after pig iron, an instrumental part in the construction of steel which used to be a large part of the local economy for decades), is likely to prove popular among Allentown and Lehigh Valley Phillies fans. The Phillies' AA team, also called the Phillies, is located in Reading, while the short-season A-level affiliate, called the Crosscutters, is located in Williamsport. The Pirates' AA team, the Curve, is located in Altoona. The short-season A-level affiliate, the State College Spikes, is located in State College. The Spikes share a stadium with the Penn State University baseball team. Other Major League Baseball teams have a presence in the state as well. The New York Yankees' AAA team, also called the Yankees, is located in Moosic, between Scranton and Wilkes-Barre in the northeastern part of the state. The Detroit Tigers' AA team, the SeaWolves, is located in Erie, and the Washington Nationals' AA affiliate, the Senators, plays in the capital of Harrisburg. Two independent-league teams, the Lancaster Barnstormers and York Revolution of the Atlantic League of Professional Baseball, are located in south-central Pennsylvania, while the Washington Wild Things of the Frontier League are located in the south-western corner of the state.

Each summer, the Little League World Series is held in South Williamsport, near where Little League Baseball was founded in Williamsport. Also, the first World Series between the Boston Pilgrims (which became the Boston Red Sox) and Pittsburgh Pirates was played in Pittsburgh in 1903.

College football is very popular in Pennsylvania. The Penn State University Nittany Lions are coached by Joe Paterno who has led Penn State to two national championships (1982 & 1986) as well as five undefeated seasons (1968, 1969, 1973, 1986 and 1994). Penn State plays its home games in the largest stadium in the United States, Beaver Stadium, which seats 107,282. In addition, the University of Pittsburgh Panthers have won nine national championships (1915, 1916, 1918, 1929, 1931, 1934, 1936, 1937 and 1976) and have played eight undefeated seasons (1904, 1910, 1915, 1916, 1917, 1920, 1937 and 1976). Pitt plays its home games at Heinz Field, a facility it shares with the Pittsburgh Steelers. Other Pennsylvania schools that have won national titles in football include Lafayette College (1896), Villanova University(2009), and the University of Pennsylvania (1895, 1897, 1904 and 1908). In professional football, the Philadelphia Eagles hold their training camp annually, each July and August, at Lehigh University, in Bethlehem.

College basketball is also popular in the state, especially in the Philadelphia area where five universities, collectively termed the Big Five, have a rich tradition in NCAA Division I basketball. National titles in college basketball have been won by the following Pennsylvania universities: La Salle University (1954), Temple University (1938), University of Pennsylvania (1920 and 1921), University of Pittsburgh (1928 and 1930) and Villanova University (1985).

Soccer is gaining popularity within the state of Pennsylvania as well. With the addition of the Philadelphia Union in the MLS, the state now boasts three teams that are eligible to compete for the Lamar Hunt U.S. Open Cup annually. The other two teams are the Pittsburgh Riverhounds and the

Harrisburg City Islanders, both of the United Soccer Leagues Second Division (USL-2). Within the American Soccer Pyramid, the MLS takes the first tier, while the USL-2 claims the third tier.

In motorsports, the Mario Andretti dynasty of race drivers hails from Nazareth in the Lehigh Valley. Notable Racetracks in Pennsylvania include the Jennerstown Speedway in Jennerstown, the Lake Erie Speedway in North East, the Mahoning Valley Speedway in Lehighton, the Motordome Speedway in Smithton, the Mountain Speedway in St. Johns, the Nazareth Speedway in Nazareth; and the Pocono Raceway in Long Pond, which is home to both the NASCAR sanctioned Pennsylvania 500 and Pocono 500 stock car races. The state is also home to Maple Grove Raceway, near Reading, which hosts major National Hot Rod Association sanctioned drag racing events each year.

There are also two motocross race tracks that host a round of the AMA Toyota Motocross Championships in Pennsylvania. [High Point Raceway]High Point [10] in located in Mt. Morris, PA, and Steel City is located in Delmont, PA.

Horse racing courses for horses in Pennsylvania consist of The Meadows Racetrack, south of Pittsburgh, Mohegan Sun at Pocono Downs, in Wilkes-Barre and Harrah's Chester Casino and Racetrack in Chester which offer harness racing, and Penn National Race Course in Grantville and Philadelphia Park, in Bensalem, and Presque Isle Downs, south of Erie, which offer thoroughbred racing. Smarty Jones, the 2004 Kentucky Derby and Preakness Stakes winner, had Philadelphia Park as his home course.

Arnold Palmer, one of the 20th century's most notable pro golfers, comes from Latrobe, while Jim Furyk, a current PGA member, grew up near in Lancaster. PGA tournaments in Pennsylvania include the 84 Lumber Classic, played at Nemacolin Woodlands Resort, in Farmington and the Northeast Pennsylvania Classic, played at Glenmaura National Golf Club, in Moosic.

Philadelphia is home to LOVE Park, once a skateboarding mecca, and across from City Hall, host to ESPN's X Games in 2001 and 2002.

Food

In his book *Yo Mama Cooks Like a Yankee*, author Sharon Hernes Silverman calls Pennsylvania the snack food capital of the world. It leads all other states in the manufacture of pretzels and potato chips. The Sturgis Pretzel House introduced the pretzel to America, and companies like Anderson Bakery Company, Intercourse Pretzel Factory, and Snyder's of Hanover are leading manufacturers in the Commonwealth. Two of the three companies that define the U.S. potato chip industry are based in Pennsylvania: Utz Quality Foods, Inc., which started making chips in Hanover, Pennsylvania in 1921, and Wise Snack Foods which started making chips in Berwick in 1921 (the third, Lay's Potato Chips, is a Texas company). Other companies such as Herr Foods, Martin's Potato Chips, Snyder's of Berlin (not associated with Snyder's of Hanover) and Troyer Farms Potato Products are popular chip manufacturers.

The U.S. chocolate industry is centered in Hershey, Pennsylvania, with Mars, Godiva, and Wilbur Chocolate Company nearby, and smaller manufacturers such as Asher's near Lansdale and Gertrude Hawk of Dunmore. Other notable companies include Just Born in Bethlehem, PA, makers of Hot Tamales, Mike and Ikes, and the Easter favorite marshmallow Peeps, Benzel's Pretzels and Boyer Brothers of Altoona, PA, which is well known for its Mallo Cups. Auntie Anne's Pretzels began as a market-stand in Downingtown, PA and now has corporate headquarters in Lancaster City. Traditional Pennsylvania Dutch foods include chicken potpie, schnitz un knepp (dried apples, hame, and dumplings), fasnachts (raised doughnuts), scrapple, pretzels, bologna, and chow-chow. Shoofly is another traditional Pennsylvanian Dutch food. D.G. Yuengling & Son, America's oldest brewery, has been brewing beer in Pottsville since 1829.

Among the regional foods associated with Philadelphia are cheesesteaks, hoagie, soft pretzels, liver on a stick, Italian water ice, scrapple, Tastykake, and strombolis. In Pittsburgh, tomato ketchup was improved by Henry John Heinz from 1876 to the early 20th century. Famous to a lesser extent than Heinz ketchup are the Pittsburgh's Primanti Brothers Restaurant sandwiches, pierogies, and city chicken. Outside of Scranton, in Old Forge there are dozens of Italian restaurants specializing in pizza made unique by thick, light crust and American cheese. Erie also has its share of unique foods, including Greek sauce, sponge candy, pepperoni balls, and ox roast. Sauerkraut along with pork and mashed potatoes is a common meal on New Year's Day in Pennsylvania.

Multi-ethnic cuisine is common[citation needed], especially in the city and Coal Region areas. Pennsylvania Dutch, Chinese, Italian, Indian, Japanese, Korean, Mexican, Pakistani, Persian, Polish, Russian, Thai, Turkish cuisine and many others can be found not only in specialty restaurants but at hundreds of community or religious festivals.

State symbols

The Ruffed Grouse

US Brig *Niagara* in port

Pennsylvania state insignia and historical facts

State motto	Virtue, liberty, and independence (Adapted in 1875, and it represents the fact that Philadelphia was the site where the Declaration of Independence was signed.)
State tree	Hemlock
State bird	Ruffed grouse
State flower	Mountain Laurel
State insect	*Photuris pennsylvanica* (Pennsylvania Firefly)
State animal	White-tailed deer
State dog	Great Dane
State fish	Brook Trout
State fossil	the trilobite *Phacops rana*
State beverage	Milk
State capital	Harrisburg
Union admission rank	2nd
State song	Pennsylvania (Formerly Hail, Pennsylvania!, until 1990)
State dance	Polka

State toy	Slinky
State ship	United States Brig *Niagara*
State electric locomotive	Pennsylvania Railroad GG1 #4849 Locomotive
State steam locomotive	Pennsylvania Railroad K4s Locomotive
State beautification plant	Crown vetch
State soil	Hazleton

Nicknames

Pennsylvania has been known as the *Keystone State* since 1802, based in part upon its central location among the original Thirteen Colonies forming the United States, and also in part because of the number of important American documents signed in the state (such as the Declaration of Independence). It was also a keystone state economically, having both the industry common to the North (making such wares as Conestoga wagons and rifles) and the agriculture common to the South (producing feed, fiber, food, and tobacco).

Another one of Pennsylvania's nicknames is the *Quaker State*; in colonial times, it was known officially as the *Quaker Province*, in recognition of Quaker William Penn's *First Frame of Government* constitution for Pennsylvania that guaranteed liberty of conscience. He knew of the hostility Quakers faced when they opposed religious ritual, taking oaths, violence, war and military service, and what they viewed as ostentatious frippery.

"The Coal State", **"The Oil State"**, **"The Chocolate State"**, and **"The Steel State"** were adopted when those were the state's greatest industries.

"The State of Independence" currently appears on many road signs entering the state.

Notable people

Main article: List of people from Pennsylvania

Gallery

Aliquippa

Allentown

Altoona

Beaver Falls

Bethlehem

Butler

Corry

Easton

Erie

Harrisburg

Jeannette

Lancaster

Lock Haven

Monessen

New
Castle

Philadelphia

Pittsburgh

Pittston City

Pottsville

Reading

Renovo

Scranton

Shamokin

Warren

Washington

Wilkes-Barre

Williamsport

York

See also

- Index of Pennsylvania-related articles
- List of Pennsylvania films and television shows
- Outline of Pennsylvania

References

- "2010 Public Transportation Fact Book" [11] (PDF). American Public Transportation Association. April 2010. Retrieved July 5, 2010.
- "Pennsylvania Department of Transportation Fact Book" [12]. Pennsylvania Department of Transportation. August 2009. Retrieved July 4, 2010.
- Waterborne Commerce Statistics Center (December 31, 2009). "Part 5: National Summaries" [13] (PDF). *Waterborne Commerce of the United States*. United States Army Corps of Engineers. Retrieved July 5, 2010.
- Trostle, Sharon, ed (2009). *The Pennsylvania Manual*. **119**. Harrisburg: Pennsylvania Department of General Services. ISBN 0-8182-0334-X.

External links

- Pennsylvania travel guide from Wikitravel
- Pennsylvania [14] at the Open Directory Project
- Gov. Andrew Curtin's Pennsylvania Reserve Volunteer Corps, Civil War 1861–1864 [15]
- Official state government site [16]
- Pennsylvania Department of Transportation [17]
- Allegheny National Forest [18]
- Pennsylvania Wilds [19]
- USGS real-time, geographic, and other scientific resources of Pennsylvania [20]
- Energy Data & Statistics for Pennsylvania [21]
- Pennsylvania State Facts [22]
- Official state tourism site [23]
- Biography of William Penn from 1829 [24]

- A History of Pennsylvania from 1905 [25]
- Free Original Documents Online: Pennsylvania State Archives 1600s to 1800s [26]
- Miller, Randall M. and William Pencak, *Pennsylvania: A History of the Commonwealth* [27]
- Interactive Pennsylvania for Kids [28]
- Pennsylvania Department of Community and Economic Development [29]
- National Association of Counties (information on each Pennsylvania County) [30]

1. REDIRECT Template:Navboxes

Geographical coordinates: 41°00′N 77°30′W

frr:Pennsylvania pnb:پنسلوانیا

Harrisburg, Pennsylvania

Harrisburg
— City —
City of Harrisburg
 Downtown Harrisburg and the Pennsylvania State Capitol, as seen from Wormleysburg, Pennsylvania
 **Seal** **Flag**
Nickname(s): "Pennsylvania's Capital City".
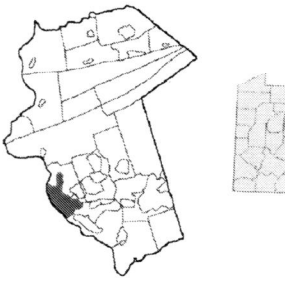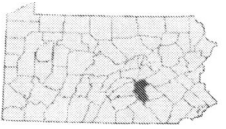 Location in Dauphin County and state of Pennsylvania

Harrisburg

Location in Pennsylvania

Coordinates: 40°16′11″N 76°52′32″W

Country	United States
Commonwealth	Pennsylvania
County	Dauphin
European settlement	About 1719
Incorporated	1791
Charter	1860
Founder	John Harris, Sr.
Named for	John Harris, Sr.
Government	
- Type	Mayor-Council
- Mayor	Linda D. Thompson (D)
- City Controller	Daniel C. Miller (D)
- City Council	
- State Senate	Jeffrey E. Piccola (R)
- State Representative	Ron Buxton (D)
Area	
- City	11.4 sq mi (26.9 km^2)
- Land	8.1 sq mi (21.0 km^2)
- Water	3.3 sq mi (8.6 km^2)
- Urban	335.4 sq mi (539.7 km^2)
Elevation	320 ft (98 m)
Population (U.S. Census Estimate, 2007)	

- City	47196
- Density	6043.2/sq mi (2333.3/km^2)
- Urban	362782
- Metro	528892 (97nd)
- CSA	647390 (56th)
- Demonym	Harrisburger
Time zone	EST (UTC-5)
- Summer (DST)	EDT (UTC-4)
ZIP codes	17101-17113, 17120-17130, 17140, 17177
Area code(s)	717
FIPS code	42-32800
GNIS feature ID	1213649
Interstates	I-76, I-78, I-81, I-83, and I-283
Waterways	Susquehanna River
Primary Airport	Harrisburg International Airport- MDT (Major/International)
Secondary Airport	Capital City Airport- CXY (Minor)
Public transit	Capital Area Transit
Website	www.harrisburgpa.gov [1]

Harrisburg is the capital of the Commonwealth of Pennsylvania, in the United States of America. As of the 2000 census, the city had a population of 48,950, making it the ninth largest city in Pennsylvania, after Philadelphia, Pittsburgh, Allentown, Erie, Reading, Scranton, Bethlehem and Lancaster. The Harrisburg-Carlisle-Lebanon combined statistical area contains 647,390 residents.

Harrisburg is the county seat of Dauphin County and lies on the east bank of the Susquehanna River, 105 miles (169 km) west-northwest of Philadelphia. The Harrisburg-Carlisle Metropolitan Statistical Area, which includes Dauphin, Cumberland, and Perry counties, had a population of 509,074 in 2000. A July 1, 2007 estimate placed the population at 528,892, making it the fifth largest Metropolitan Statistical Area in Pennsylvania after Philadelphia, Pittsburgh, Allentown-Bethlehem-Easton (the Lehigh Valley), and Scranton-Wilkes Barre. The Harrisburg-Carlisle-Lebanon Combined Statistical Area, including both the Harrisburg-Carlisle and Lebanon Metropolitan Statistical Areas, had an estimated population of 656,781 in 2007.

Harrisburg played a notable role in American history during the Westward Migration, the American Civil War, and the Industrial Revolution. During part of the 19th century, the building of the

Pennsylvania Canal and later the Pennsylvania Railroad allowed Harrisburg to become one of the most industrialized cities in the Northeastern United States. The U.S. Navy ship USS *Harrisburg*, which served from 1918 to 1919 at the end of World War I, was named in honor of the city.

In the mid-to-late 20th century, the city's economic fortunes fluctuated with its major industries consisting of government, heavy manufacturing including the production of steel, agriculture (the greater Harrisburg area is at the heart of the fertile Pennsylvania Dutch Country), and food services (nearby Hershey is home of the chocolate maker, located just 10 miles east of Harrisburg). In 1981, following contractions in the steel and dairy industries, Harrisburg was declared the second most distressed city in the nation. The city subsequently experienced a resurgence under its former mayor Stephen R. Reed, with nearly $3 billion in new investment realized during his lengthy tenure. In 2010 Forbes rated Harrisburg as the second best place to raise a family. The 2009 financial crisis and resulting recession have recently taken their toll on Harrisburg municipal finances. Harrisburg has not been able to budget for $68m in debt payments due to a local $288m incinerator project. On September 1, 2010, Harrisburg announced its intention to skip a debt payment of $3.29m on the incinerator project and the City Controller has suggested possible trouble with the City's General Obligation bonds. Chapter 9 municipal bankruptcy may well be in Harrisburg's future.

The Pennsylvania Farm Show, the largest free indoor agriculture exposition in the United States, was first held in Harrisburg in 1917 and has been held there every early to mid January since then. Harrisburg also hosts an annual outdoor sports show, the largest of its kind in North America, as well as an auto show, which features a large static display of new as well as classic cars and is renowned nationwide. Harrisburg is also known for the Three Mile Island accident, which occurred on March 28, 1979 in Londonderry Township near Middletown.

History

Main article: History of Harrisburg, Pennsylvania

Founding

Harrisburg's site along the Susquehanna River is thought to have been inhabited by Native Americans as early as 3000 BC. Known to the Native Americans as "Peixtin", or "Paxtang", the area was an important resting place and crossroads for Native American traders, as the trails leading from the Delaware to the Ohio rivers, and from the Potomac to the Upper Susquehanna intersected there. The first European contact with Native Americans in Pennsylvania was made by the Englishman, Captain John Smith, who journeyed from Virginia up the Susquehanna River in 1608 and visited with the Susquehanna tribe. In 1719, John Harris, Sr., an English trader, settled here and 14 years later secured grants of 800 acres (3.2 km^2) in this vicinity. In 1785, John Harris, Jr. made plans to lay out a town on his father's land, which he named Harrisburg. In the spring of 1785, the town was formally surveyed by William Maclay, who was a son-in-law of John Harris, Sr. In 1791, Harrisburg became incorporated and was named the Pennsylvania state capital in October 1812, and has been since.

Railroads and the American Industrial Revolution

During the first part of the 19th century, Harrisburg was a notable stopping place along the Underground Railroad, as escaped slaves would be transported across the Susquehanna River and were often fed and given supplies before heading north towards Canada. The assembling here of the Harrisburg Convention in 1827 led to the passage of the high protective-tariff bill of 1828. In 1839,

Postcard depicting Market Street in Downtown Harrisburg as it appeared in 1910. Trolley tracks are noticeable along the street.

Harrison and Tyler were nominated for President of the United States at the first national convention of the Whig Party of the United States, which was held in Harrisburg. By the 1830s Harrisburg was part of the Pennsylvania canal system and an important railroad center as well. Steel and iron became dominant industries. Steel and other industries continued to play a major role in the local economy throughout the latter part of the 19th century. The city was the center of enormous railroad traffic and supported large furnaces, rolling mills, and machine shops. The Pennsylvania Steel Company plant, which opened in nearby Steelton in 1866, was the first in the country; later operated by Bethlehem Steel.

American Civil War

Main article: Harrisburg in the American Civil War

During the American Civil War, Harrisburg was a significant training center for the Union Army, with tens of thousands of troops passing through Camp Curtin. It was also a major rail center for the Union and a vital link between the Atlantic coast and the Midwest, with several railroads running through the city and spanning the Susquehanna River. As a result of this importance, it was a target of General Robert E. Lee's Army of Northern Virginia during its two invasions. The first time during the 1862 Maryland Campaign, when Lee planned to capture the city after taking Harpers Ferry, West Virginia, but was prevented from doing so by the Battle of Antietam and his subsequent retreat back into Virginia. The second attempt was made during the Gettysburg Campaign in 1863 and was more substantial. A short skirmish took place in June 1863 at Sporting Hill, just 2 miles west of Harrisburg. This is considered by many to be the northern-most battle of the Civil War.

Early 20th century to present

In the early 20th century, several Harrisburg residents became involved in the City Beautiful movement. Mira Lloyd Dock and Horace McFarland advocated urban improvements which were influenced by European urban planning design and the World's Columbian Exposition. Specifically, their efforts greatly enlarged the Harrisburg park system, creating Riverfront Park, Reservoir Park, the Italian Lake and Wildwood Park. In addition, schemes were undertaken for the burial of electric wires, the creation of a modern sanitary sewer system, and the beautification of an expanded Capitol complex.

Many important events have helped to shape Harrisburg over the years. The Pennsylvania Farm Show, the largest indoor agriculture exposition in the United States, was first held in 1917 and has been held every January since then. The present location of the Show is the Pennsylvania State Farm Show Arena, located at the corner of Maclay and Cameron streets. In June 1972, Harrisburg was hit by a major flood from the remnants of hurricane Agnes.

Anti-nuclear protest at Harrisburg in 1979, following the Three Mile Island accident.

On March 28, 1979, the Three Mile Island nuclear plant, along the Susquehanna River located in Londonderry Township which is south of Harrisburg, suffered a partial meltdown. Although the meltdown was contained and radiation leakages were minimal, there were still worries that an evacuation would be necessary. Governor Dick Thornburgh, on the advice of Nuclear Regulatory Commission Chairman Joseph Hendrie, advised the evacuation "of pregnant women and pre-school age children ... within a five-mile radius of the Three Mile Island facility." Within days, 140,000 people had left the area.

After Harrisburg suffered years of being in bad shape economically, Stephen R. Reed was elected mayor in 1981 and served until 2009, making him the city's longest serving mayor. He immediately started projects which would attract both businesses and tourists. Several museums and hotels such as Whitaker Center for Science and the Arts, the National Civil War Museum and the Hilton Harrisburg and Towers were built during his term, along with many office buildings and residences. Several semi-professional sports franchises, including the Harrisburg Senators of the Eastern League, the defunct Harrisburg Heat indoor soccer club and the Harrisburg City Islanders of the USL Second Division began operations in the city during his tenure as mayor. While praised for the vast number of economic improvements, Reed has also been criticized for population loss and mounting debt. For example, during a budget crisis the city was forced to sell $8 million worth of Western and American-Indian artifacts collected by Mayor Reed for a never-realized museum celebrating the American West.

Geography

Topography

Harrisburg is located at 40°16′11″N 76°52′32″W (40.269789, -76.875613) in South Central Pennsylvania. According to the United States Census Bureau, the city has a total area of 11.4 square miles (29.6 km^2), of which, 8.1 square miles (21.0 km^2) of it is land and 3.3 square miles (8.6 km^2) of it (29.11%) is water. Bodies of water include Paxton Creek which empties into the Susquehanna River at Harrisburg, as well as Wildwood Lake and Italian Lake parks.

Directly to the north of Harrisburg is the Blue Mountain ridge of the Appalachian Mountains. The Cumberland Valley lies directly to the west of Harrisburg and the Susquehanna River, stretching into northern Maryland. The fertile Lebanon Valley lies to the east. Harrisburg is the northern fringe of the historic Pennsylvania Dutch Country.

The city is the county seat of Dauphin County. The adjacent counties are Northumberland County to the north; Schuylkill County to the northeast; Lebanon County to the east; Lancaster County to the south; and York County to the southwest; Cumberland County to the west; and Perry County to the northwest.

Adjacent municipalities

Harrisburg's western boundary is formed by the Susquehanna River, which also serves as the boundary between Dauphin and Cumberland counties. The city is divided into numerous neighborhoods and districts. Like many of Pennsylvania's cities and boroughs that are at "build-out" stage, there are several townships outside of Harrisburg city limits that, although autonomous, use the name *Harrisburg* for postal and name-place designation. They include the townships of: Lower Paxton, Middle Paxton, Susquehanna, Swatara and West Hanover in Dauphin County. The borough of Penbrook, located just east of Reservoir Park, was previously known as East Harrisburg. Penbrook, along with the borough of Paxtang, also located just outside of the city limits, maintain Harrisburg zip codes as well. The United States Postal Service designates 26 zip codes for Harrisburg, including 13 for official use by federal and state government agencies.

- Dauphin County
  - Lower Paxton Township (east)
  - Penbrook (northeast)
  - Paxtang (east)
  - Susquehanna Township (northeast)

- Swatara Township (southeast)
- Cumberland County
  - East Pennsboro Township (west)
  - Lemoyne (west)
  - New Cumberland (southwest)
  - Wormleysburg (west)

Climate

Climate data for Harrisburg, Pennsylvania													
Month	Jan	Feb	Mar	Apr	May	Jun	Jul	Aug	Sep	Oct	Nov	Dec	Year
Record high °F (°C)	73 (22.8)	78 (25.6)	87 (30.6)	93 (33.9)	97 (36.1)	100 (37.8)	107 (41.7)	104 (40)	102 (38.9)	97 (36.1)	84 (28.9)	75 (23.9)	107 (41.7)
Average high °F (°C)	37.5 (3.06)	40.9 (4.94)	50.9 (10.5)	62.6 (17)	72.6 (22.56)	80.8 (27.11)	85.7 (29.83)	83.7 (28.72)	75.7 (24.28)	64.3 (17.94)	52.5 (11.39)	41.7 (5.39)	62.4 (16.89)
Average low °F (°C)	23.1 (-4.94)	24.7 (-4.06)	32.5 (0.28)	41.5 (5.28)	51.4 (10.78)	60.6 (15.89)	66.0 (18.89)	64.2 (17.89)	56.7 (13.72)	44.6 (7)	36.1 (2.28)	27.8 (-2.33)	44.1 (6.72)
Record low °F (°C)	-22	-13	5 (-15)	11 (-11.7)	31 (-0.6)	40 (4.4)	49 (9.4)	45 (7.2)	30 (-1.1)	23 (-5)	10 (-12.2)	-8	-22
Precipitation inches (mm)	3.18 (80.8)	2.88 (73.2)	3.58 (90.9)	3.31 (84.1)	4.60 (116.8)	3.99 (101.3)	3.21 (81.5)	3.24 (82.3)	3.65 (92.7)	3.06 (77.7)	3.53 (89.7)	3.22 (81.8)	41.45 (1052.8)
Snowfall inches (cm)	11.4 (29)	10.4 (26.4)	6.0 (15.2)	1.7 (4.3)	0 (0)	0 (0)	0 (0)	0 (0)	0 (0)	0.2 (0.5)	3.0 (7.6)	4.5 (11.4)	37.2 (94.5)
Source: National Weather Service													

Harrisburg has a variable, four-season climate in the transition between the humid subtropical and humid continental zones (Koppen *Cfa* and *Dfa*, respectively)。 The hottest month of the year is July with an 24-hour average of 75.9 °F (24.4 °C). Summer is usually hot and humid and occasional heat waves can occur from time to time. The city averages around 15 days per year with above 90 degree temps although temperatures above 100 degrees are rare. The hottest temperature ever recorded in Harrisburg is 107 °F (42 °C) in July 1966. Summer thunderstorms also occur relatively frequently. Fall is a pleasant season when the humidity and temperatures fall to more comfortable values.

Winter in Harrisburg is cold: January averages 30.3 °F (−0.9 °C). A major snowstorm can also occasionally occur, and some winters snowfall totals can exceed 60 inches while in other winters the city may receive very little snowfall. The snowiest month recorded on record was in February 2010 when 42 inches of snow was recorded at Harrisburg International Airport. [citation needed] Overall Harrisburg receives an average of 35 inches of snow annually. The coldest temperature ever recorded in Harrisburg was in January 1994. Spring is also a nice time of year for outdoor activities. Precipitation is well-distributed and generous in most months, though May is clearly the wettest.

Cityscape

Neighborhoods

See also: List of Harrisburg neighborhoods

Center City Harrisburg, which includes the Pennsylvania State Capitol Complex, is the central core business and financial center for the greater Harrisburg metropolitan area and serves as the seat of government for Dauphin County and the Commonwealth of Pennsylvania. There are over a dozen large neighborhoods and historic districts within the city.

Architecture

Harrisburg is home to the Pennsylvania State Capitol. Completed in 1906, the central dome rises to a height of 272 feet (83 m) and was modeled on that of St. Peter's Basilica in Vatican City, Rome. The building was designed by Joseph Miller Huston and is adorned with sculpture, most notably the two groups, *Love and Labor, the Unbroken Law* and *The Burden of Life, the Broken Law* by sculptor George Grey Barnard; murals by Violet Oakley and Edwin Austin Abbey; tile floor by Henry Mercer, which tells the story of the Commonwealth of Pennsylvania. The state capitol is only the third-tallest building of Harrisburg. The five tallest buildings are 333 Market Street with a height of 341 feet (104 m), Pennsylvania Place with a height of 291 feet (89 m), the Pennsylvania State Capitol with a height of 272 feet (83 m), Presbyterian Apartments with a height of 259 feet (79 m) and the Fulton Bank Building with a height of 255 feet (78 m).

People and culture in Harrisburg

Culture

Downtown Harrisburg has two major performance centers. The Whitaker Center for Science and the Arts, which was completed in 1999, is the first center of its type in the United States where education, science and the performing arts take place under one roof. The Forum, a 1,763-seat concert and lecture hall built in 1930-31, is a state-owned and operated facility located within the State Capitol Complex. Since 1931, The Forum has been home to the Harrisburg Symphony Orchestra.

Beginning in 2001, downtown Harrisburg saw a surge of commercial nightlife development. This has been credited with reversing the city's financial decline, and has made downtown Harrisburg a destination for events from jazz festivals to Top-40 nightclubs.

Harrisburg is also the home of the annual Pennsylvania Farm Show, the largest agricultural exhibition of its kind in the nation. Farmers from all over Pennsylvania come to show their animals and participate in competitions. Livestock are on display for people to interact with and view. In 2004, Harrisburg hosted CowParade, an international public art exhibit that has been featured in major cities all over the world. Fiberglass sculptures of cows are decorated by local artists, and distributed over the city centre, in public places such as train stations and parks. They often feature artwork and designs specific to local culture, as well as city life and other relevant themes.

Demographics

Historical populations		
Year	Pop.	%±
1790	875	—
1800	1472	68.2%
1810	2287	55.4%
1820	2990	30.7%
1830	4312	44.2%
1840	5980	38.7%
1850	7834	31.0%
1860	13405	71.1%
1870	23104	72.4%
1880	30762	33.1%
1890	39385	28.0%
1900	50167	27.4%
1910	64186	27.9%
1920	75917	18.3%
1930	80339	5.8%
1940	83893	4.4%
1950	89544	6.7%
1960	79697	−11.0%
1970	68061	−14.6%
1980	53264	−21.7%

1990	52376	−1.7%
2000	48950	−6.5%
2008	47148	−3.7%
United States Census Bureau		

The U.S. Census Bureau estimates that in 2005 there were an estimated 47,472 people living in Harrisburg. In the census of 2000, there were 48,950 people, 20,561 households, and 10,917 families residing in the city. The population density was 6,035.6 people per square mile (2,330.4/km²). There were 24,314 housing units at an average density of 2,997.9/sq mi (1,157.5/km²). The racial makeup of the city was 54.83% Black or African American, 31.72% White, 0.37% Native American, 2.83% Asian, 0.07% Pacific Islander, 6.54% from other races, and 3.64% from two or more races. 11.69% of the population were Hispanic or Latino of any race. Harrisburg is the 6th most populous city in eastern Pennsylvania and 47th in the nation of Vietnamese population with 2,649 residents.

There were 20,561 households out of which 28.5% had children under the age of 18 living with them, 23.4% were married couples living together, 24.4% had a female householder with no husband present, and 46.9% were non-families. 39.3% of all households were made up of individuals and 10.4% had someone living alone who was 65 years of age or older. The average household size was 2.32 and the average family size was 3.15.

In the city the population was spread out with 28.2% under the age of 18, 9.2% from 18 to 24, 31.0% from 25 to 44, 20.8% from 45 to 64, and 10.9% who were 65 years of age or older. The median age was 33 years. For every 100 females there were 88.7 males. For every 100 females age 18 and over, there were 84.8 males.

The median income for a household in the city was $26,920, and the median income for a family was $29,556. Males had a median income of $27,670 versus $24,405 for females. The per capita income for the city was $15,787. About 23.4% of families and 24.6% of the population were below the poverty line, including 34.9% of those under age 18 and 16.6% of those age 65 or over.

The very first census taken in the United States occurred in 1790. At that time Harrisburg was a small, but substantial colonial town with a population of 875 residents. With the increase of the city's prominence as an industrial and transportation center, Harrisburg reached its peak population build up in 1950, topping out at nearly 90,000 residents. Since the 1950s, Harrisburg, along with other northeastern urban centers large and small, has experienced a declining population that is ultimately fueling the growth of its suburbs, although the decline - which was very rapid in the 1960s and 1970s - has slowed considerably since the 1980s. Unlike Western and Southern states, Pennsylvania maintains a complex system of municipalities and has very little legislation on either the annexation/expansion of cities or the consolidating of municipal entities.

Reversing fifty years of decline, 2007 Census Bureau estimates show that Harrisburg's population has actually grown. Between 2006 and 2007, Harrisburg gained 22 people.

Media

The Harrisburg area has two daily newspapers. The Patriot-News is published in Harrisburg and has a daily circulation of over 100,000. The Sentinel, which is published in Carlisle, roughly 20 miles west of Harrisburg, serves many of Harrisburg's western suburbs in Cumberland County. The Press and Journal, published in Middletown, is one of many weekly, general information newspapers in the Harrisburg area. Harrisburg has one monthly community newspaper, TheBurg. There are also numerous television and radio stations in the **Harrisburg/Lancaster/York** area, which makes up the 39th largest media market in the nation.

Newspapers

- TheBurg [2]
- Central Penn Business Journal
- Carlisle Sentinel, The
- The Patriot-News
- Press and Journal (Pennsylvania)

Television

The Harrisburg TV market is served by:

- WGAL - (NBC)
- WLYH-TV - (The CW)
- WHBG-TV - cable-only, public access
- WHP-TV - (CBS)
- WHTM-TV - (ABC)
- W35BT - (CTVN)
- WITF-TV - (PBS)
- WPMT - (Fox)
- WGCB-TV - independent, religious
- PCN-TV, is a cable television network dedicated to 24-hour coverage of government and public affairs in the commonwealth.
- Roxbury News - independent news

Radio

According to Arbitron, Harrisburg's radio market is ranked #78th in the nation.

This is a list of FM stations in the greater **Harrisburg, Pennsylvania** metropolitan area.

Callsign	MHz	Band	"Name" Format, Owner	City of license
WDCV	88.3	FM	Indie/College Rock, Dickinson College	Carlisle
WXPH	88.7	FM	WXPN relay, University of Pennsylvania	Harrisburg
WSYC	88.7	FM	Alternative, Shippensburg University	Shippensburg
WITF-FM	89.5	FM	NPR	Harrisburg
WVMM	90.7	FM	Indie/College Rock, Messiah College	Grantham
WJAZ	91.7	FM	WRTI relay, Classical/Jazz, Temple University	Harrisburg
WWKL	92.1	FM	"Hot 92", Rhythmic/CHR	Palmyra
WSJW	92.7	FM	Smooth Jazz	Starview
WTPA	93.5	FM	Classic Rock	Mechanicsburg
WRBT	94.9	FM	"Bob" Country	Harrisburg
WLAN	96.9	FM	"FM 97" Top 40	Lancaster
WRVV	97.3	FM	"The River" Classic Hits and the Best of Today's Rock	Harrisburg
WYCR	98.5	FM	98.5 The Peak	York
WQLV	98.9	FM	"Love 99" Adult Contemporary	Millersburg
WHKF	99.3	FM	"Kiss-FM" CHR	Harrisburg
WQIC	100.1	FM	Adult Contemporary	Lebanon
WROZ	101.3	FM	"The Rose" Adult Contemporary	Lancaster
WARM	103.3	FM	"Warm 103" Adult Contemporary	York
WNNK	104.1	FM	"Wink 104" Hot AC	Harrisburg
WQXA	105.7	FM	"105.7 The X" Hard Rock	York
WMHX	106.7	FM	"Mix" Adult Hits	Hershey
WGTY	107.7	FM	"Great Country"	York

This is a list of AM stations in the **Harrisburg, Pennsylvania** metropolitan area:

Callsign	kHz	Band	Format	City of license
WHP (AM)	580	AM	Conservative News/Talk	Harrisburg
WWII (AM)	720	AM	Contemporary Christian	Shiremanstown
WSBA (AM)	910	AM	News/Talk	York
WADV	940	AM	Gospel	Lebanon
WHYL	960	AM	Adult Standards	Carlisle
WIOO	1000	AM	Classic Country	Carlisle
WKBO	1230	AM	Christian Contemporary	Harrisburg
WQXA	1250	AM	Country	York
WLBR	1270	AM	Talk	Lebanon
WTCY	1400	AM	Now ESPN Radio (Formerly Adult R&B: The Touch)	Harrisburg
WTKT	1460	AM	sports: "The Ticket"	Harrisburg
WEEO (AM)	1480	AM	Oldies	Shippensburg
WLPA	1490	AM	sports	Lancaster
WWSM	1510	AM	Classic Country	Annville
WPDC	1600	AM	Spanish	Elizabethtown

Harrisburg in film

Several feature films and television series have been filmed or set in and around Harrisburg and the greater Susquehanna Valley.

See also: Harrisburg in film and television

Museums, art collections, and sites of interest

- Broad Street Market, one of the oldest continuously operating farmers markets in the United States.
- Capital Area Greenbelt, a twenty mile long greenway linking city neighborhoods, parks and open spaces
- Dauphin County Veteran's Memorial Obelisk inspired by the classic Roman/Egyptian obelisk form; located in uptown Harrisburg
- Fort Hunter Mansion and Park, located north of downtown Harrisburg on a bluff overlooking the Susquehanna River
- John Harris - Simon Cameron Mansion, a National Historic Landmark located in downtown Harrisburg along the river
- National Civil War Museum, located at Reservoir Park and affiliated with the Smithsonian Institution in Washington, D.C..

Pennsylvania Holocaust Memorial along Harrisburgs' Riverfront Park/Capital Area Greenbelt

- Pennsylvania National Fire Museum
- Pennsylvania Farm Show Complex & Expo Center, one of the largest convention/exhibition centers on the east coast
- Pennsylvania State Capitol Complex, the center of government for the commonwealth and home to the state capitol building, state archives, and state library
- Reservoir Park, the largest public park in the city
- State Museum of Pennsylvania
- Strawberry Square, across the street from the Capitol Complex, home of many state offices and a small shopping center
- Susquehanna art museum, located in downtown Harrisburg
- Whitaker Center for Science and the Arts, features an IMAX theater

Parks and recreation

- City Island and Beach
- Riverfront Park
- Italian Lake
- Wildwood Lake Park
- Reservoir Park
- Capital Area Greenbelt

Notable residents

Since the early 18th century, Harrisburg has been home to many people of note. Because it is the seat of government for the state and lies relatively close to other urban centers, Harrisburg has played a significant role in the nation's political, cultural and industrial history. *Harrisburgers* have also taken a leading role in the development of Pennsylvania's history for over two centuries. Two former U.S. Secretaries of War, Simon Cameron and Alexander Ramsey and several other prominent political figures, such as former speaker of the house Newt Gingrich, hail from Harrisburg. The actor Don Keefer was born near Harrisburg, along with the actor Richard Sanders, most famous for playing Less Nessmen in WKRP in Cincinnati . Many notable individuals are interred at Harrisburg Cemetery and East Harrisburg Cemetery.

Sports

Main article: Sports in South Central Pennsylvania

Harrisburg serves as the hub of semi-professional sports in South Central Pennsylvania. A host of teams compete in the region including three professional baseball teams, the Harrisburg Senators, the Lancaster Barnstormers, and the York Revolution. The Senators are the oldest team of the three, with the current incarnation playing since 1987. The original Harrisburg Senators began playing in the Eastern League in 1924. Playing its home games at Island Field, the team won the league championship in the 1927, 1928, and 1931 seasons. The Senators played a few more seasons before flood waters destroyed Island Field in 1936, effectively ending Eastern League participation for fifty-one years. In 1940, Harrisburg gained an Interstate League team affiliated with the Pittsburgh Pirates; however, the team remained in the city only until 1943, when it moved to nearby York and renamed the York Pirates. The current Harrisburg Senators, affiliated with the Washington Nationals, have won the Eastern League championship in the 1987, 1993, 1996, 1997, 1998, and 1999 seasons.

Club	League	Venue	Established	Championships
Harrisburg Senators	EL, Baseball	Metro Bank Park	1987	6
Central Penn Piranha	NAFL, Football	Skyline Sports Complex	1995	5
Harrisburg City Islanders	USL, Soccer	Skyline Sports Complex	2004	1
Harrisburg Stampede	AIFA, Indoor football	Pennsylvania Farm Show Complex & Expo Center	2009	0
Central PA Vipers	IWFL, Women's football	Susquehanna Township High School	2006	0
Keystone Assault	WFA, Women's football	TBA	2009	0
Harrisburg Horizon	EBA, Basketball	Manny Weaver Gym	1998	5
Harrisburg Lunatics	PIHA, Inline hockey	Susquehanna Sports Center	2001	0
Harrisburg RFC	EPRU, MARFU, Rugby	Cibort Park, Bressler	1969	1

Government

City of Harrisburg

Dr. Martin Luther King, Jr. City Government Center, the only city hall in the United States named for a civil rights leader, serves as a central location for the administrative functions of the city. Harrisburg has been served since 1970 by the "strong mayor" form of municipal government, with separate executive and legislative branches. The Mayor serves a four-year term with no term limits. As the full-time chief executive, the Mayor oversees the operation of 34 agencies, run by department and office heads, some of whom comprise the Mayor's cabinet, including the Departments of Public Safety (police and fire bureaus), Public Works, Business Administration, Parks and Recreation, Incineration and Steam Generation, Building & Housing Development and Solicitor. The city has 721 employees (2003). The current mayor of Harrisburg is Linda D. Thompson, whose term expires January 2014.

See also: List of mayors of Harrisburg

There are seven city council members, all elected at large, who serve part-time for four-year terms. There are two other elected city posts, city treasurer and city controller, who separately head their own fiscally related offices. The current city controller is Daniel C. Miller, whose term expires in January 2014.

See also: Harrisburg City Council

Property tax reform

Harrisburg is also known nationally for its use of a two tiered land value taxation. Harrisburg has taxed land at a rate six times that on improvements since 1975, and this policy has been credited by its former mayor, Stephen R. Reed, as well as by the city's former city manager during the 1980s with reducing the number of vacant structures located in downtown Harrisburg from about 4,200 in 1982 to fewer than 500 in 1995. During this same period of time between 1982 and 1995, nearly 4,700 more city residents became employed, the crime rate dropped 22.5% and the fire rate dropped 51%.

Harrisburg, as well as nearly 20 other Pennsylvania cities, employ a *two-rate* or *split-rate* property tax, which requires the taxing of the value of land at a higher rate and the value of the buildings and improvements at a lower one. This can be seen as a compromise between pure LVT and an ordinary property tax falling on real estate (land value plus improvement value). Alternatively, two-rate taxation may be seen as a form that allows gradual transformation of the traditional real estate property tax into a pure land value tax.

Nearly two dozen local Pennsylvania jurisdictions, such as Harrisburg, use two-rate property taxation in which the tax on land value is higher and the tax on improvement value is lower. In 2000, Florenz Plassmann and Nicolaus Tideman wrote that when comparing Pennsylvania cities using a higher tax rate on land value and a lower rate on improvements with similar sized Pennsylvania cities using the same rate on land and improvements, the higher land value taxation leads to increased construction within the jurisdiction.

Dauphin County

Dauphin County Government Complex, in downtown Harrisburg, serves the administrative functions of the county. The trial court of general jurisdiction for Harrisburg rests with the Court of Dauphin County and is largely funded and operated by county resources and employees.

See also: List of municipal authorities in Dauphin County, Pennsylvania

Dauphin County Courthouse located along the Susquehanna River at Front and Market Streets in downtown Harrisburg.

Commonwealth of Pennsylvania

Main article: Government of Pennsylvania

Pennsylvania State Capitol Complex, dominates the city's stature as a regional and national hub for government and politics. All administrative functions of the Commonwealth of Pennsylvania are located within the complex and at various nearby locations.

Commonwealth Judicial Center, houses Pennsylvania's three appellate courts, which are located in Harrisburg. The Supreme Court of Pennsylvania, which is the court of last resort in the state, regularly hears arguments at. The Superior Court of Pennsylvania and the Commonwealth Court of Pennsylvania are located here. Judges for these courts are elected at large.

Federal Government

Ronald Reagan Federal Building and Courthouse, located in downtown Harrisburg, serves as the regional administrative offices of the federal government. A branch of the U.S. District Court for the Middle District of Pennsylvania is also located within the courthouse.

Transport

Airports

Domestic and International airlines provide services via Harrisburg International Airport (MDT), which is located southeast of the city in Middletown. HIA is the third-busiest commercial airport in Pennsylvania, both in terms of passengers served and cargo shipments. Passenger carriers that serve HIA include US Airways, United Airlines, Delta Air Lines, Northwest Airlines, Continental Airlines, Air Canada, and AirTran Airways. Capital City Airport (CXY), a moderate-sized business class and general aviation airport, is located across the Susquehanna River in the nearby suburb of New Cumberland, south of Harrisburg. Both airports are owned and operated by the Susquehanna Area Regional Airport Authority (SARAA), which also manages the Franklin County Regional Airport in Chambersburg and Gettysburg Regional Airport in Gettysburg.

Mass transit

Harrisburg is served by Capital Area Transit (CAT) which provides public bus, paratransit, and commuter rail service throughout the greater metropolitan area. Construction of a commuter rail line designated the Capital Red Rose Corridor (previously named CorridorOne) will eventually link the city with nearby Lancaster in 2010.

Long-term plans for the region call for the commuter rail line to continue westward to Cumberland County, ending at Carlisle. In early 2005, the project hit a roadblock when the Cumberland County commissioners opposed the plan to extend commuter rail to the West Shore. Due to lack of support from the county commissioners, the Cumberland County portion, and the two new stations in Harrisburg have been removed from the project. In the future, with support from Cumberland County, the commuter rail project may extend to both shores of the Susquehanna River, where the majority of the commuting base for the Harrisburg metropolitan area resides.

In 2006, a second phase of the rail project designated CorridorTwo was announced to the general public. It will link downtown Harrisburg with its eastern suburbs in Dauphin and Lebanon counties, including the areas of Hummelstown, Hershey and Lebanon, and the city of York in York County. Future passenger rail corridors also include Route 15 from the Harrisburg area towards Gettysburg, as well as the Susquehanna River communities north of Harrisburg, and the Northern Susquehanna Valley region.

Intercity bus service

The lower level of the Harrisburg Transport Center serves as the city's intercity bus terminal. Daily bus services are provided by Greyhound, Capitol Trailways, Fullington Trailways, and Susquehanna Trailways. They connect Harrisburg to other Pennsylvania cities such as Allentown, Philadelphia, Pittsburgh, Reading, Scranton, State College, Williamsport, and York and nearby, out-of-state cities such as Baltimore, Binghamton, New York, Syracuse, and Washington, D.C., plus many other destinations via transfers.

Regional scheduled line bus service

The public transit provider in York County, Rabbit Transit, operates its RabbitEXPRESS bus service on weekdays between the city of York and both downtown Harrisburg and the main campus for Harrisburg Area Community College. The commuter-oriented service is designed to serve York County residents who work in Harrisburg, though reverse commutes are possible under the current schedule. Buses running this route make limited stops in the city of York and at two park and rides along Interstate 83 between York and Harrisburg before making various stops in Pennsylvania's capital city. As of May 2007, the RabbitEXPRESS operates three times in the morning and three times in the afternoon.

A charter/tour bus operator, R & J Transport, also provides weekday, scheduled route commuter service for people working in downtown Harrisburg. R & J, which is based in Schuylkill County, operates two lines, one between Frackville and downtown Harrisburg and the other between Minersville, Pine Grove, and downtown Harrisburg.

Rail

The Pennsylvania Railroad's main line from New York to Chicago passed through Harrisburg. The line was electrified in the 1930s, with the wires reaching Harrisburg in 1938. They went no further. Plans to electrify through to Pittsburgh and thence to Chicago never saw fruition; sufficient funding was never available. Thus, Harrisburg became where the PRR's crack expresses such as the Broadway Limited changed from electric traction to (originally) a steam locomotive, and later a diesel locomotive. Harrisburg remained a freight rail hub for PRR's successor Conrail, which was later sold off and divided between Norfolk Southern and CSX.

Freight Rail

Norfolk Southern acquired all of Conrail's lines in the Harrisburg area and has continued the city's function as a freight rail hub. Norfolk Southern considers Harrisburg one of the 3 primary hubs in its system, along with Chicago and Atlanta, and operates 2 intermodal (rail/truck transfer) yards in the immediate Harrisburg area. The Harrisburg Intermodal Yard (formerly called Lucknow Yard) is located in the north end of Harrisburg, approximately 3 miles north of downtown Harrisburg and the Harrisburg Transport Center, while the Rutherford Intermodal Yard is located approximately 6 miles east of downtown Harrisburg in Swatara Township, Dauphin County. Norfolk Southern also operates a significant classification yard in the Harrisburg area, the Enola Yard, which is located across the Susquehanna River from Harrisburg in East Pennsboro Township, Cumberland County.

Intercity Passenger Rail

Amtrak provides service to and from Harrisburg. The passenger rail operator runs its *Keystone* and *Pennsylvanian* services between New York, Philadelphia, and the Harrisburg Transportation Center daily. The *Pennsylvanian* route, which operates once daily, continues west to Pittsburgh. As of April 2007, Amtrak operates 14 weekday roundtrips and 8 weekend roundtrips daily between Harrisburg, Lancaster, and Philadelphia 30th Street Station; most of these trains also travel to and from New York Penn Station. The Keystone Corridor between Harrisburg and Philadelphia was improved in the mid-2000s, with the primary improvements completed in late 2006. The improvements included upgrading the electrical catenary, installing continuously welded rail, and replacing existing wooden railroad ties with concrete ties. These improvements increased train speeds to 110 mph along the corridor and reduced the travel time between Harrisburg and Philadelphia to as little as 95 minutes. It also eliminated the need to change locomotives at 30th Street Station (from diesel to electric and vice-versa) for trains continuing to or coming from New York. As of Federal Fiscal Year 2008, the Harrisburg Transportation Center was the 2nd busiest Amtrak station in Pennsylvania and 21st busiest in the United States.

Bridges

Harrisburg is the location of over a dozen large bridges, many up to a mile long, that cross the Susquehanna River. Several other important structures span the Paxton Creek watershed and Cameron Street, linking Center City with neighborhoods in East Harrisburg. These include the State Street Bridge, also known as the Soldiers and Sailor's Memorial Bridge, and the Mulberry Street Bridge. Walnut Street Bridge, now used only by pedestrians and cyclists, links the downtown and Riverfront Park areas with City Island but goes no further

Western span of the Walnut Street Bridge crossing the Susquehanna River, after it collapsed during the 1996 flood.

as spans are missing on its western side due to massive flooding resulting from the North American blizzard of 1996.

See also: List of crossings of the Susquehanna River

Education

Public schools

The City of Harrisburg is served by the Harrisburg School District. The school district provides education for the city's youth beginning with all-day kindergarten through twelfth grade. A multi-year restructuring plan is aimed at making the district a model for urban public schools. The district has been troubled for years with management fiascos and poor test scores. In the summer of 2007, more than 2,000 city students were enrolled in educational programs offered by the Harrisburg School District as remediation.

The city also maintains one public charter school, the Sylvan Heights Science Charter School [3]. In addition, Harrisburg is home to an arts-focused magnet school, the Capital Area School for the Arts. In 2003, SciTech High, a regional math and science magnet school affiliated with Harrisburg University, opened its doors to students. A growing number of virtual public charter schools provide residents with many alternative to the bricks and mortar public school system.

The Central Dauphin School District, the largest public school district in the metropolitan area and the 13th largest in Pennsylvania, uses several Harrisburg postal addresses for many of the districts schools.

Private schools

Harrisburg is home to an extensive Catholic educational system. There are nearly 40 parish-driven elementary schools and seven Catholic high schools within the region administered by the Roman Catholic Diocese of Harrisburg, including Bishop McDevitt High School and Trinity High School. Numerous other private schools, such as The Londonderry School [4] and The Circle School, which is a Sudbury Model school, also operate in Harrisburg. Harrisburg Academy, founded in 1784, is one of the oldest independent college preparatory schools in the nation. The Rabbi David L. Silver Yeshiva Academy [5], founded in 1944, is a progressive, modern Jewish day school. Also, Harrisburg is home to Harrisburg Christian School, founded in 1955.

Higher education

In Harrisburg

- Dixon University Center, located in Uptown, serves as the office of Chancellor and the central headquarters of the Pennsylvania State System of Higher Education (PASSHE). With a total student enrollment 110,428, PASSHE is one of the largest university systems in the United States.
- Harrisburg Area Community College: the original campus of the college, the Harrisburg Campus, and Penn Center and Midtown campus which are branches of the Harrisburg Campus are located in Harrisburg. Newer campuses are located in Gettysburg, Lancaster, Lebanon and York.
- Harrisburg University of Science and Technology, located in Center City.
- Messiah College's Harrisburg Institute, located in Center City
- Penn State Harrisburg Eastgate Center, located in Center City.
- Temple University Harrisburg Campus, located in Center City.
- Widener University Harrisburg Campus including its School of Law

Near Harrisburg

- Central Pennsylvania College, located in Summerdale, Pennsylvania.
- Dickinson College, located in Carlisle, Pennsylvania.
- Duquesne University (Capital Region Campus), located in Lemoyne, Pennsylvania.
- Elizabethtown College, located in Elizabethtown, Pennsylvania. Elizabethtown College is a consortium member of the Dixon University Center, offering seven accelerated, undergraduate degree programs in the Harrisburg area.
- Gettysburg College, located in Gettysburg, Pennsylvania.
- Lebanon Valley College, located in Annville, Pennsylvania.
- Lutheran Theological Seminary at Gettysburg, located in Gettysburg, Pennsylvania.
- Messiah College, located in Grantham, Pennsylvania.
- Millersville University, located in Millersville, Pennsylvania.
- Penn State Dickinson School of Law, located in Carlisle, Pennsylvania.
- Penn State Hershey Medical Center, located in Hershey, Pennsylvania.
- Penn State Harrisburg (Main Campus), located nearby in Middletown, Pennsylvania.
- Shippensburg University, located in Shippensburg, Pennsylvania.
- United States Army War College, located in Carlisle, Pennsylvania.
- York College of Pennsylvania, located in York, Pennsylvania.

Libraries

* Dauphin County Law Library
* Dauphin County Library System, with eight branches in Harrisburg and suburban Dauphin County
* McCormick Library of Harrisburg Area Community College
* State Library of Pennsylvania, which includes the Pennsylvania Law Library
* Medical library services of PinnacleHealth System
* Law Library, Widener University School of Law

Sister cities

Main article: List of sister cities in Pennsylvania

Harrisburg has two official sister cities as designated by Sister Cities International:

* ⬜ Ma'alot-Tarshiha, Israel.
* ▮▮ Pachuca, Hidalgo, Mexico.

Notable natives and residents

* James Boyd, a resident of Front Street, wrote a novel about the city in 1935, *Roll River*.
* Glenn Branca, an avant-garde composer and guitarist, was born here
* Bruce Brubaker, MLB player for the Los Angeles Dodgers and Milwaukee Brewers
* Phil Davis, UFC fighter
* Candace Gingrich, civil rights activist
* Newt Gingrich, former U.S. Representative from Georgia
* Danny Lansanah, NFL player for the Green Bay Packers
* LeSean McCoy, Running Back, Philadelphia Eagles (2009–Present)
* John O'Hara, a native of Pottsville, lived in Harrisburg briefly to write his novel about the city, *A Rage to Live*, published in 1949. Harrisburg, disguised as Fort Penn, appears also in other O'Hara novels.
* Bobby Troup, actor, jazz pianist, and songwriter. Known for the standard "(Get Your Kicks On) Route 66" and as Dr. Joe Early on the TV series *Emergency!*.
* Robert White, one of the Funk Brothers who played on the Motown hits in the 1960s, was born here
* Nancy Kulp was an American actress best known as "Miss Jane Hathaway" on the popular television series The Beverly Hillbillies.
* Carmen Finestra, TV producer and writer, best known for creating the 1990s sitcom Home Improvement.

See also

- Harrisburg Regional Chamber
- List of cities and towns along the Susquehanna River
- List of companies based in the Harrisburg area
- List of hospitals in Harrisburg
- List of Harrisburg neighborhoods
- National Register of Historic Places listings in Dauphin County, Pennsylvania
- New Cumberland Defense Depot
- Sports in South Central Pennsylvania

External links

- City of Harrisburg [1] (official website)
- Harrisburg Downtown Improvement District Authority [6]
- Hershey-Harrisburg Regional Visitors Bureau [7]
- Harrisburg Regional Chamber of Commerce [8]
- Harrisburg City Archives [9]
- Memorials, monuments, statues & other outdoor art in & around Harrisburg [10] (with pictures)
- Harrisburg travel guide from Wikitravel

1. REDIRECT Template:Navboxes

pnb:ہیرسبرگ

Geography of Pennsylvania

The **Geography of Pennsylvania** varies from sea level marine estuary to mountainous plateau, is significant for its natural resources and ports, and is notable for its role in the history of the United States.

Major features

Pennsylvania's nickname, the *Keystone State*, derives from the fact that the state forms a geographic bridge both between the Northeastern states and the Southern states, and between the

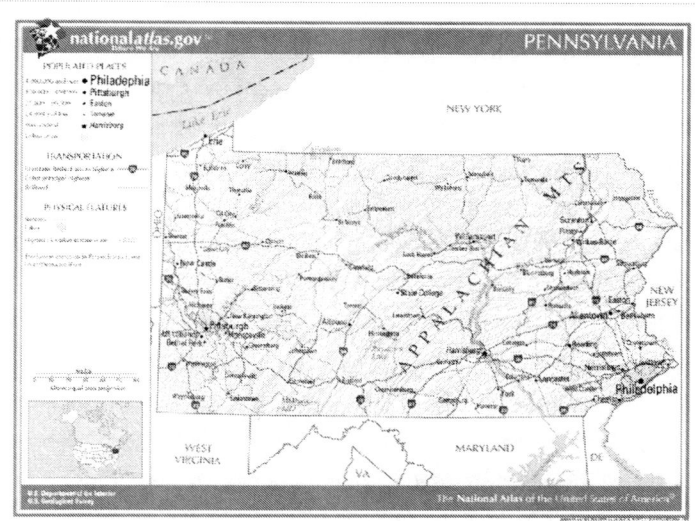

Pennsylvania cities and rivers

Atlantic seaboard and the Midwest. It even has a toehold on the Great Lakes, with the Erie triangle. It is bordered on the north and northeast by New York; on the east by New Jersey; on the south by Delaware, Maryland, and West Virginia; on the west by Ohio; and on the northwest by Lake Erie. It has a short border on Lake Erie with Canada. The Delaware, Susquehanna, Monongahela, Allegheny, and Ohio rivers are the major rivers of the state. The Lehigh River, the Youghiogheny River and Oil Creek are smaller rivers which have played an important role in the development of the state. It is one of the thirteen U.S. States that share a border with Canada.

Pennsylvania is 180 miles (290 km) north to south and 310 miles (500 km) east to west. The total land area is 44817 square miles (116080 km^2)—739200 acres (2991 km^2) of which are bodies of water. It is the 33rd largest state in the United States. The highest point of 3213 feet (979 m) above sea level is at Mount Davis. Its lowest point is at sea level on the Delaware River. Pennsylvania is in the Eastern time zone.

The Pennsylvania Dutch region

Main article: Pennsylvania Dutch Country

The Pennsylvania Dutch region in south-central Pennsylvania is a favorite for sightseers. The Pennsylvania Dutch, including the Old Order Amish, the Old Order Mennonites and at least 15 other sects, are common in the rural areas around the cities of Lancaster, York, and Harrisburg, with smaller numbers extending northeast to the Lehigh Valley and up the Susquehanna River valley. (There are actually more Old Order Amish in Holmes County, Ohio, and there are plain sect communities in at least 47 states, but many Mennonites remain, particularly in Lancaster County.) Some adherents eschew modern conveniences and use horse-drawn farming equipment and carriages, while others are virtually indistinguishable from non-Amish or Mennonites. Descendants of the plain sect immigrants who do not practice the faith may refer to themselves as *Pennsylvania Germans*.

Despite the name, the people are not from the Netherlands, but rather are from various parts of southwest Germany, Alsace and Switzerland. The word *"Dutch"* here is left over from an archaic sense of the English word, which once referred to all people speaking a West Germanic language on the European mainland. It is also often thought to be a corruption of the German word for 'German,' which is *"Deutsch."* As one might imagine, a Pennsylvania Dutch settler would have been asked what nationality he was. His reply, in German, would have been "Deutsch," which was misunderstood as 'Dutch.'

Western Pennsylvania

Main article: Western Pennsylvania

The western third of the state can be considered a separate large geophysical unit, distinctive enough that it may best be described on its own. Several important, complex factors set Western Pennsylvania apart in many respects from the east, such as the initial difficulty of access across the mountains, rivers oriented to the Mississippi River drainage system, and above all, the complex economics involved in the rise and decline of the American steel industry centered around Pittsburgh. Other factors, such as a markedly different style of agriculture, the rise of the oil industry, timber exploitation and the old wood chemical industry, and even, in linguistics, the local dialect, all make this large area sometimes seem a virtual "state within a state".

The mountains

Pennsylvania is bisected diagonally by ridges of the Appalachian Mountains from southwest to northeast. To the northwest of the folded mountains is the Allegheny Plateau, which continues into southwestern and south central New York. This plateau is so dissected by valleys that it also seems mountainous. The plateau is underlain by sedimentary rocks of Mississippian and Pennsylvanian age, which bear abundant fossils as well as natural gas and petroleum.

In 1859, near Titusville, Edwin L. Drake drilled the first oil well in the U.S. into these sediments. Similar rock layers also contain coal to the south and east of the oil and gas deposits. In the metamorphic (folded) belt, anthracite (hard coal) is mined near Wilkes-Barre and Hazelton. These fossil fuels have been an important resource to Pennsylvania. Timber and dairy farming are also sources of livelihood for midstate and western Pennsylvania. Along the shore of Lake Erie in the far northwest are orchards and vineyards.

During the most recent Ice Age, the northeastern and northwestern corners of present-day Pennsylvania were buried under the southern fringes of the Laurentide ice sheet. Glaciers extended into the Appalachian valleys of central Pennsylvania, but the ice did not overtop the mountains. At its furthest extent it spread as far south as Moraine State Park, about 40 miles (64 km) north of Pittsburgh.

The shores

Pennsylvania has 57 miles (92 km) of shoreline along the Delaware River estuary but is a landlocked state with no coastline bordering the Atlantic Ocean. The tidal marsh of this estuary has been protected as John Heinz National Wildlife Refuge at Tinicum. Pennsylvania is the only truly landlocked state of the original thirteen states, although Connecticut, located on the Long Island Sound, also has no actual coastline (The difference between coast and shore is explained in the respective articles).

Pennsylvania has one of the largest seaports in the U.S. on its narrow shore, the Port of Philadelphia. In the west the Port of Pittsburgh is also very large and even exceeds Philadelphia in rank by annual tonnage, because of the large volume of bulk coal shipped by barge down the Ohio River. Chester, downstream from Philadelphia, and Erie, the Great Lakes outlet on Lake Erie in the Erie Triangle, are smaller but still important ports.

Ecological disasters

Pennsylvania has been the site of some of the worst ecological disasters experienced in U.S. history:

- In 1889, the South Fork Dam, impounding a recreational mountain lake for sportsmen, burst after a heavy rain and destroyed the downstream factory town of Johnstown, killing over 2,200 inhabitants in the notorious Johnstown Flood (the town was later rebuilt and is a reasonably large community today in the central mountains).

- In 1948, an industrial accident in Donora released poison gases into the air, killing 68 and causing health complications for many more.

- In 1961, an exposed seam of coal at Centralia caught fire and eventually forced almost the entire community to abandon the area; the underground coal fire is still burning today and it is estimated that it can burn for another 250 years.

- In 1979, the Three Mile Island Nuclear Power Incident near the state capital of Harrisburg, while not as destructive to the community, nevertheless cost close to $1 billion to clean up and changed the national public perception of nuclear power to a much less favorable viewpoint.

Climate

Main articles: Climate of Pennsylvania and Climate change in Pennsylvania

Pennsylvania has three general climate regions, which are determined by altitude more than latitude or distance from the oceans. Most of the state falls in the humid continental climate zone. The lower elevations, including most of the major cities, has a moderate continental climate (Koppen climate classification Dfa), with cool to cold winters and hot, humid summers. Highland areas have a more severe continental climate (Koppen Dfb) with warm, humid summers and cold, more severe and snowy winters. Extreme southeastern Pennsylvania, around Philadelphia borders into a humid subtropical climate (Koppen Cfa), with milder winters and hot, humid summers.

Precipitation is abundant throughout the state, as the primary climatic influences are the Atlantic Ocean and the Gulf of Mexico, plus Arctic influences that cross over the Great Lakes.

See also

• Pennsylvania Regions

List of counties in Pennsylvania

The following is a **list of the sixty-seven counties of the Commonwealth of Pennsylvania in the United States of America.** The city of Philadelphia is coterminous with Philadelphia County, and governmental functions have been consolidated since 1854.

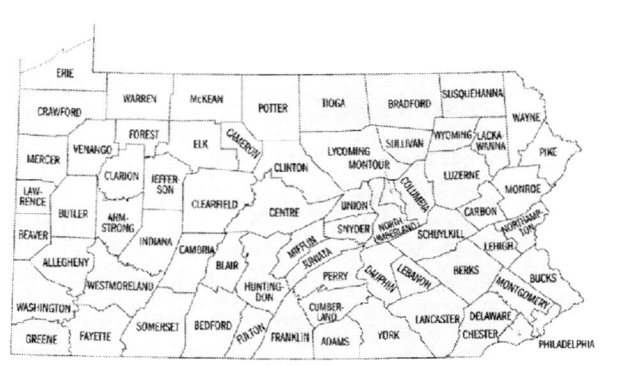

Pennsylvania counties (clickable map)

Alphabetical list

County	FIPS code	County seat	Established	Origin	Etymology	Population	Area	Map
Adams County	001 [1]	Gettysburg	1800	Parts of York County.	John Adams	91292	522 sq mi (1352 km^2)	
Allegheny County	003 [2]	Pittsburgh	1788	Parts of Washington and Westmoreland Counties.	Lenape word, of uncertain meaning, for the Allegheny River	1281666	745 sq mi (1930 km^2)	
Armstrong County	005 [3]	Kittanning	1800	Parts of Allegheny, Lycoming, and Westmoreland Counties.	John Armstrong	72392	664 sq mi (1720 km^2)	
Beaver County	007 [4]	Beaver	1800	Parts of Allegheny and Washington Counties.	Beaver River	181412	444 sq mi (1150 km^2)	
Bedford County	009 [5]	Bedford	1771	Parts of Cumberland County.	Fort Bedford, which is named for the Duke of Bedford	49984	1015 sq mi (2629 km^2)	
Berks County	011 [6]	Reading	1752	Parts of Chester, Lancaster and Philadelphia Counties.	The English county of Berkshire	373638	866 sq mi (2243 km^2)	
Blair County	013 [7]	Hollidaysburg	1846	Parts of Huntingdon and Bedford Counties.	John Blair	129144	527 sq mi (1365 km^2)	
Bradford County	015 [8]	Towanda	1810	Parts of Luzerne and Lycoming Counties; originally called Ontario County, renamed as Bradford County in 1812.	William Bradford	62761	1161 sq mi (3007 km^2)	

Bucks County	017 [9]	Doylestown	1682	One of the original counties at the formation of Pennsylvania	The English county of Buckinghamshire	597635	622 sq mi (1611 km^2)	
Butler County	019 [10]	Butler	1800	Parts of Allegheny County.	General Richard Butler	174083	795 sq mi (2059 km^2)	
Cambria County	021 [11]	Ebensburg	1804	Parts of Somerset and Huntingdon Counties.	Wales	152593	693 sq mi (1795 km^2)	
Cameron County	023 [12]	Emporium	1860	Parts of Clinton, Elk, McKean, and Potter Counties.	Simon Cameron	5974	399 sq mi (1033 km^2)	
Carbon County	025 [13]	Jim Thorpe	1843	Parts of Monroe and Northampton Counties.	Coal	58802	387 sq mi (1002 km^2)	
Centre County	027 [14]	Bellefonte	1800	Parts of Lycoming, Mifflin, Northumberland, and Huntingdon Counties.	Centre Furnance, owned by Samuel Miles and John Patton	135758	1112 sq mi (2880 km^2)	
Chester County	029 [15]	West Chester	1682	One of the original counties at the formation of Pennsylvania.	The English city of Chester in the county of Cheshire	433501	760 sq mi (1968 km^2)	
Clarion County	031 [16]	Clarion	1839	Parts of Venango and Armstrong Counties.	Clarion River	41765	609 sq mi (1577 km^2)	

Clearfield County	033 [17]	Clearfield	1804	Parts of Lycoming and Huntingdon Counties; Clearfield functioned as a part of Centre County for judiciary purposes until 1822.	The cleared fields from logging in the area	83382	1154 sq mi (2989 km^2)	
Clinton County	035 [18]	Lock Haven	1839	Parts of Lycoming and Centre Counties.	DeWitt Clinton	37914	898 sq mi (2326 km^2)	
Columbia County	037 [19]	Bloomsburg	1813	Parts of Northumberland and Luzerne Counties.	Columbia, the first popular and poetic name for the United States	64151	490 sq mi (1269 km^2)	
Crawford County	039 [20]	Meadville	1800	Parts of Allegheny County.	William Crawford	90366	1038 sq mi (2688 km^2)	
Cumberland County	041 [21]	Carlisle	1750	Parts of Lancaster County.	The historic English county of Cumberland	213674	551 sq mi (1427 km^2)	
Dauphin County	043 [22]	Harrisburg	1785	Parts of Lancaster County.	The Dauphin	251798	558 sq mi (1445 km^2)	
Delaware County	045 [23]	Media	1789	Parts of Chester County.	Delaware River	550864	191 sq mi (495 km^2)	
Elk County	047 [24]	Ridgway	1843	Parts of Jefferson, McKean, and Clearfield Counties.	Elk	35112	832 sq mi (2155 km^2)	
Erie County	049 [25]	Erie	1800	Parts of Allegheny County; attached to Crawford County until 1803.	Lake Erie	280843	802 sq mi (2077 km^2)	

Fayette County	051 [26]	Uniontown	1783	Parts of Westmoreland County.	The Marquis de Lafayette	148644	798 sq mi (2067 km^2)	
Forest County	053 [27]	Tionesta	1848	Parts of Jefferson County; attached to Jefferson County until 1857.	Chief natural feature	4946	431 sq mi (1116 km^2)	
Franklin County	055 [28]	Chambersburg	1784	Parts of Cumberland County.	Benjamin Franklin	129313	771 sq mi (1997 km^2)	
Fulton County	057 [29]	McConnellsburg	1850	Parts of Bedford County.	Robert Fulton	14261	438 sq mi (1134 km^2)	
Greene County	059 [30]	Waynesburg	1796	Parts of Washington County.	General Nathanael Greene	40672	578 sq mi (1497 km^2)	
Huntingdon County	061 [31]	Huntingdon	1787	Parts of Bedford County.	Possibly the historic English county of Huntingdonshire	45586	889 sq mi (2302 km^2)	
Indiana County	063 [32]	Indiana	1803	Parts of Lycoming and Westmoreland Counties; it was attached to Westmoreland County until 1806.	Native Americans	89605	834 sq mi (2160 km^2)	
Jefferson County	065 [33]	Brookville	1804	Parts of Lycoming County. Attached to Westmoreland County until 1806 and to Indiana County until 1830.	Thomas Jefferson	45932	657 sq mi (1702 km^2)	
Juniata County	067 [34]	Mifflintown	1831	Parts of Mifflin County.	Juniata River	22821	394 sq mi (1020 km^2)	

Lackawanna County	069 [35]	Scranton	1878	Parts of Luzerne County.	Lackawanna River	213295	465 sq mi (1204 km^2)	
Lancaster County	071 [36]	Lancaster	1729	Parts of Chester County.	The English city of Lancaster	470658	984 sq mi (2549 km^2)	
Lawrence County	073 [37]	New Castle	1849	Parts of Beaver and Mercer Counties.	The USS Lawrence	94643	363 sq mi (940 km^2)	
Lebanon County	075 [38]	Lebanon	1813	Parts of Dauphin and Lancaster Counties.	Lebanon Township; *Lebanon* is a Biblical term meaning *White Mountain*	120327	363 sq mi (940 km^2)	
Lehigh County	077 [39]	Allentown	1812	Parts of Northampton County.	Lehigh River	312090	349 sq mi (904 km^2)	
Luzerne County	079 [40]	Wilkes-Barre	1786	Parts of Northumberland County.	The Chevalier de Luzerne	319250	907 sq mi (2349 km^2)	
Lycoming County	081 [41]	Williamsport	1795	Parts of Northumberland County.	Lycoming Creek	120044	1244 sq mi (3222 km^2)	
McKean County	083 [42]	Smethport	1804	Parts of Lycoming County; Attached to Centre County until 1814 and to Lycoming County until 1826 for judicial and elective purposes. McKean was fully organized only in 1826.	Thomas McKean	45936	984 sq mi (2549 km^2)	
Mercer County	085 [43]	Mercer	1800	Parts of Allegheny County.	Hugh Mercer	120293	683 sq mi (1769 km^2)	

Mifflin County	087 [44]	Lewistown	1789	Parts of Cumberland and Northumberland Counties.	Thomas Mifflin	46486	415 sq mi (1075 km^2)	
Monroe County	089 [45]	Stroudsburg	1836	Parts of Pike and Northampton Counties.	James Monroe	138687	617 sq mi (1598 km^2)	
Montgomery County	091 [46]	Norristown	1784	Parts of Philadelphia County.	Uncertain; possibly either Richard Montgomery or the historic Welsh county of Montgomeryshire	750097	487 sq mi (1261 km^2)	
Montour County	093 [47]	Danville	1850	Parts of Columbia County.	Madame Montour	18236	132 sq mi (342 km^2)	
Northampton County	095 [48]	Easton	1752	Parts of Bucks County.	The English city of Northampton	267066	377 sq mi (976 km^2)	
Northumberland County	097 [49]	Sunbury	1772	Parts of Lancaster, Berks, Bedford, Cumberland, and Northampton Counties.	The English county of Northumberland	94556	477 sq mi (1235 km^2)	
Perry County	099 [50]	New Bloomfield	1820	Parts of Cumberland County.	Oliver Hazard Perry	43602	556 sq mi (1440 km^2)	
Philadelphia County	101 [51]	Philadelphia	1682	One of the original counties at the formation of Pennsylvania. The city and county of Philadelphia were combined in 1854 and city and county offices merged in 1952.	"Brotherly love" from Greek philos ("love") and adelphos ("brother")	1517550	143 sq mi (370 km^2)	

Pike County	103 [52]	Milford	1814	Parts of Wayne County.	Zebulon Pike	46302	567 sq mi (1469 km^2)	
Potter County	105 [53]	Coudersport	1804	From Lycoming county. Attached to Lycoming County until 1826 and to McKean County until 1835 for judicial purposes, Potter was not fully organized until 1835.	James Potter	18080	1081 sq mi (2800 km^2)	
Schuylkill County	107 [54]	Pottsville	1811	Parts of Berks and Northampton Counties.	Schuylkill River	150336	778 sq mi (2015 km^2)	
Snyder County	109 [55]	Middleburg	1855	Parts of Union County.	Simon Snyder	37546	332 sq mi (860 km^2)	
Somerset County	111 [56]	Somerset	1795	Parts of Bedford County.	The English county of Somerset	80023	1081 sq mi (2800 km^2)	
Sullivan County	113 [57]	Laporte	1847	Parts of Lycoming County; attached to Lycoming until 1848.	John Sullivan	6556	452 sq mi (1171 km^2)	
Susquehanna County	115 [58]	Montrose	1810	Parts of Luzerne County ; attached to Luzerne County until 1812.	Susquehanna River	42238	832 sq mi (2155 km^2)	
Tioga County	117 [59]	Wellsboro	1804	Parts of Lycoming County; attached to Lycoming until 1812.	Tioga River	41373	1137 sq mi (2945 km^2)	

County	No.	County seat	Est.	Formed from	Etymology	Population	Area	
Union County	119 [60]	Lewisburg	1813	Parts of Northumberland County.	The Federal union of the United States	41624	317 sq mi (821 km^2)	
Venango County	121 [61]	Franklin	1800	Parts of Allegheny and Lycoming Counties; attached to until 1805.	A corruption of the Native word "onenge", meaning "otter"	57565	683 sq mi (1769 km^2)	
Warren County	123 [62]	Warren	1800	Parts of Allegheny and Lycoming counties; attached to Crawford County until 1805 and then to Venango until Warren was formally organized in 1819.	General Joseph Warren	43863	898 sq mi (2326 km^2)	
Washington County	125 [63]	Washington	1781	Parts of Westmoreland County.	George Washington	202897	861 sq mi (2230 km^2)	
Wayne County	127 [64]	Honesdale	1798	Parts of Northampton County.	Anthony Wayne	47722	751 sq mi (1945 km^2)	
Westmoreland County	129 [65]	Greensburg	1773	Parts of Bedford County.	Possibly the historic English county of Westmorland	369993	1036 sq mi (2683 km^2)	
Wyoming County	131 [66]	Tunkhannock	1842	Parts of Luzerne County.	The Delaware word xwé:waməŋk, meaning "at the big river flat"	28080	405 sq mi (1049 km^2)	
York County	133 [67]	York	1749	Parts of Lancaster County.	The English city of York	381751	910 sq mi (2357 km^2)	

See also

• Pennsylvania counties by per capita income

Climate of Pennsylvania

The **climate of Pennsylvania** is diverse due to the multitude of geographic features found within the state.Pennsylvania rarly has overcast. Straddling two major climate zones, the southeastern corner of Pennsylvania has the warmest climate. Greater Philadelphia lies at the southernmost tip of the Humid continental climate zone, with some characteristics of the Humid subtropical climate that lies in Delaware and Maryland to the south. Moving west toward the mountainous interior of the state, the climate becomes markedly colder, the number of cloudy days increases, and winter snowfall amounts are greater.

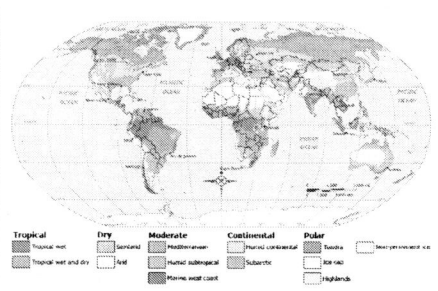

Worldwide climate classifications

Temperature

City	Jan	Feb	Mar	Apr	May	Jun	Jul	Aug	Sep	Oct	Nov	Dec
Monthly Normal High and Low Temperatures For Various Pennsylvania Cities												
Scranton	34/18	37/20	47/28	59/38	71/48	78/57	83/61	81/60	72/53	61/42	49/34	39/24
Erie	33/20	36/21	45/28	56/38	67/49	76/59	80/64	79/63	72/56	61/46	49/36	39/27
Pittsburgh	37/20	39/21	50/29	62/38	71/48	80/56	85/62	83/60	76/53	64/41	53/33	42/25
Harrisburg	38/23	41/25	51/33	63/42	73/51	81/61	86/66	84/64	76/57	64/45	53/36	42/28

Philadelphia	39/25	42/28	51/35	62/44	72/55	81/64	86/70	84/69	77/61	66/49	55/40	44/31

Most interior lowland areas have a moderate humid continental climate (Koppen climate classification *Dfa*), with hot, humid summers and cool to cold winters. Highland areas in the Appalachians have a more severe humid continental climate (Koppen *Dfb*), with colder, snowy winters and somewhat cooler summers. The southeastern area has a humid subtropical climate (Koppen *Cfa*) with somewhat milder winters.

Precipitation

Western areas of the state, particularly cities near Lake Erie, can receive over 100 inches (254 cm) of snowfall annually, and the entire state receives an average of 41 inches (1041 mm) of rainfall every year. Floods are more common in March and April than other months of the year.

Tropical cyclones

Tropical cyclones threaten the state during the summer and fall, with their main impact being rainfall. Although Hurricane Agnes was barely a hurricane at landfall in Florida, its major impact was over the Mid-Atlantic region, where Agnes combined with a non-tropical low to produce widespread rains of 6 inches (150 mm) to 12 inches (300 mm) with local amounts up to 19 inches (480 mm) in western Schuylkill County in Pennsylvania . These rains produced widespread severe flooding from Virginia northward to New York, with other flooding occurring over the western portions of the Carolinas.

Philadelphia has received sustained winds approaching hurricane-force from tropical cyclones in the past.

Climate change in Pennsylvania

Pennsylvania Governor Edward Rendell has approved a bill that establishes a $500 million fund to support renewable energy projects. Special Session House Bill 1 authorizes the Commonwealth Financing Authority to borrow $500 million, most of which will be split into six funding sources relating to energy efficiency and renewable energy: $80 million in grants and loans for solar energy projects; $100 million in grants, loans, and rebates for up to 35% of the cost of solar energy projects at residences and small businesses; $165 million in grants and loans for alternative energy projects, excluding solar energy, at businesses and local government facilities; $25 million for wind energy and geothermal energy projects; $40 million to help start-up businesses involved in energy efficiency technologies; and $25 million in grants and loans to improve the energy efficiency of new and existing homes and small business buildings. An additional $65 million will go toward pollution control technologies and to help low-income families pay their energy bills.

In addition to the $500 million fund, the bill creates a Consumer Energy Program that is funded at $15 million for the next 3 fiscal years, then gradually decreases to $8 million by the 2015-2016 fiscal year, for a total of $100 million. Of that, $92.5 million will support loans, grants, and rebates for up to 25% of the cost of energy efficiency improvements to homes and small businesses, while $5 million will support low-interest loans for energy efficiency improvements to homes. An additional $50 million will be available over the next 8 years to support tax credits for 15% of the cost of alternative energy projects, capped at $1 million per year for each project.

Governor Rendell also approved two bills on July 10 that relate to biofuels. House Bill 1202 could add as much as 1 billion gallons of advanced biofuels to the state's fuel supply. It requires all retail diesel fuel sold in the state to contain 2% biodiesel, once the in-state production of biodiesel reaches 40 million gallons per year, increasing incrementally to a 20% biodiesel requirement, once the in-state production of biodiesel reaches 400 million gallons per year (but only if vehicle manufacturers approve the use of 20% biodiesel). Likewise, all retail gasoline sold in the state must contain 10% ethanol, once the in-state production of cellulosic ethanol reaches 350 million gallons per year. The state already has a biodiesel production capacity of 60 million gallons per year, so the 2% biodiesel requirement could go into effect soon, if production is high enough. To encourage biodiesel production, Special Session Senate Bill 22 will offer a subsidy of 75 cents per gallon of biodiesel produced, capped at $1.9 million per year for each producer. The bill also expands a hybrid vehicle rebate program to include plug-in hybrids and other alternative fuel vehicles.

See also

- Johnstown Flood
- List of Pennsylvania weather records
- List of wettest known tropical cyclones in Pennsylvania
- Wind power in Pennsylvania

History of Pennsylvania

The **History of Pennsylvania** is as varied as any in the American experience and reflects the *salad bowl* vision of the United States. Before Pennsylvania was settled by Europeans, the area was home to the Delaware (also known as Lenni Lenape), Susquehannock, Iroquois, Eries, Shawnee and other Native American tribes. Most of these tribes were driven off or reduced to remnants as a results of the European colonization.

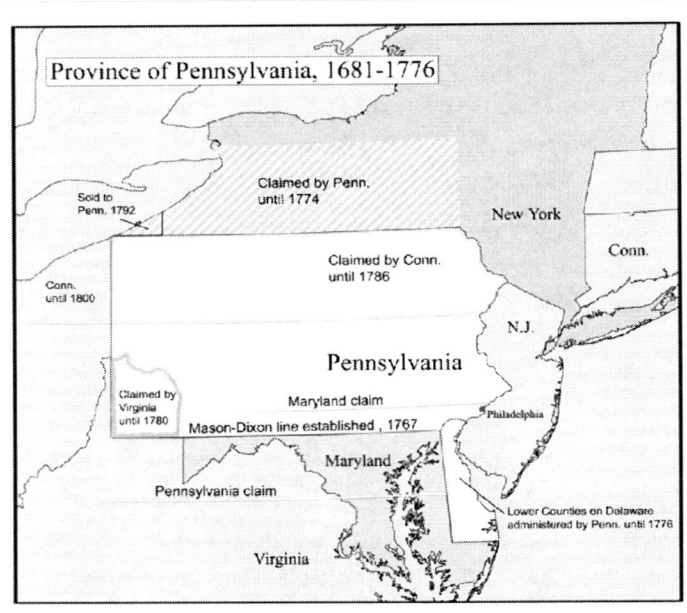

A map of the Province of Pennsylvania.

Dutch and Swedish influence

Main article: New Sweden

Before the 1600's, the area known as present-day Pennsylvania was mapped by the Spanish and labeled *L'arcadia*, or "wooded coast", during Giovanni da Verrazzano's voyage in 1524 . Eventually, the Delaware River watershed was claimed by the British based on the explorations of John Cabot in 1497, Captain John Smith and others, and was named for Thomas West, 3rd Baron De La Warr, the Governor of Virginia from 1610 until 1618. At that time the area was of the Colony of Virginia.

However, the Dutch thought they also had a claim, based on the 1609 explorations of Henry Hudson, and under the auspices of the Dutch West India Company were the first Europeans to actually occupy the land. They established trading posts in 1624 at Burlington Island, opposite Bristol, Pennsylvania, and then in 1626 at Fort Nassau, now Gloucester City, New Jersey. Peter Minuit was the Dutch Director-General during this period and probably spent some time at the Burlington Island post, thereby familiarizing himself with the region.

Minuit had a falling out with the directors of the Dutch West India Company, was recalled from New Netherland, and promptly made his services available to his many friends in Sweden, then a major power in European politics. They established a New Sweden Company and, following much negotiation, Minuit led a group under the flag of Sweden to the Delaware River in 1638. They established a trading post at Fort Christina, now in Wilmington, Delaware. Minuit claimed possession of the western side of the Delaware River, saying he had found no European settlement there. Unlike the Dutch West India Company, the Swedes intended to actually bring settlers to their outpost and begin a colony.

Minuit drowned in a hurricane on the way home that same year, but the Swedish colony continued to grow gradually. By 1644 Swedish and Finnish settlers were living along the western side of Delaware River from Fort Christina to the Schuylkill River. New Sweden's best known governor, Johan Björnsson Printz, moved his residence to what is now Tinicum Township, Pennsylvania, nearer the center of the settlements.

The Dutch never gave up their claim to the area, however, and under Peter Stuyvesant they attacked the Swedish communities and in 1655 reincorporated the area back into New Netherland. Before long though, the Dutch as well were forcibly removed by the British, asserting their earlier claim. In 1664, James, the Duke of York, and brother of King Charles II, outfitted an expedition that easily ousted the Dutch from both the Delaware and Hudson Rivers and leaving the Duke of York the proprietary authority in the whole area.

British colonial period

Main article: Province of Pennsylvania

On March 4, 1681, Charles II of England granted a land tract to William Penn for the area that now includes Pennsylvania because of a £16,000 (around £2,100,000 in 2008, adjusting for retail inflation) debt the King owed to William's father. Penn then founded a colony there as a place of religious freedom for Quakers, and named it for the Latin *sylvania* meaning "woods".

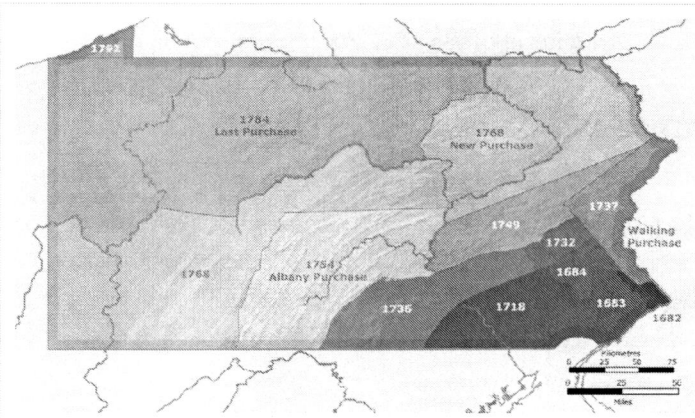

Land purchases from Native Americans.

A large tract of land north and west of Philadelphia, in Montgomery, Chester, and Delaware Counties, was settled by Welsh Quakers and called the "Welsh Tract". Even today many cities and towns in that area bear the names of Welsh municipalities.

The colony's reputation of religious freedom also attracted significant populations of German and Scots-Irish settlers who helped to shape colonial Pennsylvania and later went on to populate the neighboring states further west.

In order to give his new province access to the ocean, Penn had leased the proprietary rights of the King's brother, James, Duke of York to what became known as the "three lower counties" on the Delaware. The Province of Pennsylvania was never merged with the Lower Counties because the Duke of York, and therefore Penn, never had a clear title to it. He did govern them both, however, and his deputy governors were assigned to both as well. In Penn's *Frame of Government of 1682*, he tried to establish a combined assembly by providing for equal membership from each county and requiring legislation to have the assent of both the Lower Counties and the Upper Counties of Chester, Philadelphia and Bucks. The meeting place also alternated between Philadelphia and New Castle. Once Philadelphia began to grow its leaders resented having to go to New Castle and gain agreement of the assemblymen from the sparsely populated Lower Counties and so there was a mutual agreement in 1704 for the two assemblies to meet separately from thenceforth.

French and Indian War

Further information: Great Britain in the Seven Years War

The western portions of Pennsylvania were among disputed territory between the colonial British and French during the French and Indian War. The French established numerous fortifications in the area, including the pivotal Fort Duquesne on top of which the city of Pittsburgh was built. Britain's victory in the war secured Pennsylvania's frontier, as the Ohio Country came under formal British control following the Treaty of Paris in 1763. Shortly after this Pontiac's Rebellion began, which led to the British government passing the Proclamation Act barring any further settlement west of a certain point.

American Revolution

See: Battle of Brandywine, Battle of Germantown, Valley Forge.

Most of Pennsylvania's residents generally supported the protests and dismay common to all 13 colonies after the Proclamation of 1763 and the Stamp Act. Pennsylvanians originally supported the idea of common action, and sent delegates to the Stamp Act Congress in 1765. When difficulties continued, they sent delegates to the first Continental Congress and its later meetings, and even hosted the Congress in Philadelphia.

Statehood and constitutional government

After elections in May 1776 returned old guard Assemblymen to office, the Second Continental Congress encouraged Pennsylvania to call delegates together to discuss a new form of governance. Delegates met in June in Philadelphia, where events (the signing of the Declaration of Independence) soon overtook Assemblymen's efforts to control the delegates and the outcome of their discussions. On July 8 attendees elected delegates to write a state constitution. A Committee was formed with Benjamin Franklin as chair and George Bryan and James Cannon as prominent members. The convention proclaimed a new constitution on September 28, 1776 and called for new elections.

Elections later in 1776 turned out the old Assemblymen out from power. But the new constitution was problematic as it was possibly too democratic in its lack of a governor or upper legislative house to provide checks against popular movements. It also required test oaths, which kept the opposition from taking office. The constitution called for a unicameral legislature or Assembly. Executive authority rested in a *Supreme Executive Council* whose members were to be appointed by the assembly. In elections during 1776 radicals gained control of the Assembly. By early 1777, they selected an executive council, and Thomas Wharton, Jr. was named as the President of the Council. This constitution was never formally adopted, so government was on an ad-hoc basis until a new constitution could be written fourteen years later.

Pennsylvania ratified the U.S. Constitution at the Philadelphia Convention on December 12, 1787, the second state to do so after Delaware. The state's name is spelled "Pensylvania" in the Constitution. A new state constitution was formed in 1790.

Westward expansion and land speculation

After Revolutionary war soldiers received depreciation land grants for military service, the Pennsylvania General Assembly passed a general land act on April 3, 1792 authorizing the sale and distribution of the large remaining tracts of land east and west of the Allegheny River in hopes of sparking development of the vast territory. The process was an uneven affair prompting much speculation but little settlement, with most soldiers selling their shares sight unseen under market value and many investors were ultimately ruined. East Allegheny district consisted of lands in Potter, McKean, Cameron, Elk, and Jefferson counties, at the time worthless tracts. West Allegheny district was made up of lands in Erie, Crawford, Warren, and Venango counties, relatively good investments at the time. Three great land companies participated in the land speculation that followed. Holland Land Company and its agent, Theophilus Cazenove, acquired 1000000 acres (4000 km^2) of East Allegheny district land and 500000 acres (2000 km^2) of West Allegheny land from Pennsylvania Supreme Court Justice James Wilson. The Pennsylvania Population Company and its President, Pennsylvania State Comptroller General John Nicholson, controlled 500000 acres (2000 km^2) of land, mostly in Erie County and the Beaver Valley. The North American Land Company and its patron, Robert Morris, held some Pennsylvania lands but was mostly vested in New York State.

Antebellum and Civil War

Main article: Pennsylvania in the American Civil War

Pennsylvania was the target of several raids by the Confederate States Army, including cavalry raids in 1862 and 1863 by J.E.B. Stuart, in 1863 by John Imboden, and in 1864 by John McCausland in which his troopers burned the city of Chambersburg.

Pennsylvania also saw the Battle of Gettysburg, near Gettysburg. Many historians consider this battle the major turning point of the American Civil War. Dead from this battle rest at Gettysburg National Cemetery, site of Abraham Lincoln's Gettysburg Address.

A number of smaller engagements were also fought in Pennsylvania, including the Battle of Hanover, Battle of Carlisle, Battle of Hunterstown, and the Battle of Fairfield, all during the Gettysburg Campaign.

Industrial Power, 1865-1900

In the latter half of the 19th century, the U.S. oil (kerosene) industry was born in western Pennsylvania, which supplied the vast majority of U.S. kerosene for years thereafter, and saw the rise and fall of oil boom towns, like Titusville. See the Pennsylvanian oil rush.

Ethnicity and Labor 1865-1945

During this time, America saw the arrival of millions of immigrants, mainly Europeans. Pennsylvania and New York received the bulk of them. Many of these poor immigrants took jobs in factories, steel mills, and coal mines throughout the state.

Depression and War 1929-1950

During the Depression, the Commonwealth attempted to fund public works through passage of the **Pennsylvania State Authority Act** in 1936. The Act caused the incorporation of the **General State Authority**, which would purchase land from the state and add improvements to that land using state loans and grants. The state expected to receive Federal grants and loans to fund the project. The Pennsylvania Supreme Court, in *Kelly v Earle*, found the Act violated the state constitution.

Decline of manufacturing and mining: 1950-75

During the 20th century Pennsylvania's existing iron industries expanded into a major center of steel production. Shipbuilding and numerous other forms of manufacturing

WPA poster 1935

flourished in the eastern part of the state, and coal mining was also extremely important in many regions. In the late 19th century and early 20th century, Pennsylvania received very large numbers of immigrants from Europe seeking work; dramatic, sometimes violent confrontations took place between organized labor and the state's industrial concerns. The state was hard-hit by the decline of the steel industry and other heavy U.S. industries during the late 20th century.

In 1962, the Republican party which had lost the two previous gubernatorial elections and seen the state's electoral votes go Democratic in the 1960 presidential election, became convinced that a moderate like Bill Scranton would have enough bipartisan appeal to revitalize the party. He ran for Governor of Pennsylvania against Richardson Dilworth, the mayor of Philadelphia. The ticket was balanced by having Raymond P. Shafer, who would succeed him as governor, as his running mate. After one of the most acrimonious campaigns in state history, the Scranton/Shafer team won a landslide victory in the election besting their opponents by nearly half a million votes out of just over than 6.6 million cast.

As governor 1963-67, Scranton signed into law sweeping reforms in the state's education system including creation of the state community college system, the state board of education, and the state Higher Education Assistance Agency. Furthermore, he created a program designed to promote the state in national and international markets and to increase the attractiveness of the state's products and services.

The Service State: 1975-Present

Pennsylvania has suffered severely from the fall of steel and coal. Economic failure, severe population loss in many areas, closed-up factories, and much more. However, beginning in the late 1970s, Pennsylvania began to turn around and make a recovery. At every new census, the state grew faster than the previous ten years. Many new immigrants, especially from Asia and Latin America, have arrived for many reasons. Dirty, lifeless towns have become vibrant, growing places. Jobs and companies have begun transferring their headquarters to the state, and Pennsylvania has one of the best economies in the nation. With the turnaround from manufacturing, the state has turned to service industries. Healthcare, retail, transportation, and tourism are some of the state's biggest industries of this era. Recent studies showed that in the next decade, Pennsylvania could have a population growth similar to that of Georgia currently.

Politics

Bob Casey was the governor, 1987-1995—Casey was an Irish American Democrat "pol" of the old school, the son and grandson of coal miners, who championed unions and believed in government as a beneficent force. Casey pushed through the legislature the "Pennsylvania Abortion Control Act," which placed limitations on abortion, including the notification of parents of minors, a twenty-four-hour waiting period, and a ban on partial-birth procedures except in cases of risk to the mother's life. Planned Parenthood of Southeastern Pennsylvania sued, with Casey as the named defendant, asserting that the law violated Roe v. Wade. The case went to the Supreme Court in April, 1992. The Court decided Planned Parenthood v. Casey on June 29, upholding all of Pennsylvania's contested restrictions but one (a requirement for spousal notification) and affirming the right of states to restrict abortions. At the national level Governor Casey was the most prominent pro-life Democrat and he demanded publicly to give a minority plank on abortion at the 1992 Democratic National Convention. He was refused, and protested loudly. In 1994, Casey refused to endorse Harris Wofford, the Democrat he had appointed to the Senate and who was running for re-election. The reason was Casey rejected Wofford's pro-choice views. The result was a deep split in the state Democratic party that helped elect conservative Republican Rick Santorum in 1994. Casey's critics within the Democratic Party accused him of treason. The Democratic divisiveness over abortion did not fade away seat so in 2006, five years after Casey's death, national Democratic leaders promoted Casey's son Bob Casey, Jr. for Senator as a way of defusing the issue and attracting disaffected pro-life Democrats; the son defeated Santorum by a landslide.

See also

Main article: Historical outline of Pennsylvania

- History of the Mid-Atlantic States
- History of the Northeastern United States
- History of Erie, Pennsylvania
- History of Harrisburg, Pennsylvania
- History of the Townships of Lycoming County, Pennsylvania
- History of Pittsburgh

- History of Philadelphia
- Pennsylvania Historical and Museum Commission
- Jewish history in Pennsylvania
- History of slavery in Pennsylvania
- History of Veterinary Medicine in Pennsylvania
- History of Williamsport, Pennsylvania

References

Surveys

- Miller, Randall M. and William A. Pencak, eds. *Pennsylvania: A History of the Commonwealth* (2002) detailed scholarly history
- Beers, Paul B. *Pennsylvania Politics Today and Yesterday* (1980)*
- Klein, Philip S and Ari Hoogenboom. *A History of Pennsylvania* (1973).
- Weigley, Russell. *Philadelphia: A 300-Year History* (1982)

Pre 1900

- Buck, Solon J., Clarence McWilliams and Elizabeth Hawthorn Buck. *The Planting of Civilization in Western Pennsylvania* (1939), social history online edition [1]
- Dunaway, Wayland F. *The Scotch-Irish of Colonial Pennsylvania* (1944) online edition [2]
- Higginbotham, Sanford W. *The Keystone in the Democratic Arch: Pennsylvania Politics, 1800-1816* (1952)
- Illick Joseph E. *Colonial Pennsylvania: A History* (1976) onlineedition [3]
- Ireland, Owen S. *Religion, Ethnicity, and Politics: Ratifying the Constitution in Pennsylvania* (1995)
- Kehl, James A. *Boss Rule in the Gilded Age: Matt Quay of Pennsylvania* (1981) onlineedition [4]
- Klees, Fredric. *The Pennsylvania Dutch* (1950)
- Klein, Philip Shriver. *Pennsylvania Politics, 1817-1832: A Game without Rules* (1940)
- McCullough, David. *The Johnstown Flood* (1987)
- Mueller, Henry R. *The Whig Party in Pennsylvania* (1922)
- Snyder, Charles Mccool. *The Jacksonian Heritage: Pennsylvania Politics, 1833-1848* (1958) online edition [5]
- William A. Sullivan; *The Industrial Worker in Pennsylvania, 1800-1840* Pennsylvania Historical and Museum Commission, 1955 online edition [6]

- Tinkcom, Harry Marlin. *The Republicans and Federalists in Pennsylvania, 1790-1801: A Study in National Stimulus and Local Response* (1950) online edition [7]
- Williamson, Harold F. and Arnold R. Daum. *The American Petroleum Industry: The Age of Illumination, 1859-1899* (1959)
- Wood, Ralph. et al. *The Pennsylvania Germans* (1942) online edition [8]
- Karin Wulf; *Not All Wives: Women of Colonial Philadelphia.* Cornell University Press, 2000 online edition [9]

Since 1900

- John Bodnar; *Immigration and Industrialization: Ethnicity in an American Mill Town, 1870–1940,* (1977), on Steelton online edition [10]
- Thomas Dublin and Walter Licht, *The Face of Decline: The Pennsylvania Anthracite Region in the Twentieth Century* Cornell University Press, (2005). ISBN 0-8014-8473-1.
- Kenneth J. Heineman; *A Catholic New Deal: Religion and Reform in Depression Pittsburgh,* 1999 online edition [11]
- Lamis, Renée M. *The Realignment of Pennsylvania Politics since 1960: Two-Party Competition in a Battleground State* (University Park: Pennsylvania State University Press, 2009) 398 pp. isbn 978-0-271-03419-5
- M. Nelson McGeary, *Gifford Pinchot: Forester-Politician* (1960) Republican governor 1923–1927 and 1931–1935
- Warren, Kenneth. *Big Steel: The First Century of the United States Steel Corporation, 1901-2001* (2002)

Primary sources

- Vincent P. Carocci, *A Capitol Journey: Reflections on the Press, Politics, and the Making Of Public Policy In Pennsylvania.* (2005) memoir by senior aide to Gov Casey in 1990s excerpts online [12]
- Casey, Robert P. *Fighting for Life: The Story of a Courageous Pro-Life Democrat Whose Own Brush with Death Made Medical History.* Dallas, Texas: Word Publishing (1996). Autobiography. Hardcover: ISBN 0-8499-1224-5, ISBN 978-0-8499-1224-5.
- W. E. B. Dubois; *The Philadelphia Negro: A Social Study* (1899) online edition [13]
- Albert Cook Myers; ed., *Narratives of Early Pennsylvania, West New Jersey and Delaware, 1630–1707,* (1912) online edition [14]

External links

- ExplorePAHistory.com [15]
- History of Pennsylvania on the Pennsylvania legislature site [16]
- Pennsylvania State Archives web site [17]
- View the Pennsylvania State Archives Online [18]
- Pennsylvania Historical and Museum Commission Publications [19]
- 1776 Constitution text [20]
- "Pennsylvania's Anarchist Experiment: 1681-1690," [21] Prof. Murray N. Rothbard, excerpt from *Conceived in Liberty*, Vol. 1 (Auburn, Alabama: The Ludwig von Mises Institute, 1999)
- Pennsylvania Indian Tribes [22] Listing of Native American tribes with a historical presence in Pennsylvania

List of towns and boroughs in Pennsylvania

List of towns and boroughs in Pennsylvania, arranged by type and in alphabetical order.

Towns

- Bloomsburg

Home Rule Municipalities

- City of Allentown (Lehigh County)
- Borough of Bellevue (Allegheny County)
- Borough of Bethel Park (Allegheny County)
- Borough of Bradford Woods (Allegheny County)
- Borough of Bryn Athyn (Montgomery County)
- Borough of Cambridge Springs (Crawford County)
- City of Carbondale (Lackawanna County)
- Borough of Chalfont (Bucks County)
- Township of Cheltenham (Montgomery County)
- City of Chester (Delaware County)
- Township of Chester (Delaware County)
- City of Clairton (Allegheny County)
- City of Coatesville (Chester County)
- City of DuBois (Clearfield County)
- Borough of Edinboro (Erie County)
- Elk Township (Chester County)

- City of Farell (Mercer County)
- Township of Ferguson (Centre County)
- City of Franklin (Venango County)
- City of Greensburg (Westmoreland County)
- Borough of Greentree (Allegheny County)
- Township of Hampton (Allegheny County)
- Township of Hanover (Lehigh County)
- Township of Haverford (Delaware County)
- City of Hermitage (Mercer County)
- Township of Horsham (Montgomery County)
- City of Johnstown (Cambria County)
- Borough of Kingston (Luzerne County)
- Township of Kingston (Luzerne County)
- Borough of Latrobe (Westmoreland County)
- City of Lebanon (Lebanon County)
- Township of McCandless (Allegheny County)
- City of McKeesport (Allegheny County)
- Middletown Township (Delaware County)
- Borough of Monroeville (Allegheny County)
- Township of Mount Lebanon (Allegheny County)
- Borough of Murrysville (Westmoreland County)
- Borough of Norristown (Montgomery County)
- Township of O'Hara (Allegheny County)
- Township of Penn Hills (Allegheny County)
- Township of Peters (Washington County)
- City of Philadelphia (Philadelphia County)
- Township of Pine (Allegheny County)
- City of Pittsburgh (Allegheny County)
- Township of Plymouth (Montgomery County)
- Portage Borough (Cambria County)
- Township of Radnor (Delaware County)
- City of Reading (Berks County)
- Township of Richland (Allegheny County)
- City of St. Marys (Elk County)
- Salisbury Township (Lehigh County)
- City of Scranton (Lackawanna County)
- Borough of State College (Centre County)
- Township of Tredyffrin (Chester County)

- Borough of Tyrone (Blair County)
- Township of Upper Darby (Delaware County)
- Township of Upper Providence (Delaware County)
- Township of Upper St. Clair(Allegheny County)
- City of Warren (Warren County)
- Borough of West Chester (Chester County)
- Township of West Deer (Allegheny County)
- Borough of Whitehall (Allegheny County)
- Whitehall Township (Lehigh County)
- Township of Whitemarsh (Montgomery County)
- City of Wilkes-Barre (Luzerne County)
- Township of Wilkes-Barre (Luzerne County)
- Borough of Youngsville (Warren County)

Boroughs

Contents: Top · 0–9 · A B C D E F G H I J K L M N O P Q R S T U V W X Y Z

A

- Abbottstown
- Adamsburg
- Adamstown
- Addison
- Akron
- Alba
- Albion
- Alburtis
- Aldan
- Alexandria
- Allenport
- Ambler
- Ambridge
- Apollo
- Applewold
- Archbald
- Arendtsville
- Armagh

- Arona
- Ashland
- Ashley
- Ashville
- Aspinwall
- Atglen
- Athens
- Atwood
- Auburn
- Austin
- Avalon
- Avis
- Avoca
- Avondale
- Avonmore

B

- Baden
- Baldwin
- Bally
- Bangor
- Barkeyville
- Bath
- Beallsville
- Bear Creek Village
- Bear Lake
- Beaver
- Beaver Meadows
- Beavertown
- Bechtelsville
- Bedford
- Beech Creek
- Bell Acres
- Bellefonte
- Belle Vernon
- Bellevue
- Bellwood

- Ben Avon
- Ben Avon Heights
- Bendersville
- Benson
- Bentleyville
- Benton
- Berlin
- Bernville
- Berrysburg
- Berwick
- Bessemer
- Bethany
- Bethel Park
- Big Beaver
- Biglerville
- Big Run
- Birdsboro
- Birmingham
- Blain
- Blairsville
- Blakely
- Blawnox
- Bloomfield
- Blooming Valley
- Blossburg
- Bolivar
- Bonneauville
- Boswell
- Bowmanstown
- Boyertown
- Brackenridge
- Braddock
- Braddock Hills
- Bradford Woods
- Brentwood
- Briar Creek
- Bridgeport
- Bridgeville

- Bridgewater
- Brisbin
- Bristol
- Broad Top City
- Brockway
- Brookhaven
- Brookville
- Brownstown
- Brownsville
- Bruin
- Burgettstown
- Burlington
- Burnham
- Burnside

C

- California
- Callensburg
- Callery
- Callimont
- Cambridge Springs
- Camp Hill
- Canonsburg
- Canton
- Carlisle
- Carmichaels
- Carnegie
- Carrolltown
- Carroll Valley
- Cassandra
- Casselman
- Cassville
- Castle Shannon
- Catasauqua
- Catawissa
- Centerport
- Centerville

- Centerville
- Central City
- Centralia
- Centre Hall
- Chalfant
- Chalfont
- Chambersburg
- Chapman
- Charleroi
- Cherry Tree
- Cherry Valley
- Chester Heights
- Chester Hill
- Chest Springs
- Cheswick
- Chicora
- Christiana
- Churchill
- Clarendon
- Clarion
- Clark
- Clarks Green
- Clarks Summit
- Clarksville
- Claysville
- Clearfield
- Cleona
- Clifton Heights
- Clintonville
- Clymer
- Coal Center
- Coaldale
- Coaldale
- Coalmont
- Coalport
- Cochranton
- Cokeburg
- Collegeville

- Collingdale
- Columbia
- Colwyn
- Confluence
- Conneaut Lake
- Conneautville
- Connoquenessing
- Conshohocken
- Conway
- Conyngham
- Coopersburg
- Cooperstown
- Coplay
- Coraopolis
- Cornwall
- Corsica
- Coudersport
- Courtdale
- Crafton
- Cranesville
- Creekside
- Cresson
- Cressona
- Cross Roads
- Curwensville

D

- Daisytown
- Dale
- Dallas
- Dallastown
- Dalton
- Danville
- Darby
- Darlington
- Dauphin
- Dawson

- Dayton
- Deemston
- Deer Lake
- Delaware Water Gap
- Delmont
- Delta
- Denver
- Derry
- Dickson City
- Dillsburg
- Donegal
- Donora
- Dormont
- Dover
- Downingtown
- Doylestown
- Dravosburg
- Driftwood
- Dublin
- Duboistown
- Dudley
- Dunbar
- Duncannon
- Duncansville
- Dunlevy
- Dunmore
- Dupont
- Duryea
- Dushore

E

- Eagles Mere
- East Bangor
- East Berlin
- East Brady
- East Butler
- East Conemaugh
- East Greenville
- East Lansdowne
- East McKeesport
- East Petersburg
- East Pittsburgh
- East Prospect
- East Rochester
- East Side
- East Stroudsburg
- Eastvale
- East Vandergrift
- East Washington
- Eau Claire
- Ebensburg
- Economy
- Eddystone
- Edgewood
- Edgeworth
- Edinboro
- Edwardsville
- Ehrenfeld
- Elco
- Elderton
- Eldred
- Elgin
- Elizabeth
- Elizabethtown
- Elizabethville
- Elkland
- Ellport
- Ellsworth

- Ellwood City
- Elverson
- Emlenton
- Emmaus
- Emporium
- Emsworth
- Enon Valley
- Ephrata
- Erwinna
- Ernest
- Etna
- Evans City
- Everett
- Everson
- Exeter
- Export

F

- Factoryville
- Fairchance
- Fairfield
- Fairview
- Falls Creek
- Fallston
- Fawn Grove
- Fayette City
- Felton
- Ferndale
- Finleyville
- Fleetwood
- Flemington
- Folcroft
- Ford City
- Ford Cliff
- Forest City
- Forest Hills
- Forksville

- Forty Fort
- Fountain Hill
- Foxburg
- Fox Chapel
- Frackville
- Frankfort Springs
- Franklin
- Franklin Park
- Franklintown
- Fredonia
- Freeburg
- Freedom
- Freeland
- Freemansburg
- Freeport
- Friendsville

G

- Galeton
- Gallitzin
- Garrett
- Geistown
- Georgetown
- Gettysburg
- Gilberton
- Girard
- Girardville
- Glasgow
- Glassport
- Glen Campbell
- Glendon
- Glenfield
- Glen Hope
- Glenolden
- Glen Rock
- Goldsboro
- Gordon

- Grampian
- Gratz
- Great Bend
- Greencastle
- Green Hills
- Green Lane
- Greensboro
- Green Tree
- Greenville
- Grove City

H

- Halifax
- Hallam
- Hallstead
- Hamburg
- Hanover
- Harmony
- Harrisville
- Hartleton
- Harveys Lake
- Hastings
- Hatboro
- Hatfield
- Hawley
- Hawthorn
- Haysville
- Heidelberg
- Hellertown
- Herndon
- Highspire
- Hollidaysburg
- Homer City
- Homestead
- Homewood
- Honesdale
- Honey Brook

- Hookstown
- Hooversville
- Hop Bottom
- Hopewell
- Houston
- Houtzdale
- Howard
- Hughestown
- Hughesville
- Hulmeville
- Hummelstown
- Hunker
- Huntingdon
- Hyde Park
- Hydetown
- Hyndman

I

- Indiana
- Indian Lake
- Industry
- Ingram
- Irvona
- Irwin
- Ivyland

J

- Jackson Center
- Jacobus
- Jamestown
- Jeddo
- Jefferson
- Jefferson Hills
- Jenkintown
- Jennerstown
- Jermyn
- Jersey Shore

- Jessup
- Jim Thorpe
- Johnsonburg
- Jonestown, Lebanon County
- Juniata Terrace

K

- Kane
- Karns City
- Kenhorst
- Kennett Square
- Kingston
- Kistler
- Kittanning
- Knox
- Knoxville
- Koppel
- Kulpmont
- Kutztown

L

- Laceyville
- Laflin
- Lake City
- Landingville
- Landisburg
- Lanesboro
- Langhorne
- Langhorne Manor
- Lansdale
- Lansdowne
- Lansford
- Laporte
- Larksville
- Laureldale
- Laurel Mountain
- Laurel Run

- Lawrenceville
- Leechburg
- Leesport
- Leetsdale
- Lehighton
- Lemoyne
- Lenhartsville
- Le Raysville
- Lewisberry
- Lewisburg
- Lewis Run
- Lewistown
- Liberty
- Ligonier
- Lilly
- Lincoln
- Linesville
- Lititz
- Little Meadows
- Littlestown
- Liverpool
- Loganton
- Loganville
- Long Branch
- Lorain
- Loretto
- Lumber City
- Luzerne
- Lykens
- Lyons

M

- McAdoo
- McClure
- McConnellsburg
- McDonald
- McEwensville
- McKean
- McKees Rocks
- McSherrystown
- Macungie
- McVeytown
- Madison
- Mahaffey
- Mahanoy City
- Malvern
- Manchester
- Manheim
- Manns Choice
- Manor
- Manorville
- Mansfield
- Mapleton
- Marcus Hook
- Marianna
- Marietta
- Marion Center
- Marion Heights
- Marklesburg
- Markleysburg
- Mars
- Martinsburg
- Marysville
- Masontown
- Matamoras
- Mayfield
- Mechanicsburg
- Mechanicsville
- Media

- Mercer
- Mercersburg
- Meshoppen
- Meyersdale
- Middleburg
- Middleport
- Middletown
- Midland
- Midway
- Mifflin
- Mifflinburg
- Mifflintown
- Milesburg
- Milford
- Millbourne
- Mill Creek
- Millersburg
- Millerstown
- Millersville
- Mill Hall
- Millheim
- Millvale
- Mill Village
- Millville
- Milton
- Minersville
- Modena
- Mohnton
- Monaca
- Monroe
- Mont Alto
- Montgomery
- Montoursville
- Montrose
- Moosic
- Morrisville
- Morton
- Moscow

- Mount Carbon
- Mount Carmel
- Mount Gretna
- Mount Holly Springs
- Mount Jewett
- Mount Joy
- Mount Lebanon
- Mount Oliver
- Mount Penn
- Mount Pleasant
- Mount Pocono
- Mount Union
- Mountville
- Mount Wolf
- Muncy
- Munhall
- Municipality of Monroeville
- Municipality of Murrysville
- Myerstown

N

- Nanty-Glo
- Narberth
- Nazareth
- Nescopeck
- Nesquehoning
- New Albany
- New Alexandria
- New Baltimore
- New Beaver
- New Berlin
- New Bethlehem
- New Brighton
- New Britain
- New Buffalo
- Newburg
- Newburg

- New Centerville
- New Columbus
- New Cumberland
- New Eagle
- Newell
- New Florence
- New Freedom
- New Galilee
- New Holland
- New Hope
- New Lebanon
- New Milford
- New Morgan
- New Oxford
- New Paris
- New Philadelphia
- Newport
- New Ringgold
- Newry
- New Salem
- New Stanton
- Newton Hamilton
- Newtown
- Newville
- New Washington
- New Wilmington
- Nicholson
- Northampton
- North Apollo
- North Belle Vernon
- North Braddock
- North Catasauqua
- North Charleroi
- North East
- Northern Cambria
- North Irwin
- Northumberland
- North Wales

- North York
- Norwood
- Nuangola

O

- Oakdale
- Oakland
- Oakmont
- Ohiopyle
- Ohioville
- Oklahoma
- Old Forge
- Olyphant
- Orangeville
- Orbisonia
- Orrstown
- Orwigsburg
- Osborne
- Osceola Mills
- Oswayo
- Oxford

P

- Paint
- Palmerton
- Palmyra
- Palo Alto
- Parkesburg
- Parkside
- Parryville
- Patterson Heights
- Patton
- Paxtang
- Pen Argyl
- Penbrook
- Penn
- Penn Hills

- Penndel
- Penn Lake Park
- Pennsburg
- Pennsbury Village
- Perkasie
- Perryopolis
- Petersburg
- Petrolia
- Philipsburg
- Phoenixville
- Picture Rocks
- Pillow
- Pine Grove
- Pitcairn
- Platea
- Pleasant Hills
- Pleasantville
- Pleasantville
- Plum
- Plumville
- Plymouth
- Point Marion
- Polk
- Portage
- Port Allegany
- Port Carbon
- Port Clinton
- Portersville
- Portland
- Port Matilda
- Port Royal
- Port Vue
- Pottstown
- Pringle
- Prompton
- Prospect
- Prospect Park
- Punxsutawney

Q

- Quakertown
- Quarryville

R

- Railroad
- Rainsburg
- Ramey
- Rankin
- Red Hill
- Red Lion
- Renovo
- Reynoldsville
- Rices Landing
- Richland
- Richlandtown
- Ridgway
- Ridley Park
- Riegelsville
- Rimersburg
- Ringtown
- Riverside
- Roaring Spring
- Robesonia
- Rochester
- Rockhill Furnace
- Rockledge
- Rockwood
- Rome
- Roscoe
- Roseto
- Rose Valley
- Roseville
- Rosslyn Farms
- Rouseville
- Royalton
- Royersford

- Rural Valley
- Rutledge

S

- Saegertown
- St. Clair
- St. Clairsville
- St. Lawrence
- St. Petersburg
- Salisbury
- Salladasburg
- Saltillo
- Saltsburg
- Sandy Lake
- Sankertown
- Saxonburg
- Saxton
- Sayre
- Scalp Level
- Schellsburg
- Schuylkill Haven
- Schwenksville
- Scottdale
- Selinsgrove
- Sellersville
- Seven Fields
- Seven Springs
- Seven Valleys
- Seward
- Sewickley
- Sewickley Heights
- Sewickley Hills
- Shade Gap
- Shamokin Dam
- Shanksville
- Sharon Hill
- Sharpsburg

- Sharpsville
- Sheakleyville
- Shelocta
- Shenandoah
- Shickshinny
- Shillington
- Shinglehouse
- Shippensburg
- Shippenville
- Shippingport
- Shiremanstown
- Shirleysburg
- Shoemakersville
- Shrewsbury
- Silverdale
- Sinking Spring
- Slatington
- Sligo
- Slippery Rock
- Smethport
- Smicksburg
- Smithfield
- Smithton
- Snow Shoe
- S.N.P.J.
- Snydertown
- Somerset
- Souderton
- South Bethlehem
- South Coatesville
- South Connellsville
- South Fork
- South Greensburg
- South Heights
- Southmont
- South New Castle
- South Philipsburg
- South Renovo

- South Waverly
- Southwest Greensburg
- South Williamsport
- Spartansburg
- Speers
- Springboro
- Spring City
- Springdale
- Spring Grove
- Starrucca
- State College
- Steelton
- Stewartstown
- Stillwater
- Stockdale
- Stockertown
- Stoneboro
- Stoystown
- Strasburg
- Strattanville
- Strausstown
- Stroudsburg
- Sugarcreek
- Sugar Grove
- Sugar Notch
- Summerhill
- Summerville
- Summit Hill
- Susquehanna Depot
- Sutersville
- Swarthmore
- Swissvale
- Swoyersville
- Sykesville
- Sylvania

T

- Tamaqua
- Tarentum
- Tatamy
- Taylor
- Telford
- Terre Hill
- Thompson
- Thompsontown
- Thornburg
- Three Springs
- Throop
- Tidioute
- Timblin
- Tioga
- Tionesta
- Topton
- Towanda
- Tower City
- Townville
- Trafford
- Trainer
- Trappe
- Tremont
- Trevose
- Troutville
- Troy
- Trumbauersville
- Tullytown
- Tunkhannock
- Tunnelhill
- Turbotville
- Turtle Creek
- Twilight
- Tyrone

U

- Uhlerstown
- Ulysses
- Union City
- Union Dale
- Unionville
- Upland
- Upper Black Eddy
- Ursina
- Utica

V

- Valencia
- Valley-Hi
- Vanderbilt
- Vandergrift
- Vandling
- Venango
- Verona
- Versailles
- Vintondale
- Volant

W

- Wall
- Wallaceton
- Walnutport
- Wampum
- Warrior Run
- Washingtonville
- Waterford
- Watsontown
- Wattsburg
- Waymart
- Waynesboro
- Waynesburg

- Weatherly
- Weissport
- Wellersburg
- Wellsboro
- Wellsville
- Wernersville
- Wesleyville
- West Alexander
- West Brownsville
- West Chester
- West Conshohocken
- West Easton
- West Elizabeth
- Westfield
- West Grove
- West Hazleton
- West Homestead
- West Kittanning
- West Lawn
- West Leechburg
- West Liberty
- West Mayfield
- West Middlesex
- West Middletown
- West Mifflin
- Westmont
- West Newton
- Westover
- West Pittston
- West Reading
- West Sunbury
- West View
- West Wyoming
- West York
- Wheatland
- Whitaker
- Whitehall
- White Haven

- White Oak
- Wilkinsburg
- Williamsburg
- Williamstown
- Wilmerding
- Wilmore
- Wilson
- Windber
- Wind Gap
- Windsor
- Winterstown
- Womelsdorf
- Woodbury
- Woodcock
- Wormleysburg
- Worthington
- Worthville
- Wrightsville
- Wyalusing
- Wyoming
- Wyomissing
- Wyomissing Hills

Y

- Yardley
- Yatesville
- Yeadon
- Yoe
- Yorkana
- York Haven
- York Springs
- Youngstown
- Youngsville
- Youngwood

Z

• Zelienople

See also

• Pennsylvania
• List of cities in Pennsylvania
• List of cities in the United States
• List of townships in Pennsylvania
• List of places in Pennsylvania

List of cities in Pennsylvania

List of the 57 cities in Pennsylvania, arranged in alphabetical order.

Contents: Top · 0–9 · A B C D E F G H I J K L M N O P Q R S T U V W X Y Z

A

• Aliquippa
• Allentown
• Altoona
• Arnold

B

• Beaver Falls
• Bethlehem
• Bradford
• Butler
• Boiling Springs

C

- Carbondale
- Chester
- Clairton
- Coatesville
- Connellsville
- Corry

D

- DuBois
- Duquesne

E

- Easton
- Erie

Ellwood City

F

- Farrell
- Franklin (Venango County)

G

- Greensburg

H

- Harrisburg
- Hazleton
- Hermitage
- Hershey

J

- Jeannette
- Johnstown

L

- Lancaster
- Latrobe
- Lebanon
- Levittown
- Lock Haven
- Lower Burrell

M

- McKeesport
- Meadville
- Monessen
- Monongahela
- Morrisville

N

- Nanticoke
- New Castle
- New Kensington

O

- Oil City

P

- Parker
- Philadelphia
- Pittsburgh
- Pittston
- Pottsville

R

- Reading

S

- St. Marys
- Scranton
- Shamokin
- Sharon
- Sunbury

T

- Titusville

U

- Uniontown

W

- Warren
- Washington
- Wilkes-Barre
- Williamsport

Y

- York

See also

- Pennsylvania
- List of towns and boroughs in Pennsylvania
- List of places in Pennsylvania
- List of Ghost Towns in Pennsylvania

Education in Pennsylvania

There are numerous elementary, secondary, and higher institutions of learning in Pennsylvania. Pennsylvania is home to 501 public school districts, thousands of private schools, many publicly funded colleges and universities, and over 100 private institutions of higher education.

In general, under state law, school attendance in Pennsylvania is mandatory for a child from the age of 8 until the age of 17, or until graduation from an accredited high school, whichever is earlier.

As of 2005, 83.8% of Pennsylvania residents age 18 to 24 have completed high school. Among residents age 25 and over, 86.7% have graduated from high school. Additionally, 25.7% have gone on to obtain a bachelor's degree or higher.

Primary and Secondary Education

See Also: List of school districts in Pennsylvania or List of high schools in Pennsylvania

Pennsylvania's public schools are operated and funded under the authority of the General Assembly and local school boards, whose members are elected. There are many types of public schools, including elementary, intermediate, middle school, junior high, high, junior-senior high, vocational-technical, and charter schools. Each public school is headed by a school principal, who reports to the superintendent of schools appointed by the board of the school district.

There are 500 public school districts in Pennsylvania, consisting of 3,287 schools and 120 charter schools. Two school districts do not have high schools. As of the 2005-2006 school year, there were 1,871,060 students enrolled in public schools in Pennsylvania, of whom 74.6% were Caucasian, 15.9% were African-American, 6.8% were Hispanic, 2.6% were Asian/Pacific Islander, and 0.2% were Native Americans. The average per pupil expenditure was $10,738, and the pupil/teacher ratio was 15.2:1.

As of the 2007-2008 school year, there were 265,545 students enrolled in private K-12 schools in Pennsylvania.

State students consistently do well in standardized testing. In 2007, Pennsylvania ranked 14th in mathematics, 12th in reading, and 10th in writing for 8th grade students.

In 2004-2005, Pennsylvania elementary and secondary schools ranked 8th in revenue and 11th in spending out of 50 states and the federal district. In 2009 Pennsylvania spends $25 billion dollars in public education when federal, state and local taxation dollars are combined.

Approved Private Schools and Charter Schools for the Blind and Deaf

The Commonwealth of Pennsylvania has 36 Approved Private Schools including the Charter Schools for the Blind and Deaf. Students attending these schools come from across the commonwealth. The private schools are licensed by the State Board of Private Academic Schools. They provide a free appropriate special education for students with severe disabilities. The cost of tuition for these schools is paid 60% by the state and 40% by the local school district where the student is a resident. Pennsylvania currently has four PA chartered and 30 non-charter APSs for which the Department approves funding. These schools provide a program of special education for over 4,000 day and residential students. Parents are not charged for the services at the school. The majority of these schools are located in the southeastern region and southwestern region of Pennsylvania.

Public Cyber Charter Schools

In 2009 there are 11 public cyber charter schools available to Pennsylvania students K-12. These public schools receive funding from the state and federal government. Students attend through online enrollment. The local school district remits the payment for the tuition costs. Cyber school students are provided with a computer, books and materials by the cyber school entity. The students meet the same academic requirements, under No Child Left Behind, as traditional bricks and mortar schools.

In 2006-07, there were approximately 15,838 Pennsylvania students enrolled in cyber charter schools. The cyber charter schools are required to submit annual reports to the Pennsylvania Department of Education

By Pennsylvania law, all K-12 students in the district, including those who attend a private nonpublic school, cyber charter school, charter school and those homeschooled, are eligible to participate in the extracurricular programs including all athletics. They must meet the same eligibility rules as the students enrolled in the district's schools.

Dual enrollment

The state's Dual Enrollment program permits high school students to take courses, at local higher education institutions, to earn college credits. Students remain enrolled at their high school. The courses count towards high school graduation requirements and towards earning a college degree. The students continue to have full access to activities and programs at the high school, including the graduation ceremony. The college credits are offered at a deeply discounted rate. The state offers a small grant to assist students in costs for tuition, fees and books. The amount of funding for the district varies widely across the Commonwealth. Under the Pennsylvania Transfer and Articulation Agreement, many Pennsylvania colleges and universities accept these credits for students who transfer to their institutions. Over 400 schools district offered this program in 2009.

Sports

Many schools participate in intramural sports, and most outside competitions are sponsored by the Pennsylvania Interscholastic Athletic Association, which hosts 23 statewide championships in 16 different sports.

Academic Achievement Assessment

Each year, the state conducts a series of tests (called assessments) to evaluate the progress students are making in attaining essential content and skills. All public schools including: school districts, charter schools and cyber charter schools are required to participate. Some private schools have elected to participate.

The PSSAs began in 1998 as a state education initiative. Reading and mathematics were tested in 5th, 8 and 11th grades. With the passage of No Child Left Behind, the state added reading and mathematics testing in 3rd, 4th, 6th, and 7th grades. The content of the tests are based on the Pennsylvania Academic Standards. A writing assessment was added that examines student skills in informational writing and persuasive writing. The schools were provided with a writing rubric and sample prompts to guide their instruction along with specialized training for teachers. In 2007, the science tests were administered to 4th, 8th and 11th grades. The results were provided to the schools, but not made public. Beginning in 2008, the science test results were made public.

Results on the PSSAs are reported as: Advanced, Proficient, Basic and Below Basic. The scores that constitute each level were established by working groups of Pennsylvania teachers when the examines are developed. The Pennsylvania Department of Education reports these results to the schools and each student's parents. Additionally, they PDE reports them to the community via an Academic Achievement Report Card website. These results are reported for the entire state, by each school district, by each school, by each grade in that school and by subgroups. These subgroups include: race, gender, student's family income, special needs and English language learners. The report cards also provide graduation rates for each school district, school attendance rates and teacher qualifications.

Beginning in 2009, the Department of Education began reporting the results for each individual student as a part of the PVAAS report. (Pennsylvania Value Added Assessment System). This permits the state, the school district and the school to track each student's progress from one year to the next. Growth in achievement, regardless of the level of proficiency reached, is the focus of this assessment system. When students make 10% progress over last year, the school is credited with adequate yearly progress.

2009 State wide Graduation Rate and Attendance Rate

All Students - 89%, Attendance rate - 94%

Males - 88%, Attendance rate - 94%

Females - 91%, Attendance rate - 94%

White - 93%, Attendance rate - 95%

Black - 77%, Attendance rate - 91%

Latino/Hispanic - 72%, Attendance rate - 92%

Asian - 93%, Attendance rate - 96%

Native American - 83%, Attendance rate - 92%

Individual Education Plan - 83%, Attendance rate - 92%

(Special needs) English Language Learners - 73%, Attendance rate - 93%

Economically disadvantaged - 79%, Attendance rate - 92%

State wide Reading 11th grade results

2009 - 65% on grade level

2008 - 65%

2007 - 65%

2006 - 65%

2005 - 65%

2004 - 61%

State wide Math 11th grade results

2009 - 56% on grade level

2008 - 56%

2007 - 53%

2006 - 52%

2005 - 51%

2004 - 49%

College Remediation

According to a Pennsylvania Department of Education study released in January 2009, more than 40% of Pennsylvania high schools' graduates required remediation in mathematics and reading before they were prepared to take college level courses in the Pennsylvania State System of Higher Education or community colleges.

College Graduation Rate

Less than 66% of Pennsylvania high school graduates, who enroll in a four-year college in Pennsylvania, earn a bachelor's degree within six years. Among Pennsylvania high school graduates pursuing an associate degree, only one in three graduate in three years. Per the Pennsylvania Department of Education, one in three recent high school graduates who attend Pennsylvania's public universities and community colleges takes at least one remedial course in math, reading or English.

Homeschooling

In 1988, the Pennsylvania General Assembly passed Act 169, which allows parents or guardians to homeschool their children as an option for compulsory school attendance. This law specifies the requirements and responsibilities of the parents and the school district where the family lives.

Higher education

See Also: List of colleges and universities in Pennsylvania

There are dozens of notable private liberal arts colleges and universities located throughout Pennsylvania, as well as many publicly supported community colleges and universities. The state provides funding to (1) the Commonwealth System of Higher Education, consisting of four universities; (2) the Pennsylvania State System of Higher Education, consisting of 14 universities; and (3) 14 community colleges.

Commonwealth System of Higher Education

The Commonwealth System of Higher Education consists of four prominent universities, which are publicly supported but are operated and controlled independently. These institutions are:

- Lincoln University (Pennsylvania), which serves approximately 2,000 students.
- Pennsylvania State University, one of the ten largest public universities in the United States, which serves more than 84,000 undergraduate and graduate students at 24 campuses, the largest of which is in State College, Pennsylvania.
- Temple University, which serves over 34,000 undergraduate and graduate students on several campuses in the Greater Philadelphia area.
- University of Pittsburgh, which serves approximately 34,000 undergraduate and graduate students in western Pennsylvania.

Pennsylvania State System of Higher Education

The Pennsylvania State System of Higher Education consists of 14 universities in which more than 112,500 students are enrolled. It is led by a 20-member Board of Governors, each of whom serves a four-year term, with the exception of three students, who are chosen from among the universities' student government association presidents and serve until graduation. The members include individuals selected by the Governor of Pennsylvania, and four legislators chosen by the majority and minority leaders of the State Senate and House of Representatives. The Governor of Pennsylvania or a designee also is a Board member, as is the state Secretary of Education.

Community Colleges

Pennsylvania community colleges served 189,000 students in credit programs and over 256,000 students in non-credit programs during the 2005-2006 school year. On average, annual 2005-2006 tuition and fees were $2,327. Many community college students transfer to four-year programs at colleges and universities.

Financial Aid

The Pennsylvania Higher Education Assistance Agency is a financial aid organization which provides grants, administers loans, and affords other services to post-secondary students. The agency has consistently been listed by the U.S. Department of Education as having one of the lowest default rates among all major guarantors through its highly successful default prevention initiatives.

History

The fourth-oldest institution of higher learning in America, and arguably the oldest university, is the University of Pennsylvania, founded by Benjamin Franklin in 1740.

Data from the indentured servant contracts of German immigrant children in Pennsylvania from 1771-1817 showed that the number of children receiving education increased from 33.3% in 1771-1773 to 69% in 1787-1804. Additionally, the same data showed that the ratio of school education versus home education rose from .25 in 1771-1773 to 1.68 in 1787-1804. The increase in the number of children being educated, and the fact that more students were being educated in school rather than at home, could help explain how near-universal literacy was achieved by 1840.

Lincoln University, founded in 1854 and later named for President Abraham Lincoln, was the nation's first historically black university to provide arts and sciences education and degrees to African-American students.

Until the Civil War, almost all education was conducted either in private schools or at home. Public schools first came on the scene in the second half of the nineteenth century.

The forerunner to the Pennsylvania Department of Education was created in 1834. The State Board of Education, which adopts regulations for the Department, was created in 1963.

Governance

Many regulations and programs regarding elementary, secondary, and higher education are administered by the Pennsylvania Department of Education, which is led by the Secretary of Education appointed by the Governor and confirmed by the State Senate.

The current Secretary of Education is Dr. Gerald L. Zahorchak, who was nominated by Governor Edward Rendell on October 5, 2005, and confirmed by the Senate on February 7, 2006. Dr. Zahorchak, a career educator, previously served as the deputy secretary for elementary and secondary education, and as the superintendent of the Greater Johnstown School District.

The State Board of Education is the principal administrative regulatory body for elementary, secondary, and higher education in the state. It has numerous responsibilities, including approving or disapproving an application for the creation of a new school district, or change in the boundaries of an existing school district; applying for and administering federal grants for education; adopting master plans for basic and higher education; and adopting policies for the Secretary of Education to apply in regulating schools and universities.

The State Board of Education has 22 members, ten of whom serve as the Board's Council of Basic Education and ten of whom serve on the Board's Council of Higher Education. Seventeen members are appointed by the Governor, with the approval of the Senate, and each serves a six-year term. Four members of the Board are members of the General Assembly who serve as long as they hold majority and minority chairs of the House and Senate Education Committees. The current chairperson of the State Board of Education, also appointed by the Governor, is Joe Torsella. The Secretary of Education serves as the chief executive officer of the Board and does not vote as a member of the Board.

The state is divided into 29 intermediate units, which provide services to the 501 public school districts and 2,400 non-public institutions.

State Education Budget

The state budget provides for extensive financing and regulation of education programs. The state budget allotted over $11.4 billion for education-related programs in the 2008-2009 fiscal year. Governor Rendell's proposed 2009-2010 budget suggests a 1.5% increase in education expenditures.

The Rendell Administration has successfully proposed a number of education-related programs, including funding of pre-kindergarten and full kindergarten education. On February 3, 2009, in his annual budget presentation, Governor Rendell proposed a tuition relief program to make college more affordable for Pennsylvania residents. The proposal would benefit families earning up to $100,000 a year who have students attending any of Pennsylvania's 14 community colleges or the 14 public universities in the Pennsylvania State System of Higher Education. When the proposal was made, Education Secretary Zahorchak stated that the plan would start in the fall of 2009 with incoming freshmen and benefit more than 170,000 students once it is fully implemented. He also predicted that the plan would help approximately 10,000 students who would not otherwise be able to afford college or who would leave Pennsylvania to attend college. The proposal suggests funding through revenues collected from the legalization and regulation of video poker in bars and clubs in Pennsylvania.

See also

- Pennsylvania Department of Education

Philadelphia Zoo

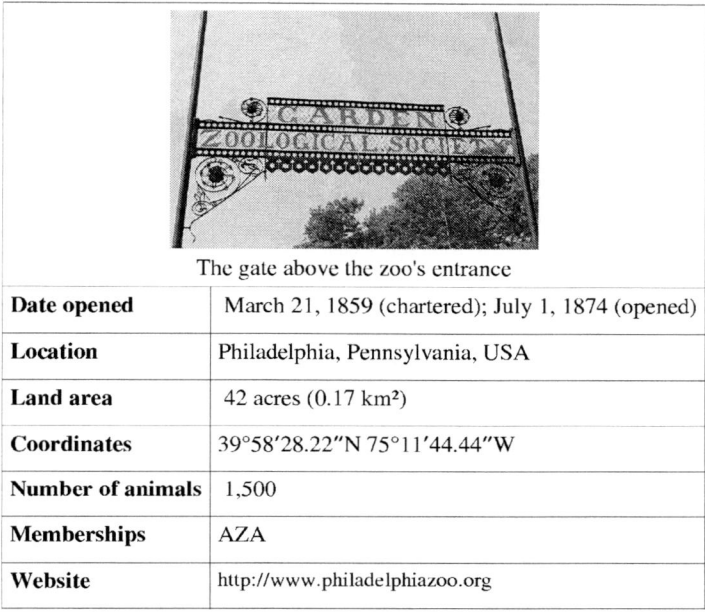

The gate above the zoo's entrance

Date opened	March 21, 1859 (chartered); July 1, 1874 (opened)
Location	Philadelphia, Pennsylvania, USA
Land area	42 acres (0.17 km²)
Coordinates	39°58′28.22″N 75°11′44.44″W
Number of animals	1,500
Memberships	AZA
Website	http://www.philadelphiazoo.org

The **Philadelphia Zoo**, located in Philadelphia, Pennsylvania, on the west bank of the Schuylkill River, was the first zoo in the United States. Chartered by the Commonwealth of Pennsylvania on March 21, 1859, its opening was delayed by the American Civil War until July 1, 1874. It opened with 1,000 animals and an admission price of 25 cents.

The Philadelphia Zoo is one of the premier zoos in the world for breeding animals that have been found difficult to breed in captivity. The zoo also works with many groups around the world to protect the natural habitats of the animals in their care.

The zoo is 42 acres (170000 m^2) and is home to more than 1,300 animals, many of which are rare and endangered. The zoo features a children's zoo, a balloon ride, a paddleboat lake, a rainforest themed carousel, and many interactive and educational exhibits.

Recent events

In the early morning of December 24, 1995, a fire in the *World of Primates* building killed 23 animals, including a family group of six lowland gorillas, a family group of three orangutans, four white-handed gibbons, and ten lemurs (two ruffed, six ringtail, and two mongoose). All were members of endangered species. The animals died in their sleep from smoke inhalation (carbon-monoxide poisoning); none were burned. Ten primates housed in an adjoining building, the Discovery House, survived. At the time of the fire, detection

Entrance

equipment existed in only 20% of the zoo buildings; the primates building, which had been constructed in 1985, was not one of them. In the ten months following the fire, the zoo installed fire detection equipment in all animal buildings.

On July 1, 1999, the zoo opened a new primate exhibit, the *PECO Primate Reserve*. It features 2.5 acres (10000 m^2) of indoor and outdoor exhibits with ten species of primates, including Sumatran Orangutans, lowland gorillas, lemurs, langurs, and gibbons.

In 2006 the zoo opened a new, $20-million big cat exhibit, **Big Cat Falls**, sponsored by Bank of America. Showcasing the animals in scenes reminiscent of their natural habitats, this exhibit allows visitors to get very close to the cats, sometimes separated only by a pane of glass. Visitors can see 12 endangered big cats from around the world, including three new snow leopard cubs, three new cougar kittens, and a new black jaguar cub.

The elephants at the Philadelphia Zoo have been phased out. In July 2009, the last two elephants, both African, departed.

On May 25, 2007, three Amur Tiger cubs were born at the Philadelphia Zoo to mother Kira and father Dmitri (also spelled "Dimitri"). The three female cubs, named Changbai, Koosaka, and Terney, were introduced to the public August 16, 2007.

On June 9, 2008, Petal, the oldest African elephant in a United States zoo, died at the age of 52.

On March 21, 2009, the zoo opened its 150th Anniversary Year-Long Celebrations.

On May 30, 2009, the zoo opened the McNeil Avian Center, a renovation of its classic bird house. It features two species that are extinct in the wild: the Guam Rail and the Micronesian Kingfisher. A theatre presents a fourteen-minute, 4D-movie about avian migration, following the migration of an animated oriole named Otis.

McNeil Avian Centre (photo June 2010)

On October 2, 2009, the Zoo welcomed a baby Sumatran Orangutan, subsequently named "Batu". Batu, a female, is the first-born child to 15-year-old father Sugi and 18-year-old mother Tua. She is also the first baby orangutan to be born in the PECO Primate Reserve, which opened in 1999. The Zoo, however, does have a history of successfully breeding orangutans, being the first zoo in the nation to have a successful birth in 1928.

On April 10, 2010, the Zoo's seasonal *"Creatures of Habitat"* opened, a unique exhibit featuring 9 animal stations throughout the Zoo, each featuring an endangered animal, and each consisting of statue(s) made completely out of Lego bricks. Each statue was created by Sean Kenney, the first of only nine LEGO-certified artists in the world.

On July 17, 2010, the Zoo welcomed a new female baby giraffe to first-time parents Stella, 7, and Gus, 4 after a gestation period of over 15 months. This is the first giraffe birth at the Philadelphia Zoo in over a decade.

Features of the zoo

- The Rare Animal Conservation Center: Interactive graphics and up-close views of some of the world's most endangered animals: giant Rodrigues fruit bats, naked mole rats, blue-eyed lemurs, tree-kangaroos, and more.
- The Reptile and Amphibian House: Features over 125 species of amphibians and reptiles, including giant tortoises and the venomous King Cobra.
- Small Mammal House: Features many species of small mammals, such as meerkats, echidnas, pygmy marmosets, vampire bats, and many others.
- McNeil Avian Center: An aviary finished in 2009 featuring many species of birds, mainly from Africa, the Pacific Islands, South America, and other places. Some species include the Micronesian

The Channel 6 Zooballoon above the Philadelphia Zoo with the pre-2008 balloon.

Kingfisher, Guam Rail, Rhinoceros Hornbill, Mariana Fruit Dove, Victoria Crowned Pigeon, and many others. There is also a 4-D Migration Theater telling the story of an oriole named Otis's migration.

- Bird Valley: A section near the McNeil Avian Center featuring an artificial creek running down a small hill. It's home to waterfowl, Humboldt penguins, flamingos,and Turkey vultures.
- Bank of America: Big Cat Falls: Features numerous species of wild cats including African Lions, Black Jaguars, Amur Tigers, and Pumas. It was in this area of the zoo that Rocky Balboa proposed to Adrian in Rocky II, although that original site, the Carnivora House, has been revamped and renovated into its current Big Cat Falls.
- Carnivore Kingdom: Features a family of six rare, playful Giant Otters, Snow Leopards, Red Pandas, and Canadian Lynx in unique naturalistic environments.
- African Plains: Features Ostriches, a White Rhino, Mhorr Gazelle, reticulated giraffes, an Addax, and zebras.
- Exotic South American animals: Features such animals as Giant Anteaters and capybaras.
- Educational programs are offered for children age three and older. Summer camps are offered for grade school aged children.
- The Animal Health Center: The Philadelphia Zoo hosts one of the nation's busiest and most comprehensive animal hospital and health-care facilities.
- The Channel 6 Zooballooon: a tethered helium balloon, rises 400 feet (120 m) in the air to offer a view of the Zoo, the Schuylkill River, and the Philadelphia Center City skyline. The balloon is sponsored, in part, by WPVI-TV.
- The only breeding giant otters in North America. The zoo was also the first to exhibit them in 1996 and the first and only to breed them in 2004.

Gallery

The zoo's welcome sign.

A flock of Flamingos.

A Cheetah in his enclosure.

A Pygmy Marmoset at the Small Mammals exhibit.

Polar bear inside her enclosure.

The WPVI Zoo Balloon, from ground level. In late 2008, the zoo changed the color and design of the balloon.

Red-shanked Douc

See also

- Fairmount Park

References

- Dewan, Vikram.*Best for the animals, best for the zoo* [1] *Philadelphia Daily News*, December 4, 2006, retrieved December 4, 2006.

External links

- Official website of "America's First Zoo" [2]
- Aerial photographs [3] at the Historic American Buildings Survey
- Listing and photographs [4] at the Historic American Buildings Survey

List of airports in Pennsylvania

This is a **list of airports in Pennsylvania** (a U.S. state), grouped by type and sorted by location. It contains all public-use and military airports in the state. Some private-use and former airports may be included where notable, such as airports that were previously public-use, those with commercial enplanements recorded by the FAA or airports assigned an IATA airport code.

Currently, Pennsylvania has 15 commercial airports, 106 general aviation airports, 7 general aviation heliports, 3 ultralight airports, 1 gliderport, and 2 general aviation seaplane bases. The largest commercial airline in Pennsylvania is US Airways. The airline has its largest hub at Philadelphia and majority operations in Pittsburgh and serves most of the other commercial airports in the state.

: Airports - See also - References

Airports

This list contains the following information:

- **City served** - The city generally associated with the airport. This is not always the actual location since some airports are located in smaller towns outside of the city they serve.
- **FAA** - The location identifier assigned by the Federal Aviation Administration (FAA). These are linked to each airport's page from the Pennsylvania Dept. of Transportation - Bureau of Aviation [1].
- **IATA** - The airport code assigned by the International Air Transport Association (IATA). Those that do not match the FAA code are shown in bold.
- **ICAO** - The location indicator assigned by the International Civil Aviation Organization (ICAO).
- **Airport name** - The official airport name. Those shown in bold indicate the airport has scheduled service on commercial airlines.
- **Role** - One of four FAA airport categories, as per the 2009-2013 National Plan of Integrated Airport Systems (NPIAS) Report:
  - P: *Commercial Service - Primary* are publicly owned airports that receive scheduled passenger service and have more than 10,000 passenger boardings (*enplanements*) each year. Each primary airport is sub-classified by the FAA as one of the following four "hub" types:
    - L: *Large Hub* that accounts for at least 1% of total U.S. passenger enplanements.
    - M: *Medium Hub* that accounts for between 0.25% and 1% of total U.S. passenger enplanements.
    - S: *Small Hub* that accounts for between 0.05% and 0.25% of total U.S. passenger enplanements.
    - N: *Non-Hub* that accounts for less than 0.05% of total U.S. passenger enplanements, but more than 10,000 annual enplanements.

- CS: *Commercial Service - Non-Primary* are publicly owned airports that receive scheduled passenger service and have at least 2,500 passenger boardings each year.
- R: *Reliever* airports are designated by the FAA to relieve congestion at a large commercial service airport and to provide more general aviation access to the overall community.
- GA: *General Aviation* airports are the largest single group of airports in the U.S. airport system.
- **Enpl**. - The number of *enplanements* (commercial passenger boardings) that occurred at the airport in calendar year 2008, as per FAA records.

City served	FAA IATA		ICAO	Airport name	Role	Enpl.
				Commercial Service - Primary Airports		
Allentown	ABE [2]	ABE	KABE	**Lehigh Valley International Airport**	P-S	392,039
Erie	ERI [3]	ERI	KERI	**Erie International Airport** (Tom Ridge Field)	P-N	124,667
Harrisburg / Middletown	MDT [4]	MDT	KMDT	**Harrisburg International Airport**	P-S	635,627
Latrobe	LBE [5]	LBE	KLBE	**Arnold Palmer Regional Airport**	P-N	18,946
Philadelphia	PHL [6]	PHL	KPHL	**Philadelphia International Airport**	P-L	15,586,852
Pittsburgh	PIT [7]	PIT	KPIT	**Pittsburgh International Airport**	P-M	4,292,546
State College	UNV [8]	SCE	KUNV	**University Park Airport**	P-N	133,777
Wilkes-Barre / Scranton	AVP [9]	AVP	KAVP	**Wilkes-Barre/Scranton International Airport**	P-N	219,745
Williamsport	IPT [10]	IPT	KIPT	**Williamsport Regional Airport**	P-N	23,901
				Commercial Service - Non-Primary Airports		
Altoona	AOO [11]	AOO	KAOO	**Altoona-Blair County Airport**	CS	11,051
Bradford	BFD [12]	BFD	KBFD	**Bradford Regional Airport**	CS	4,898
DuBois / Falls Creek	DUJ [13]	DUJ	KDUJ	**DuBois Regional Airport** (was DuBois-Jefferson County Airport)	CS	3,230

Johnstown	JST [14]	JST	KJST	**John Murtha Johnstown-Cambria County Airport**	CS	7,634
Lancaster	LNS [15]	LNS	KLNS	**Lancaster Airport**	CS	1,673
				Reliever Airports		
Beaver Falls	BVI [16]	**BFP**	KBVI	Beaver County Airport	R	6
Butler	BTP [17]	BTP	KBTP	Butler County Airport (K.W. Scholter Field)	R	6
Coatesville	MQS [18]	**CTH**	KMQS	Chester County G. O. Carlson Airport	R	113
Doylestown	DYL [19]	DYL	KDYL	Doylestown Airport	R	12
Harrisburg	CXY [20]	**HAR**	KCXY	Capital City Airport	R	59
Monongahela / Belle Vernon	FWQ [21]		KFWQ	Rostraver Airport	R	
Philadelphia	PNE [22]	PNE	KPNE	Northeast Philadelphia Airport	R	410
Philadelphia / Blue Bell	LOM [23]	**BBX**	KLOM	Wings Field	R	269
Pittsburgh / West Mifflin	AGC [24]	AGC	KAGC	Allegheny County Airport	R	278
Pottstown	PTW [25]	PTW	KPTW	Pottstown Limerick Airport	R	5
Toughkenamon	N57 [26]			New Garden Airport	R	
West Chester	OQN [27]	OQN	KOQN	Brandywine Airport	R	11
				General Aviation Airports		
Allentown	XLL [28]		KXLL	Allentown Queen City Municipal Airport	GA	
Bedford	HMZ [29]		KHMZ	Bedford County Airport	GA	

Bloomsburg	N13 [30]			Bloomsburg Municipal Airport	GA	
Chambersburg	N68 [31]			Franklin County Regional Airport (was Chambersburg Municipal)	GA	2
Clarion	AXQ [32]		KAXQ	Clarion County Airport	GA	8
Clearfield	FIG [33]		KFIG	Clearfield-Lawrence Airport	GA	
Collegeville	N10 [34]			Perkiomen Valley Airport	GA	
Connellsville	VVS [35]		KVVS	Joseph A. Hardy Connellsville Airport (was Connellsville Airport)	GA	
Corry	8G2 [36]			Corry-Lawrence Airport	GA	
East Stroudsburg	N53 [37]	**ESP**		Stroudsburg-Pocono Airport	GA	
Ebensburg	9G8 [38]			Ebensburg Airport	GA	
Franklin	FKL [39]	FKL	KFKL	**Venango Regional Airport** (Chess Lamberton Field)	GA	681
Gettysburg	W05 [40]	**GTY**		Gettysburg Regional Airport (was Gettysburg Airport & Travel Ctr)	GA	
Greenville	4G1 [41]			Greenville Municipal Airport	GA	
Grove City	29D [42]			Grove City Airport	GA	
Hazleton	HZL [43]	HZL	KHZL	Hazleton Municipal Airport	GA	2
Honesdale	N30 [44]			Cherry Ridge Airport	GA	
Indiana	IDI [45]	IDI	KIDI	Indiana County Airport (Jimmy Stewart Field)	GA	7
Jeannette	5G8 [46]			Greensburg-Jeannette Regional Airport	GA	

Lehighton	22N [47]			Jake Arner Memorial Airport	GA	7
Lock Haven	LHV [48]	LHV	KLHV	William T. Piper Memorial Airport	GA	5
Meadville	GKJ [49]	**MEJ**	KGKJ	Port Meadville Airport	GA	24
Mount Pleasant	P45 [50]			Mount Pleasant-Scottdale Airport	GA	
Mount Pocono	MPO [51]	MPO	KMPO	Pocono Mountains Municipal Airport	GA	
New Castle	UCP [52]		KUCP	New Castle Municipal Airport	GA	4
Philipsburg	PSB [53]	PSB	KPSB	Mid-State Airport	GA	
Pottstown	N47 [54]			Pottstown Municipal Airport	GA	5
Pottsville	ZER [55]		KZER	Schuylkill County Airport (Joe Zerbey Airport)	GA	5
Punxsutawney	N35 [56]			Punxsutawney Municipal Airport	GA	5
Quakertown	UKT [57]	UKT	KUKT	Quakertown Airport	GA	
Reading	RDG [58]	RDG	KRDG	Reading Regional Airport (Carl A. Spaatz Field)	GA	2,170
Reedsville	RVL [59]	**RED**	KRVL	Mifflin County Airport	GA	5
Selinsgrove	SEG [60]	SEG	KSEG	Penn Valley Airport	GA	9
Shamokin / Elysburg	N79 [61]			Northumberland County Airport	GA	
Somerset / Friedens	2G9 [62]			Somerset County Airport	GA	5
St. Marys	OYM [63]	**STQ**	KOYM	St. Marys Municipal Airport	GA	

Tarentum	9G1 [64]			Rock Airport	GA	
Titusville	6G1 [65]			Titusville Airport	GA	
Towanda	N27 [66]			Bradford County Airport	GA	
Washington	AFJ [67]	**WSG**	KAFJ	Washington County Airport	GA	78
Waynesburg	WAY [68]	WAY	KWAY	Greene County Airport	GA	
Wellsboro	N38 [69]			Wellsboro Johnston Airport (was Grand Canyon Airport)	GA	
Wilkes-Barre	WBW [70]	WBW	KWBW	Wilkes-Barre Wyoming Valley Airport	GA	
York / Thomasville	THV [71]	THV	KTHV	York Airport	GA	25
Zelienople	PJC [72]		KPJC	Zelienople Municipal Airport	GA	
				Other Public-Use Airports (not listed in NPIAS)		
Bally	7N8			Butter Valley Golf Port		
Bellefonte	N96 [73]			Bellefonte Airport		
Bethel	8N1 [74]			Grimes Airport		
Brogue	9W8 [75]			Baublitz Commercial Airport (was Baublitz Airport)		
Butler	3G9 [76]			Butler Farm Show Airport		
Canadensis	8N4 [77]			Flying Dollar Airport		
Carlisle	N94 [78]			Carlisle Airport		

Centre Hall	N74 [79]			Penn's Cave Airport		
Centre Hall	N16 [80]			Centre Airpark		
Columbia	8N7 [81]			McGinness Airport (McGinness Field)		
Cresco	48P			Rocky Hill Ultralight Flightpark (was BBI Ultralight Flightpark)		
Danville	8N8 [82]			Danville Airport		
Easton	N43 [83]			Braden Airpark		
Eighty Four	22D [84]			Bandel Airport		
Erwinna	9N1 [85]			Van Sant Airport (Vansant Airport)		
Essington	9N2	PSQ		Philadelphia Seaplane Base		
Factoryville	9N3 [86]			Seamans Field		
Fairfield	W73 [87]			Mid Atlantic Soaring Center		
Finleyville	G05 [88]			Finleyville Airpark		
Fredericksburg	9N7 [89]			Farmers Pride Airport		
Freeport	P37 [90]			McVille Airport		
Germansville	P91 [91]			Flying M Aerodrome		
Hanover	6W6 [92]			Hanover Airport		
Irwin / McKeesport	31D [93]			Inter County Airport		
Jersey Shore	P96 [94]			Jersey Shore Airport		

Kralltown	07N [95]			Bermudian Valley Airpark		
Lebanon	08N [96]			Keller Brothers Airport		
Lehighton	14N [97]			Beltzville Airport		
Mars	P09			Lakehill Airport		
Mifflintown	P34 [98]			Mifflintown Airport		
Monroeville	4G0 [99]			Pittsburgh-Monroeville Airport		
Montrose	P32			Husky Haven Airport (formerly private-use, FAA: PA52)		
Morgantown	O03 [100]			Morgantown Airport		
Mount Joy / Marietta	N71 [101]			Donegal Springs Airpark		
Myerstown	9D4 [102]			Deck Airport		
Newry	7G4 [103]			Blue Knob Valley Airport		
Palmyra	58N [104]			Reigle Airport (Reigle Field)		
Perkasie	CKZ [105]	KCKZ		Pennridge Airport		
Philadelphia	P72			Penn's Landing Heliport		26
Philipsburg	1N3 [106]			Albert Airport		
Pittsfield	P15 [107]			Brokenstraw Airport		
Seven Springs / Champion	7SP [108]			Seven Springs Airport		
Shippensburg	N42 [109]			Shippensburg Airport		

Slatington	69N [110]			Slatington Airport		
Smoketown / Lancaster	S37 [111]			Smoketown Airport		
Sunbury	H11			Sunbury Seaplane Base		
Sterling	70N [112]			Spring Hill Airport		
Stewartstown	0P2 [113]			Shoestring Aviation Airfield (Shoestring Aviation Airport)		
Sunbury	71N [114]			Sunbury Airport		
Tower City	74N [115]			Bendigo Airport		
Tunkhannock	76N [116]			Skyhaven Airport		
Unionville / Julian	79N [117]			Ridge Soaring Gliderport		
Wattsburg	3G1 [118]			Erie County Airport		
Wellsville	2N5 [119]			Kampel Airport		
Williamsburg	6G6 [120]			Cove Valley Airport		
				Other Military Airports		
Fort Indiantown Gap	MUI	MUI	KMUI	Muir Army Airfield		
Willow Grove	NXX	NXX	KNXX	NAS JRB Willow Grove		381
				Notable Private-Use Airports		
Annville	4PA0			Millard Airport (formerly public-use, FAA: N76 [121])		
Bellefonte	03PS			Ziggy's Field		1
Breinigsville	29PA			Gardner Airport		
Farmington	PA88			Nemacolin Airport		

				Notable Former Airports		
Burgettstown	P64			Miller Airport (closed) [122]		
Galeton	5G6			Cherry Springs Airport (closed 2007)		
Harrisburg				Olmsted Air Force Base (closed 1969)		
Hershey				Hershey Airpark (closed 1981) [123]		
Indian Lake	5G2			Indian Lake Airport (closed 1999)		
Kutztown	N31 [124]			Kutztown Airport (closed 2009) [125]		
Morris	PN0			Echo Airport (closed) [126]		
Mount Union	MUU [127]		KMUU	Huntingdon County Airport (closed) [128]		
Pittsburgh				Greater Pittsburgh International Airport (closed 1992)		
State College	SCE			State College Air Depot (closed 1986-1994?) [129]		
Valencia				Glade Mill Airport (closed)		
Warminster	NJP		KNJP	NAWC Warminster (closed 1990s)		

Footnotes:

See also

- Essential Air Service
- Pennsylvania World War II Army Airfields
- Susquehanna Area Regional Airport Authority (SARAA), governing authority of four airports in south-central Pennsylvania.
- Wikipedia:WikiProject Aviation/Airline destination lists: North America#Pennsylvania

References

Federal Aviation Administration (FAA):

- FAA Airport Data (Form 5010) [1] from National Flight Data Center (NFDC), also available from AirportIQ 5010 [2]
- National Plan of Integrated Airport Systems for 2009–2013 [3], updated 15 October 2008
- Passenger Boarding (Enplanement) Data for CY 2008 [4], updated 18 December 2009

Pennsylvania Department of Transportation (PENNDOT):

- Bureau of Aviation [1]

Other sites used as a reference when compiling and updating this list:

- Aviation Safety Network [5] - used to check IATA airport codes.
- Great Circle Mapper: Airports in Pennsylvania [6] - used to check IATA and ICAO airport codes.
- Abandoned & Little-Known Airfields: Pennsylvania [7] - used for information on former airports.

Sports in Pennsylvania

Pennsylvania sports includes numerous professional sporting teams, events, and venues located in the U.S. state of Pennsylvania.

Football

Football is the most popular sport in Pennsylvania, especially in the Lehigh Valley, Northeastern Pennsylvania, Central Pennsylvania, and Western Pennsylvania. In fact, Western PA is the home to some of the earliest moments in football history, as the first professional football game was played in Pittsburgh in 1895, with the first-ever professional player (William "Pudge" Heffelfinger) playing a game in the city just three years earlier.

Today, football is popular on all levels, from high school, college, and professionally. The high school games get regular attention in the local newspapers and regularly draw over 10,000 fans to the games. At the college level, the most popular football teams are the Penn State Nittany Lions (of State College), the Pitt Panthers (of Pittsburgh), and, despite being one of the college game's worst teams, the Temple Owls (of Philadelphia). The Penn State-Pitt rivalry, in fact, was once one of the biggest rivalries in the college game until a scheduling dispute ended the rivalry in 2000. The Army–Navy Game has also been played in Philadelphia on a regular basis, with their games only occasionally played on other sites, such as the 2007 matchup being played in Baltimore.

Professionally, the Pittsburgh Steelers and Philadelphia Eagles of the NFL are also hugely popular. Both teams have fan bases across the entire state, and in the case of the Steelers, are one of the most popular sports teams in the United States, if not the world. (This is likely due to that team's dominance in the NFL during the 1970s.) While the Eagles are not quite as popular as the Steelers outside Pennsylvania (as well as nearby states to Philadelphia such as New Jersey and Delaware), they still maintain a passionate fan base in the state and across the United States as they are one of the more popular teams in the NFL. Often one of the most rowdy in the NFL, the Eagles fanbase is known for their passion and dedication. In fact, the Eagles' old home field, Veterans Stadium, was the first sports stadium in the United States to have a jail cell as a result of the rowdiness of the fans, but was removed only a couple years later after incidents settled down. Both fanbases though are considered to be among the best traveled fanbases in the NFL. During games in which the teams are on the road, Steelers fans and Eagles fans alike migrate to the opposing team's stadium and always have a strong presence, and in some cases, their numbers have made opposing teams feel as if they are not in their home stadium—a testament to the die-hard fanbases of professional football in Pennsylvania.

Pittsburgh was also the home to one of the first Arena Football League franchises, the Pittsburgh Gladiators, in 1987. Although the team moved to Tampa, Florida in 1991 (where they currently exist as the Tampa Bay Storm), arena football remains in the state, with the Philadelphia Soul playing in the main AFL while the Wilkes-Barre/Scranton Pioneers play in the AFL's minor league af2. The AFL is also considering returning to Pittsburgh with an expansion team in the near future upon the completion of the new arena for the NHL's Pittsburgh Penguins.

Baseball

Along with football, baseball is one of the more popular sports in Pennsylvania. The state has both major league and minor league baseball teams.

Major league teams are: the Philadelphia Phillies, the 2008 World Series champions, and the Pittsburgh Pirates.

Pennsylvania also has its share of minor-league baseball teams. These are: the Lehigh Valley IronPigs and the Scranton/Wilkes-Barre Yankees in Triple-A, the Reading Phillies, the Harrisburg Senators, the Erie SeaWolves, and the Altoona Curve in Double-A, and the State College Spikes and Williamsport Crosscutters in Short-Season A.

Basketball

Pennsylvania is home to the Philadelphia 76ers of the NBA, also being the only one of the big four sports in Pennsylvania not to have a team in both Philadelphia and Pittsburgh. Pennsylvania's many NCAA college teams, like the Villanova Wildcats and the Pittsburgh Panthers, make a large impact, rather than NBA teams.

Ice hockey

Pennsylvania is home to more professional ice hockey teams than any other U.S. state, except New York. In all, seven professional hockey teams call Pennsylvania home: the Philadelphia Flyers and Pittsburgh Penguins of the National Hockey League; the Hershey Bears and Wilkes-Barre/Scranton Penguins of the American Hockey League; the Johnstown Chiefs and Reading Royals of the ECHL; and the Indiana Ice Miners of the Mid-Atlantic Hockey League. The Hershey Bears are the oldest existing AHL franchise, joining the league in 1938. The Erie Otters of the junior Ontario Hockey League also play in Pennsylvania. The Otters are one of only three OHL teams located outside of Canada.

Hersheypark Arena in Hershey, Pennsylvania, home to the Hershey Bears of the American Hockey League from 1936 to 2002

Due in large part to Pennsylvania's cold winter climate and the state's geographic location in the Northeast, hockey is fairly popular throughout the state.

A number of notable current and former professional hockey players are Pennsylvania natives: Mike Richter, one of the most successful American-born goaltenders in NHL history; Pete Babando; Bob Beers; Jay Caufield; Ryan Malone; Gerry O'Flaherty; George Parros; Jesse Spring; and R.J. Umberger. Legendary amateur hockey player Hobey Baker, namesake of U.S. college hockey's Hobey Baker Memorial Award, was also born in Pennsylvania.

Soccer

Chester, Pennsylvania is home to the Philadelphia Union of Major League Soccer.

Collegiate teams

NCAA Division I

- Bucknell Bisons
- Drexel Dragons
- Duquesne Dukes
- Lafayette Leopards
- La Salle Explorers

- Lehigh Mountain Hawks
- Penn State Nittany Lions*
- Robert Morris Colonials
- Saint Francis Red Flash
- Saint Joseph's Hawks
- Temple Owls*
- Pennsylvania Quakers
- Pittsburgh Panthers*
- Villanova Wildcats

indicates a member of Division I FBS; the highest level of college football in the United States.

Olympians

- Giddeon Massie of Quakertown member, 2004 Bicycling team
- John Woodruff of Connellsville Gold Medal, 1936, in 800-meters event
- Catherine "Kit" Klein of Harrisburg Gold and Bronze, 1932 Olympics, 1936 Olympics, speed skater, World Record - 1000 meters (1935), World Record - 3000 meters (1936), 1936 World Champion.
- Candy Young-Sanders of Beaver Falls, qualified for the boycotted 1980 Olympics, 100m hurdles
- Roger Kingdom of Monroeville, Gold medal in both 1984 and 1988 Olympics, 110m hurdles
- Kurt Angle 1996 freestyle wrestling gold medalist.
- Kim Gallagher, American track & field Olympian in the 800 meters in 1984and 1988. She also holds National High School Records and PIAA State Records and was a Penn Relays champion.
- Lauryn Williams 2004, silver medal winner, women's 100m track, native of Rochester, Pennsylvania.
- Marty Nothstein of Trexlertown Gold Medal, 2000, Cycling
- Angie Loy of Elliottsburg Eighth Place, 2008, Field Hockey

Bicycle racing

Floyd Landis, of Farmersville won the 2006 Tour de France. The sanctioning body alleges that Landis had abnormal hormone ratios in his system, and engaged in prohibited doping, and intends to strip him of his title. Landis denies engaging in doping and is legally challenging the action.

Pennsylvania hosts the Pro Cycling Tour "Commerce Bank Triple Crown of Cycling" bicycle races each June, with the Tom Bamford Lancaster Classic, the Reading Classic, and the The Philadelphia International Championship Bike Race. The PCT is sanctioned by USA Cycling, the national governing body for cycling in the U.S.

Pennsylvania also hosts the Univest Grand Prix professional bicycle race each year in September, sanctioned by the Union Cycliste Internationale, the worldwide governing body for cycling. The road race starts and finishes in Souderton, while the criterium is located in Doylestown.

The Lehigh Valley Velodrome annually hosts a USA Cycling Elite Nationals qualifying event.

Motorsports

Motorsports are popular in Pennsylvania. The Mario Andretti dynasty of race drivers hails from Nazareth.

Asphalt oval tracks

Asphalt ovals in Pennsylvania include Jennerstown Speedway in Jennerstown, Lake Erie Speedway in North East, Mahoning Valley Speedway in Lehighton, Motordome Speedway in Smithton, Mountain Speedway in St. Johns, Nazareth Speedway in Nazareth, and Pocono Raceway in Long Pond.

Dirt track racing

Dirt ovals include Dunn Hill 2 Speedway in Monroeton, Allegheny Mountain Raceway in Kane, Bedford Speedway in Bedford, Big Diamond Raceway in Minersville, Blanket Hill Speedway in Kittanning, Borger's Speedway in Saylorsburg, Bradford Speedway in Bradford, Central Pennsylvania Speedway in Clearfield, Challenger Raceway in Indiana, Clinton County Raceway in Lock Haven, Clyde Martin Memorial Speedway in Schaefferstown, Dog Hollow Speedway in Strongstown, Eriez Speedway in Erie, Farmington VFD Speedway in Farmington, Gamblers Raceway Park in Clearfield, Grandview Speedway in Bechtelsville, Greenwood Valley Action Track in Millville, Hamlin Speedway in Hamlin, Hesston Speedway in Huntingdon, Hill Valley Speedway in Orbisonia, Hummingbird Speedway in Falls Creek, Lake Moc-A-Tek Speedway in Lakeville, Latrobe Speedway in Latrobe, Lernerville Speedway in Sarver, Lincoln Speedway in Abbottstown, Linda's Speedway in Jonestown (Lebanon County), Marion Center Speedway in Marion Center, Mckean County Raceway in East Smethport, Mercer Raceway Park in Mercer, Path Valley Speedway Park in Spring Run, Penn Can Speedway in Susquehanna, Pittsburgh's Pa Motor Speedway in Imperial, Port Royal Speedway in Port Royal, Redline Raceway in Troy, Roaring Knob Motorsports Complex in Markleysburg, Selinsgrove Speedway in Selinsgrove, Shippensburg Speedway in Shippensburg, Silver Spring Speedway in Mechanicsburg [Operated 1953-2005], Snydersville Raceway in Snydersville, Susquehanna Speedway in Newberrytown, The Fairgrounds At Kutztown in Kutztown, Thunder Valley Raceway in Central City, Trail-Way Speedway in Hanover, Tri-City Speedway in Franklin, Williams Grove Speedway in Mechanicburg, and Windber Speedway in Windber.

Drag strips

Drag Strips include Beaver Springs Dragway in Beaver Springs, Lucky Drag City in Wattsburg, Maple Grove Raceway in Mohnton, Numidia Raceway in Numidia, Pittsburgh Raceway Park in New Alexandria, and South Mountain Dragway in Boiling Springs.

Road racing

Road Courses include Beaverun Motorsports Complex in Wampum, and Pittsburgh Vintage Grand Prix in Pittsburgh.

Horse events

Harness racing

The Meadows Racetrack, in Pittsburgh, Mohegan Sun at Pocono Downs, in Wilkes-Barre and Summerside Raceway in Summerside offer harness racing in Pennsylvania.

Thoroughbred racing

Penn National Race Course in Grantville and Philadelphia Park, in Bensalem which offer thoroughbred racing.

Famous horses

Smarty Jones, the 2004 Kentucky Derby winner, was owned by Roy Chapman and wife Patricia. Roy Chapman had built a chain of car dealerships known as the Chapman Auto Group in southeast and south central Pennsylvania. Smarty Jones was bred at Chapman's Someday Farm (Patricia explains the name: "Some day we were going to do this and some day we were going to do that. And my husband said, 'I think we ought to call it Someday Farm,' so we did.") near Philadelphia, and had Philadelphia Park as his home course.

Barbaro, the 2006 Kentucky Derby winner, came from Mr. and Mrs. Roy Jackson's Lael Stables in West Grove. After suffering injuries in the Preakness Stakes on May 20, 2006, Barbaro was treated in the Intensive Care Unit of George D. Widener Hospital, at the University of Pennsylvania's New Bolton Center in Kennett Square. He was also being treated for laminitis. As of September 12, 2006, the horse was being hand-grazed daily, and his vital signs and appetite were excellent. In November, his cast was removed, and his prognosis seemed good. Sadly, he developed further complications in January 2007, and after a final surgery that month, he was euthanized on January 29 after his owners concluded that his pain and suffering were too great to continue treatment.

Golf

Leading golfers

Arnold Palmer, one of the leading 20th-century pro golfers, comes from Latrobe, and Jim Furyk, one of the leading 21-century pro golfers, grew up near Lancaster.

Major tournaments

PGA tournaments in Pennsylvania include the 84 Lumber Classic, played at Nemacolin Woodlands Resort, in Farmington and the Northeast Pennsylvania Classic, played at Glenmaura National Golf Club, in Scranton.There is also the PGT (Pittsburgh Golfers Tour) which is people from all over the east coast joining a club where the owner schedules tournaments all over the state.

Gaming

Casinos

Casinos recently became legal in the state of Pennsylvania. Some are located at horse racing venues, while some stand alone. These casinos are: Harrah's Chester Casino and Racetrack, Mohegan Sun at Pocono Downs, Philadelphia Park Casino and Racetrack, Hollywood Casino at Penn National Race Course, Presque Isle Downs and Casino, Meadows Racetrack & Casino, Mount Airy Casino Resort, Sands Casino Resort Bethlehem, and Rivers Casino. Three other casinos are planned but have not yet begun construction.

Poker

The legal status of Poker is developing. The decision cited below was rendered on January 16, 2009.

Texas Hold 'em Poker

Texas Hold' em Poker was found not to be gambling under the Pennsylvania Crimes Code by Judge Thomas A. James Jr. in the case of Commonwealth of Pennsylvania vs Walter Watkins.

The case involved a $1/$2 table stakes Texas Hold 'em Poker game with a dealer making tips. The organizers were charged with 20 counts of violating Section 5513 sections (a)(2), (a)(3), and (a)(4), related to "unlawful gambling", and had materials related to the games confiscated by police as "gambling devices".

Section 5513 of the Pennsylvania Code makes it a misdemeanor of the first degree for a person to invite or allows other people to gather in a place of his control for the purpose of "unlawful gambling".

In his decision, Judge Thomas A. James Jr. stated, "[T]here are three elements of gambling: consideration, chance and reward." The judge found through a four pronged test that skill predominates over chance, and that Texas Hold' em is a game of skill, therefore not gambling.

Specifically, the decision states:

> The court finds that Texas Hold 'em poker is a game where skill predominates over chance. Thus, it is not "unlawful gambling' under the Pennsylvania Crimes Code.

Section 5512(d), which provides definitions, states:

> As used in this section the term "unlawful" means not specifically authorized by law.

Section 5513 states: (emphasis added)

> § 5513. Gambling devices, gambling, etc.

> (a) Offense defined.--A person is guilty of a misdemeanor of the first degree if he:

> (1) intentionally or knowingly makes, assembles, sets up, maintains, sells, lends, leases, gives away, or offers for sale, loan, lease or gift, any punch board, drawing card, slot machine or any device to be used for gambling purposes, **except playing cards**; (2) allows persons to collect and assemble for the purpose of unlawful gambling at any place under his control; (3) solicits or invites any person to visit any unlawful gambling place for the purpose of gambling; or (4) being the owner, tenant, lessee or occupant of any premises, knowingly permits or suffers the same, or any part thereof, to be used for the purpose of unlawful gambling.

Other Poker Games

The decision above may be limited to Texas Hold 'em.

In the 1949 case of Commonwealth of Pennsylvania V. Silverman, the Pennsylvania Supreme Court ruled that the "Sporadic or casual act of playing cards or betting is not an indictable offense in Pennsylvania."

In 2004, Lackawanna County District Attorney Andy Jarbola was quoted as saying, "it's legal to gather with friends to play poker but it's not legal when the 'house' or an outside party profits from the game."

In 2005, York County District Attorney Stan Rebert was asked about illegal poker games in the York area by the York Daily Record. He replied that he had not heard of any and that it's not something that he would worry about. "Casual gambling ... that is not illegal," he said, "It's kind of a fine line."

Previous legal challenges and legislative initiatives have taken place, but until recently, none have changed the status of poker in Pennsylvania.

- HB2121 [1] would authorize table games, including poker, in Pennsylvania's recently authorized casinos.
- HB947 [2] would authorize poker tournaments to be held by the holders of licenses for small games of chance.
- In Lewistown, three members of the Brooklyn Hose Fire Co. were charged with unlawful gambling for the poker tournaments held there.

- In Greensburg, a defense attorney who had $10,000 and equipment confiscated from his office from poker tournaments is suing for their return. The attorney has not been charged and insists that poker tournaments are legal games of skill.

The Pennsylvania Liquor Control Board has published an FAQ page [3] on the legalities of Texas Hold'em Poker for licensed establishments.

See also

- Lacrosse in Pennsylvania
- Sports in South Central Pennsylvania

Overview of Bethlehem

Bethlehem, Pennsylvania

Bethlehem, Pennsylvania
— City —
Downtown Bethlehem in 2007

Seal

Nickname(s): The Christmas City, The Steel City

Location in Lehigh and Northampton Counties, Pennsylvania

Bethlehem, Pennsylvania

Location within Pennsylvania

Coordinates: 40°37′34″N 75°22′32″W

Country	United States
Commonwealth	Pennsylvania
Counties	Lehigh and Northampton
Founded	1741

Government	
- Type	Mayor-Council
- Mayor	John B. Callahan
Area	
- City	19.4 sq mi (50.3 km^2)
- Land	19.3 sq mi (49.9 km^2)
- Water	0.2 sq mi (0.4 km^2)
- Urban	289.50 sq mi (749.79 km^2)
- Metro	730.0 sq mi (1174.82 km^2)
Elevation	360 ft (109.728 m)
Population (2000)	
- City	71329
- Density	3,704.4/sq mi (594.0/km^2)
- Urban	576408
- Metro	740395
Time zone	EST (UTC-5)
- Summer (DST)	EDT (UTC-4)
ZIP Codes	18015-18018, 18020, 18025
Website	bethlehem-pa.gov [1]

Bethlehem is a city in Lehigh and Northampton Counties in the Lehigh Valley region of eastern Pennsylvania, in the United States. As of the 2000 census, the city had a total population of 71,329, (2008 estimate 72,241), making it the sixth largest city in Pennsylvania, after Philadelphia, Pittsburgh, Allentown, Erie, and Reading.

Bethlehem lies in the center of the Lehigh Valley, a region of 731 square miles (1,893 km²) that is home to more than 800,000 people. The Valley embraces a trio of cities (Bethlehem, Allentown and Easton) within two counties

Graveyard with Bethlehem Steel in background, 1935. Photo by Walker Evans.

(Lehigh and Northampton), making it Pennsylvania's third-largest metropolitan area. Smaller than Allentown but larger than Easton, Bethlehem is the Lehigh Valley's second most populous city.

There are three general sections of the city, North Bethlehem, South Bethlehem and West Bethlehem. Each of these sections blossomed at different times in the city's development and each contains areas recognized under the National Register of Historic Places.

Main Street, downtown Bethlehem, 2007

In July 2006, *Money* magazine included Bethlehem as one of its "Top 100 Best Places to Live." It placed number 88.

History

The areas along the Delaware River and its tributaries in eastern Pennsylvania were long inhabited by indigenous peoples of various cultures. By the time of European contact, these areas were the historic territory of the Algonquian-speaking Lenape Nation, which had two main language families, the Unami and the Munsee. They traded with the Dutch and then English colonists in the mid-Atlantic area.

South Bethlehem in 1935, looking north to houses and Bethlehem Steel

On Christmas Eve in 1741, David Nitschmann and Count Nicolaus von Zinzendorf, leading a small group of Moravians, founded the mission community of Bethlehem along the banks of the Monocacy Creek by the Lehigh River in the colony of Pennsylvania. They named the settlement after the town of Bethlehem in Judea, the birthplace of Jesus Christ. Originally it was a typical Moravian Settlement Congregation, where the Church owned all the property. Until the 1850s, only members of the Moravian Church were permitted to live in Bethlehem. The historic Brethren's House, Sisters' House, Widows' House and *Gemeinhaus* (Congregation House) with the Old Chapel are remnants of this period of communal living.

The Moravians ministered to regional Lenape Native Americans through their mission in the area, as well as further east in the New York colony. In the historic Bethlehem God's Acre cemetery, converted Lenape were buried alongside the Moravians.

In 1762, Bethlehem built the first water works in America to pump water for public usage. While George Washington and his troops stayed in Valley Forge, his personal effects were stored at the farm of James Burnside in Bethlehem. This is now a historical museum (Burnside Plantation).

The prosperous village was incorporated into a free borough in the County of Northampton in 1845. After the Unity Synod of 1848, Bethlehem became the headquarters of the Northern Province of the Moravian Church in North America.

On March 27, 1900, the Bach Choir of Bethlehem presented the United States debut of German Lutheran Johann Sebastian Bach's Mass in B Minor in the city's Central Moravian Church.

Christmas star

On December 7, 1937, at a grand ceremony during the Great Depression, Mrs. Marion Brown Grace pulled a large switch to turn on the new Christmas street lights and a large wooden star. Mrs. Grace was the daughter of former South Bethlehem burgess, Charles F. Brown, and wife of Eugene Grace, President of Bethlehem Steel Corporation. Hundreds of citizens attended the ceremony and thousands more listened to the speeches and musical performances on the radio. This was the first year the Bethlehem Chamber of Commerce adopted the nickname "Christmas City, USA".

Bethlehem Steel works, May 1881.
Watercolor by Joseph Pennell.

The *Bethlehem Globe-Times* paid for the large wooden star erected on the top of South Mountain, at a cost of $460.

The star of Bethlehem viewed from Main Street at night

The star was attached to two wooden poles and was smaller than the current star. The star was created with four wooden planks, overlapped to create an eight point star. The dimensions were 60' high, 51' wide lit by 150 bulbs, 50 watts each. The installation of the star was done by PP&L and Bethlehem Water Department. The star was erected on the top of South Mountain, on property owned by the Water Department, located in Lower Saucon Township.

The Hotel Bethlehem was an appropriate location for such a ceremony, as it was the site of the first building in Bethlehem, a two-room log house. On Christmas Eve in 1741, the original settlers conducted their evening worship in this building. As their benefactor, Count Zinzendorf, observed the farm animals that shared the space and listened to their hymn, "Not Jerusalem, But Lowly Bethlehem", he proclaimed the name of the settlement to be Bethlehem. The people gathered at the 1937 ceremony heard the same words when the Bach Choir sang the old German hymn, "Jesu, Rufe Mich (Jesus, Call Thou Me)," by Adam Drese.

In 1939 the wooden star was replaced with a star made of Bethlehem steel, at a cost of $5000. It had eight rays with the main horizontal ray extended eighty-one feet and the main vertical ray was fifty-three feet long. In 1967, the star was redesigned, and Plexiglas was installed to protect the 250 light bulbs, 50 watts each. It was installed on the old steel frame. This was ninety-one feet high and twenty-five feet wide at the base, with a depth of five feet, set in concrete. In the summer of 2006, the city repaired the base. A crew of municipal electricians changes the bulbs every two years. Beginning in the mid-1990s, the star was lit from 4:30 p.m. until midnight, every day of the year. This schedule continues today. During World War II, from 1941 to 1945 none of the Christmas decorations in Bethlehem were lit. City officials said the lit star made "too good of an air raid target" and "during the global strife it didn't seem right for the lights to be all lit up when our boys were out in the darkness fighting for us." When lit, the star can be seen from as far as Wind Gap, 20 miles (32 km) away. The star has become an important symbol for Bethlehem.

Center of United States heavy industry

Bethlehem became a center of heavy industry and trade during the industrial revolution. Bethlehem Steel, founded in 1857, began producing the first wide-flange structural shapes made in the United States. The company was the first to produce the now-ubiquitous "I-beam" used in construction of steel-framed buildings, including skyscrapers. It manufactured construction materials for numerous New York and other city skyscrapers, as well as major bridges.

The company was a major supplier of armor plate and ordnance products during World War I and World War II, including the manufacture of 1100 warships. After roughly 140 years of metal production at its Bethlehem plant, Bethlehem Steel ceased operations there in 1995. Overseas competition and declining demand had ended the business.

Geography

According to the United States Census Bureau, the city has a total area of 19.4 square miles (50.3 km²), of which, 19.3 square miles (49.9 km²) of it is land and 0.2 square miles (0.4 km²) of it (0.88%) is water.

Because large volumes of water were required in the steelmaking process, the city purchased 22,000 acres (89 km²) of land in the Pocono Mountains, where its water is stored in reservoirs.

The Lehigh River in Bethlehem in 2007.

Climate

Bethlehem's climate falls in the humid continental climate zone. Summers are typically hot and humid, fall and spring are generally mild, and winter is cold. Precipitation is distributed throughout the year, with thunderstorms in the summer, showers in spring and fall, and snow in winter. The average high temperature varies widely, from 34 °F (1 °C) in January to 84.5 °F (29.2 °C) in July. The highest recorded temperature was 105 °F (41 °C), while the lowest recorded temperature was −16 °F (−27 °C).

Monocacy Creek near downtown Bethlehem in 2007.

Climate data for Bethlehem													
Month	Jan	Feb	Mar	Apr	May	Jun	Jul	Aug	Sep	Oct	Nov	Dec	Year
Record high °F (°C)	72 (22.2)	76 (24.4)	87 (30.6)	94 (34.4)	97 (36.1)	100 (37.8)	105 (40.6)	105 (40.6)	99 (37.2)	93 (33.9)	81 (27.2)	72 (22.2)	105 (40.6)
Average high °F (°C)	35 (1.7)	39 (3.9)	49 (9.4)	60 (15.6)	71 (21.7)	79 (26.1)	84 (28.9)	82 (27.8)	74 (23.3)	63 (17.2)	51 (10.6)	40 (4.4)	60.6 (15.89)
Average low °F (°C)	19 (-7.2)	21 (-6.1)	29 (-1.7)	38 (3.3)	48 (8.9)	58 (14.4)	63 (17.2)	61 (16.1)	53 (11.7)	41 (5)	33 (0.6)	24 (-4.4)	40.7 (4.83)
Record low °F (°C)	-16 (-26.7)	-12 (-24.4)	-5 (-20.6)	12 (-11.1)	29 (-1.7)	39 (3.9)	38 (3.3)	41 (5)	31 (-0.6)	19 (-7.2)	3 (-16.1)	-9 (-22.8)	-16 (-26.7)
Precipitation inches (mm)	3.50 (88.9)	2.75 (69.9)	3.56 (90.4)	3.49 (88.6)	4.47 (113.5)	3.99 (101.3)	4.27 (108.5)	4.35 (110.5)	4.37 (111)	3.33 (84.6)	3.70 (94)	3.39 (86.1)	45.17 (1147.3)
Source: The Weather Channel													

Cityscape

Neighborhoods

Bethlehem is divided into four main areas: Center City, West Side, East Side, and South Side. The West Side is located in Lehigh County, while the other three neighborhoods are located in Northampton county.

- Center City is bounded by the Monocacy Creek to the west, Hanover and Bethlehem townships (both Northampton County) to the north, and Stefko Boulevard to the east.
- The West Side begins at the city's western border with Allentown and continues east to the Monocacy Creek and north to Hanover Township (Lehigh County).
- The East Side is bordered to the west by Center City and to the east by Bethlehem Township and Freemansburg. The East Side includes the Pembroke Village area.
- The South Side's borders are Fountain Hill to the west, the Lehigh River to the north, South Mountain to the south, and Hellertown to the east.

Demographics

Historical populations		
Census	Pop.	%±
1850	1516	—
1860	2866	89.1%
1870	4512	57.4%
1880	5193	15.1%
1890	6762	30.2%
1900	7293	7.9%
1910	12837	76.0%
1920	50358	292.3%
1930	57892	15.0%
1940	58490	1.0%
1950	66340	13.4%
1960	75408	13.7%
1970	72686	−3.6%
1980	70419	−3.1%

1990	71428		1.4%
2000	71329		−0.1%
Est. 2009	73338		2.8%

As of the 2009 American Community Survey 1-Year Estimates, there were 73,338 people living in the city. 78.9% were White, 7.9% were Black, 1.6% were Asian, 0.3% were Native American, 0.0% were Pacific Islander, 8.9% were of some other race, and 2.4% were from two or more races. Hispanic or Latino were 22.7% of the population of any race

As of the 2008 United States Census Bureau estimates Bethlehem had 71,608 residents. 78.8% of the population was White American, 4.8% African American, 2.9% Asian, 0.1% Native American, 0.0% Pacific Islander, 10.3% were of some other race, and 3.1% were of two or more races. Hispanic or Latino were 22.9% of the population, with 17.6% being of Puerto Rican descent. 5.0% of all housing units were vacant. 15.9% of all people were living below the poverty line.

As of the census of 2000, there were 71,329 people residing in the city, including 17,094 families and 28,116 households. The population density was 3,704.4 people per square mile (1,429.9/km²). There were 29,631 housing units at an average density of 1,538.8/sq mi (594.0/km²). The racial makeup of the city was 81.85% White, 3.64% African American, 0.26% Native American, 2.22% Asian, 0.03% Pacific Islander, 9.44% from other races, and 2.56% from two or more races. Hispanic or Latino of any race were 18.23% of the population. There were 28,116 households out of which 26.3% had children under the age of 18 living with them, 44.1% were married couples living together, 12.8% had a female householder with no husband present, and 39.2% were non-families. 32.3% of all households were made up of individuals and 14.4% had someone living alone who was 65 years of age or older. The average household size was 2.34 and the average family size was 2.95.

In the city the population was spread out with 21.0% under the age of 18, 14.4% from 18 to 24, 26.6% from 25 to 44, 20.1% from 45 to 64, and 17.9% who were 65 years of age or older. The median age was 36 years. For every 100 females there were 91.5 males. For every 100 females age 18 and over, there were 88.6 males.

The median income for a household in the city was $35,815, and the median income for a family was $45,354. Males had a median income of $35,190 versus $25,817 for females. The per capita income for the city was $18,987. About 11.1% of families and 15.0% of the population were below the poverty line, including 20.7% of those under age 18 and 8.8% of those age 65 or over.

The city is served by Lehigh Valley International Airport, which also serves Allentown, Pennsylvania and the greater Lehigh Valley.

Economy

See also: Transportation in the Lehigh Valley

In December 2006, Las Vegas Sands Corp was awarded a Category 2 Slot Machine License by the Pennsylvania Gaming Control Board. LVSC began work on the site, categorized as both the largest brownfield redevelopment project in the nation and the largest casino development investment made to date in the Commonwealth. Its mission was to create reinvestment and urbanization in the area. At a projected cost of $743 million, the historic Bethlehem Steel plant is being redeveloped as a fully integrated resort, to include 3,000 slot machines, over 300 luxury hotel rooms, 9 restaurants, 200000 square feet (19000 m^2) of premium retail outlet shopping, and 46000 square feet (4300 m^2) of flexible multi-purpose space. In 2007, the casino resort company of Las Vegas Sands began the construction of Sands Casino Resort Bethlehem. The Sands Casino has been projected to bring in approximately one million dollars in revenue per day as of 2009.

Another major economic anchor to the city is St. Luke's Hospital located in the Fountain Hill section of the city. That Hospital and Health Network is the second largest of its type in the Lehigh Valley.

Politics and government

The city government is composed of a mayor and a seven-person city council. The current mayor of Bethlehem is John B. Callahan, who was elected to his second term in November 2005. His election marks the 10th consecutive year a Democrat has held the city's highest office.

Callahan is a member of the Mayors Against Illegal Guns Coalition, a bi-partisan group with a stated goal of "making the public safer by getting illegal guns off the streets." The Coalition is co-chaired by Boston Mayor Thomas Menino and New York City Mayor Michael Bloomberg.

Federally, Bethlehem is part of Pennsylvania's 15th congressional district, represented by Republican Charlie Dent, elected in 2004.

Crime

Bethlehem has a significantly lower crime rate than that of Allentown and Easton. In 2008, Bethlehem had an overall crime index of 244.4, while Allentown's crime index was 510.4 and Easton's crime index was 379.2. The United States' average was 320.9. Also, Bethlehem's violent crime rate was more than half of Allentown's rate. Bethlehem's crime is often concentrated in low-income areas, such as the Pembroke Village neighborhood.

Bethlehem	
Crime rates (2008)	
Crime type	**Rate***
Homicide:	0
Forcible rape:	16.5
Robbery:	147.5
Aggravated assault:	146.1
Violent crime:	310.2
Burglary:	550.1
Larceny-theft:	2,598.7
Motor vehicle theft:	190.2
Arson:	6.9
Property crime:	3,339.0
Notes * Number of reported crimes per 100,000 population. 2008 population: 72,537	
Source: 2008 FBI UCR Data [2]	

Education

Colleges and universities

Bethlehem is home to two institutes of higher education. Lehigh University, located on South Mountain on the city's South Side, has 4,800 undergraduates and 2,100 graduate students. The university, which was founded in 1865, was ranked #35 in U.S. News & World Report's 2010 ratings of America's best colleges.

Moravian College's south campus in Bethlehem.

Moravian College, located in the center city area, is a small, highly respected liberal arts college. Founded in 1742 as Bethlehem Female Seminary, Moravian is the sixth oldest

college in the nation. Besides undergraduate programs, the college also includes the Moravian Theological Seminary, a graduate school with approximately 100 students from more than a dozen religious denominations.

Northampton Community College is also located in neighboring Bethlehem Township.

Primary and secondary education

Bethlehem is home to the Bethlehem Area School District (BASD), which covers a 40-square-mile (100 km^2) area that includes the city, the boroughs of Fountain Hill and Freemansburg, and Bethlehem and Hanover Townships. The district operates two high schools for grades 9-12: Liberty High School near center city and Freedom High School in neighboring Bethlehem Township.

The district also has four public middle schools for grades 6-8: Broughal Middle School, East Hills Middle School, Nitschmann Middle School, and Northeast Middle School. In addition, BASD maintains 19 public elementary schools for grades K-5. Lehigh Valley Charter High School for the Performing Arts (LVPA) is also operated by the district, though it accepts students in grades 9-12 from throughout Northampton and surrounding counties.

Bethlehem has two private high schools: Bethlehem Catholic High School, which serves grades 9-12, and Moravian Academy, which serves all primary and secondary school grades. Notre Dame High School, located just north of the city, also serves grades 9 through 12.

Bethlehem Catholic, Freedom and Liberty all compete athletically in Pennsylvania's Lehigh Valley Conference.

Media

Main article: Media in Lehigh Valley, Pennsylvania

Bethlehem's daily newspaper, *The Globe-Times*, ceased publication in 1991. *The Morning Call*, based in Allentown, and *The Express-Times*, based in Easton, are now the city's dominant newspapers. The newspapers used to have offices on Bethlehem's historic Main Street, separated by only a couple of buildings, but the *Express-Times* has moved several blocks away. Other smaller newspapers include the *Bethlehem Press*; an award-winning weekly, *Pulse Weekly*, based in Allentown; *Eastern Pennsylvania Business Journal*, based in Bethlehem; and *Lehigh Valley Sports Extra*, a popular all-sports monthly newspaper founded in 2001.

Religious broadcaster WBPH is the only television station licensed in Bethlehem, though WLVT Channel 39, a PBS affiliate, has its operations in the city. WFMZ Channel 69, an independent station, is based in neighboring Allentown. Bethlehem is part of the Philadelphia DMA and its cable systems also receive select radio and television broadcasts from New York City.

Bethlehem has two licensed commercial radio stations, variety WGPA AM, and hard rock WZZO FM (though the latter's facilities are in Whitehall Township). There is also one non-commercial station, WLVR FM, operated by Lehigh University. In addition, public radio station WDIY FM, while licensed in Allentown, maintains its facilities in Bethlehem. There are numerous other stations broadcast from

Allentown and Easton representing a variety of commercial formats, as well as several translators of public stations from Philadelphia and New Jersey.

Sports

In the early part of the 20th century, Bethlehem was a hotbed of American soccer, with the corporate Bethlehem Steel team, named Bethlehem Steel F.C. after the company, winning the 1918-19 championship in the National Association Football League (NAFL), and then winning what amounted to national championships three more times during the next decade (1920-21 in the NAFL; 1926-27 in the American Soccer League I; and in 1928-29 winning the EPSL II). The Bethlehem Steel sides consisted largely of British imported players and also had the distinction of being the first American professional soccer team to play in Europe, which it did during its tour of Sweden in 1919. The team also won the U.S. Open Cup, now called the Lamar Hunt U.S. Open Cup after billionaire sports franchise owner Lamar Hunt, five times beginning in 1915, and for the last time in 1926.

Club	League	Venue	Established	Championships
Lehigh Valley Steelhawks	IFL, Indoor football	Stabler Arena	2011	0

The Philadelphia Eagles of the National Football League hold their pre-season training camp each summer at the football facilities of Bethlehem's Lehigh University. The Eagles camp in Bethlehem is among the most highly-attended training camps in the entire NFL, drawing thousands of fans to each practice. During training camp, Eagles' practices typically are held twice daily (at 8:45am and 2:45pm) and are usually open to the public. An estimated 10,000 fans attended Eagles practice daily, the highest of any NFL team's training camp, in the summer of 2006.

Bethlehem also is home to Lehigh University's Stabler Arena, which hosts numerous athletic and music events. Stabler is home to the Indoor Football League's Lehigh Valley Steelhawks and to Lehigh University collegiate basketball.

Bethlehem Steel F.C., founded in 1911, was one of the most successful early American soccer clubs. Bethlehem Steel won the American Cup in 1914, 1916, 1917, 1918, 1919 and 1924. Additionally, they won the National Cup, currently the U.S. Open Cup, in 1915, 1916, 1918, 1919, and 1926, the Allied Amateur Cup in 1914 and the Lewis Cup in 1928. The team folded in 1930.

The Lehigh Valley RFC rugby union team play their matches in Bethlehem at Monocacy Park.

Bethlehem-area high schools compete athletically in the Lehigh Valley Conference.

Recreation and entertainment

The city is famous for its annual Musikfest, a largely free, ten-day music festival that draws over a million people to the city each August. Other festivals include The Celtic Classic, which celebrates Celtic culture, food and music, and the SouthSide Film Festival, a non-competitive, not-for-profit film festival. The city has also been the past, and current host of the North East Art Rock Festival, or NEARFest, a popular 3-day Progressive rock music event.

The Bethlehem Area Public Library is a popular destination for recreation and entertainment. The Banana Factory houses studios of area artists and is open to the public every first Friday of the month. Touchstone Theatre, also on the SouthSide, houses the Valley's only professional resident theatre company, producing and presenting original theatre performances.

Historic Bethlehem features many specialized boutiques, spas and nightclubs along its main streets.

On the first Friday of the month, the businesses of the Southside Shopping District hosts First Friday, a celebration of arts and culture. Stores, restaurants and art galleries stay open late and offer special discounts, refreshments, gallery openings and more.

Lehigh University's Zoellner Arts Center offers a variety of musical and dramatic events through the year.

The city is the location of Pennsylvania's largest casino, the Sands Casino Resort Bethlehem, located on the former Bethlehem Steel property.

The Lehigh Canal provides hiking and biking opportunities along the canal towpath which follows the Lehigh River in Bethlehem.

The western part of the former Bethlehem Steel site was selected as a filming location for the movie *Transformers 2: Revenge of the Fallen*, which was released in 2009. In the film, the Steel's blast furnaces and surrounding area are used for the opening sequence of the film to represent Shanghai.

City parks

Bethlehem owns 39 park sites, encompassing 568 acres (2.3 km^2). Among the city's parks are Buchannan Park, Elmwood Park, Illick's Mill Park, Johnston Park, Monocacy Park, Rockland Park, Rose Garden, Sand Island, Saucon Park, Sell Field, South Mountain Park, Triangle Park, West Side Park, and Yosko Park.

Notable natives and residents

Main article: List of people from the Lehigh Valley

- Jeff Andretti, is an American race car driver.
- John Andretti, professional race car driver, raced in NASCAR, and currently races in the IndyCar Series.
- Michael Andretti, professional racing team owner, former professional race car driver.
- David A. Bader, Georgia Tech professor.
- Chuck Bednarik, former professional football player, Philadelphia Eagles, Pro Football Hall of Fame member.
- Michael Behe, biochemist at Lehigh University, advocate of intelligent design.
- Stephen Vincent Benét, American writer.
- Pete Carril, former professional and collegiate basketball coach.
- Alexandra Chando, actress, *As The World Turns*.
- H.D., writer, poet.
- Russell Davenport, publisher and writer.
- Jimmy DeGrasso, former drummer, Megadeth.
- Richard Diehl, archaeologist, academic and Mesoamericanist scholar.
- Edwin Drake, oil driller.
- Jonathan Frakes, director and actor, *Star Trek: The Next Generation*.
- Eugene Grace, industrialist, President of Bethlehem Steel, 1916-1945.
- Mel Harris, actress, ABC's *thirtysomething*.
- George Hrab, musician.
- Dwayne "The Rock" Johnson, professional wrestler and actor.
- Gelsey Kirkland, ballerina.
- Nathan Homer Knorr, religious leader and 3rd president, Jehovah's Witnesses.
- Gary Lavelle, former professional baseball player, Oakland Athletics, San Francisco Giants and Toronto Blue Jays.
- Barry W. Lynn, executive director of Americans United for Separation of Church and State.
- Alix Olson, spoken word poet.
- Billy Packer, CBS basketball analyst.
- Daniel Roebuck, actor, ABC's *Lost*.
- Thom Schuyler, country music singer and songwriter
- Charles M. Schwab, industrialist, former President of U.S. Steel, later incorporated as Bethlehem Steel in 1904.
- Sheetal Sheth, actress, *Looking for Comedy in the Muslim World*.
- John Spagnola, former professional football player, Green Bay Packers, Philadelphia Eagles and Seattle Seahawks.

- Donald Smaltz, lawyer
- Gary Mark Smith, artist, author, and global street photographer.
- Sarah Strohmeyer, novelist, creator of *Bubbles*.
- Jonathan Taylor Thomas, actor, ABC's *Home Improvement*.

Related communities

Sister cities

Main article: List of sister cities in Pennsylvania

- **Murska Sobota**, Slovenia
- **Tondabayashi**, Japan
- **Schwäbisch Gmünd**, Germany

Twin cities

- **Allentown, Pennsylvania**
- **Easton, Pennsylvania**

External links

- Official website [1].
- Official visitor website [3].
- Bethlehem travel guide from Wikitravel.
- *Bethlehem, Pennsylvania: A Moravian Settlement in Colonial America,* a National Park Service Teaching with Historic Places (TwHP) lesson plan [4].

Lehigh County, Pennsylvania

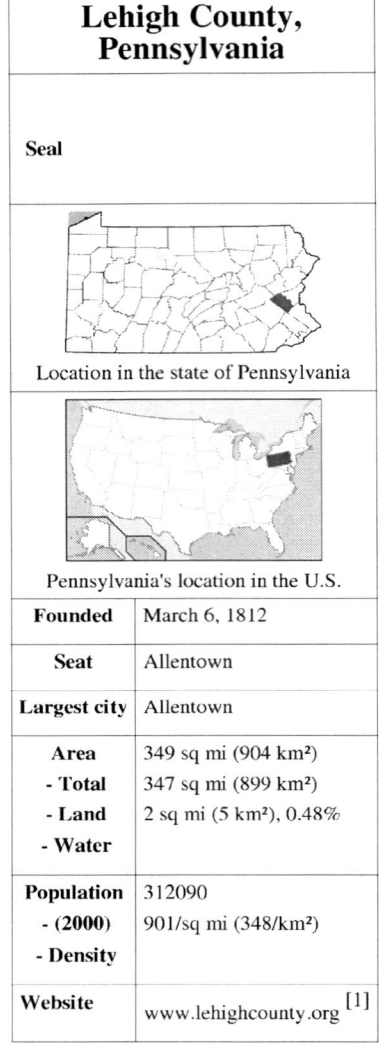

Lehigh County, Pennsylvania	
Seal	
Location in the state of Pennsylvania	
Pennsylvania's location in the U.S.	
Founded	March 6, 1812
Seat	Allentown
Largest city	Allentown
Area	349 sq mi (904 km²)
- Total	347 sq mi (899 km²)
- Land	2 sq mi (5 km²), 0.48%
- Water	
Population	312090
- (2000)	901/sq mi (348/km²)
- Density	
Website	www.lehighcounty.org [1]

Lehigh County is a county located in the Lehigh Valley region of the eastern part of the U.S. state of Pennsylvania. As of the 2000 U.S. Census, the county's population was 312,090. Its county seat is Allentown, the state's third largest city behind Philadelphia and Pittsburgh. In addition to Allentown, the county includes the western section of the city of Bethlehem, six boroughs and 14 townships.

The county, which was first settled around 1730, was formed in 1812 with the division of Northampton County into two counties. It is named after the Lehigh River, whose name is derived from the Delaware Indian term Lechauweki or Lechauwekink, meaning "where there are forks".

Geography

Topography

According to the U.S. Census Bureau, the county has a total area of 347 square miles (902 km²), of which 347 square miles (898 km²) is land and 2 square miles (4 km²) (0.48%), water.

The Lehigh Valley, which includes all of Lehigh and Northampton counties, is bounded on the north by Blue Mountain, a ridge of the Appalachian mountain range with an altitude of 1,300 to 1700 feet (520 m), and on the south by South Mountain, a ridge of 700 to 1100 feet (340 m) that cuts through the southern portions of the two counties. The highest point in Lehigh County

The Lehigh River near Slatington at the Lehigh County–Northampton County line.

is Bake Oven Knob, a mass of Tuscarora conglomeratic rocks that rise about 100 feet above the main ridge of the Blue Mountain in northwestern Heidelberg Township.

Lehigh County is in the Delaware River watershed. While most of the county is drained by the Lehigh River and its tributaries, the Schuylkill River also drains regions in the south of the county via the Perkiomen Creek and the northwest via the Maiden Creek.

Adjacent counties are Carbon County to the north; Northampton County to the northeast and east; Bucks County to the southeast; Montgomery County to the south; and Berks County and Schuylkill County to the west.

Climate

See also: Climate of Allentown, Pennsylvania

Most of the county's climate is considered to fall in the humid continental climate zone. Summers are typically hot and muggy, fall and spring are generally mild, and winter is cold. Precipitation is almost uniformly distributed throughout the year.

For the city of Allentown, January lows average −6 °C (21.2 °F) and highs average 1.3 °C (34.3 °F). The lowest officially recorded temperature was −26.7 °C (−16 °F) in 1912 . July lows average 17.6 °C (63.7 °F) and highs average 29.2 °C (84.6 °F), with an average relative humidity (morning) of 82%. The highest temperature on record was 40.6 °C (105.1 °F) in 1966 . Early fall and mid winter are generally driest, with October being the driest month with only 74.7 mm of average precipitation.

Snowfall is variable, with some winters bringing light snow and others bringing numerous significant snowstorms. Average snowfall is 82.3 centimetres (32.4 in) per year, with the months of January and

February receiving the highest at just over 22.86 centimetres (9.00 in) each. Rainfall is generally spread throughout the year, with eight to twelve wet days per month, at an average annual rate of 110.54 centimetres (43.52 in).

Month	Jan	Feb	Mar	Apr	May	Jun	Jul	Aug	Sep	Oct	Nov	Dec	Year
Avg high temperature °F (°C)	35 (1)	38 (3)	48 (8)	61 (16)	71 (21)	80 (26)	85 (29)	82 (27)	75 (23)	64 (17)	52 (11)	40 (4)	61 (16)
Avg low temperature °F (°C)	20 (-6)	21 (-6)	29 (-1)	39 (3)	49 (9)	59 (15)	64 (17)	62 (16)	54 (12)	43 (6)	34 (1)	24 (-4)	42 (5)
Precipitation in. (cm)	3.2 (8)	2.9 (7)	3.6 (9)	3.7 (9)	4.1 (10)	3.5 (8)	4.3 (10)	4.3 (10)	3.9 (9)	3.0 (7)	3.8 (9)	3.6 (9)	44.1 (112)
Source: Weatherbase [2]													

Demographics

Historical populations		
Census	Pop.	%±
1900	93893	—
1910	118832	26.6%
1920	148101	24.6%
1930	172893	16.7%
1940	177533	2.7%
1950	198207	11.6%
1960	227536	14.8%
1970	255304	12.2%
1980	272349	6.7%
1990	291130	6.9%
2000	312090	7.2%
Est. 2009	343519	10.1%

As of the 2006-2008 American Community Survey, there were 336,738 people living in Lehigh County. 82.0% were White, 5.0% were African American, 2.8% were Asian, 0.1% were Native American, 0.0% were Pacific Islander, 8.2% were of some other race, and 1.8% were of 2 or more races. 15.3% of the population was Hispanic or Latino of any race.

The skyline of Allentown, Pennsylvania in Lehigh County, 2008.

As of the census of 2000, there were 312,090 people, 121,906 households, and 82,164 families residing in the county. The population density was 900 people per square mile (348/km²). There were 128,910 housing units at an average density of 372 per square mile (144/km²). The racial makeup of the county was 87.02% White, 3.56% Black or African American, 0.18% Native American, 2.10% Asian, 0.04% Pacific Islander, 5.28% from other races, and 1.83% from two or more races. 10.22% of the population were Hispanic or Latino of any race. 27.1% were of German, 7.9% Italian, 7.7% Irish, 6.2% Pennsylvania German and 5.6% American ancestry according to Census 2000. 85.0% spoke English, 8.4% Spanish and 1.2% Arabic as their first language.

There were 121,906 households out of which 30.60% had children under the age of 18 living with them, 53.00% were married couples living together, 10.50% had a female householder with no husband present, and 32.60% were non-families. 27.10% of all households were made up of individuals and 11.20% had someone living alone who was 65 years of age or older. The average household size was 2.48 and the average family size was 3.02.

In the county, the population was spread out with 23.90% under the age of 18, 8.10% from 18 to 24, 29.20% from 25 to 44, 23.00% from 45 to 64, and 15.80% who were 65 years of age or older. The median age was 38 years. For every 100 females there were 93.20 males. For every 100 females age 18 and over, there were 89.60 males.

Politics and government

As of January 2010, there are 223,867 registered voters in Lehigh County [3].

- Democratic: 112,412 (50.21%)
- Republican: 76,904 (34.35%)
- Other Parties: 34,551 (15.43%)

Lehigh County and neighboring Northampton County are part of Pennsylvania's 15th Congressional district. The 15th Congressional district is a contentious swing district with neither Republicans nor Democrats winning the district consistently. Despite the advantage in Democratic registration in the district, voters elected Republicans Charlie Dent in 2004, 2006 and 2008 and, previously, Pat Toomey in 1998, 2000, and 2002. In 2004, the county narrowly voted for John Kerry over George W. Bush for President, and in 2008 the county gave all statewide Democratic candidates significant leads and Barack Obama a victory of more than 15 points over John McCain, 57.1% to 41.5%.

All five statewide winners carried it in November 2004. Although the Republican Party has historically been dominant in county-level politics, the Democratic Party has made substantial inroads this decade. In 2005, Bethlehem Mayor Don Cunningham unseated incumbent County Executive Jane Ervin to become the first Democrat to be elected to the office. Four of the nine commissioner seats and all row offices except for the District Attorney have held by Democrats since winning two at-large seats in November 2007. Lehigh County has a home-rule charter with four at-large and five district commissioners. In 2006 Lehigh County voters approved a county-charter amendment to combine the offices of Clerk of Courts, Register of Wills, and Recorder of Deeds into the office of the Clerk of Judicial Records. Clerk of Courts Andrea Naugle won the new office in November 2007.

Commissioners

Office	Holder	Party
County Commissioner (chairman)	Dean Browning	Republican
County Commissioner	Thomas C. Creighton III	Republican
County Commissioner	Percy Dougherty	Republican
County Commissioner	Glenn Eckhart	Republican
County Commissioner	Gloria Hamm	Democratic
County Commissioner	David S. Jones Sr.	Democratic
County Commissioner	Vacant	Democratic
County Commissioner (vice-chairman)	Daniel McCarthy	Democratic
County Commissioner	Andy Roman	Republican

Other county offices

Office	Holder	Party
Clerk of Judicial Records	Andrea Naugle	Democratic
County Executive	Don Cunningham	Democratic
Controller	Thomas Slonaker	Democratic
Coroner	Scott Grim	Democratic
District Attorney	James B. Martin	Republican
Sheriff	Ronald Rossi	Democratic

Pennsylvania House of Representatives

District	Representative	Party
131	Karen D. Beyer	Republican
132	Jennifer Mann	Democratic
133	Joseph F. Brennan	Democratic
134	Doug Reichley	Republican
135	Steve Samuelson	Democratic
183	Julie Harhart	Republican
187	Gary Day	Republican

Pennsylvania State Senate

District	Representative	Party
16	Pat Browne	Republican
18	Lisa Boscola	Democratic
24	Bob Mensch	Republican
29	Dave Argall	Republican

United States House of Representatives

- Jim Gerlach, Republican, Pennsylvania's 6th congressional district (Upper Macungie 3rd district only)
- Charles Dent, Republican, Pennsylvania's 15th congressional district (all other precincts)

Municipalities

Under Pennsylvania law, there are four types of incorporated municipalities: cities, boroughs, townships, and, in at most two cases, towns. The following cities, boroughs and townships are located in Lehigh County:

Cities

See also: List of Allentown neighborhoods

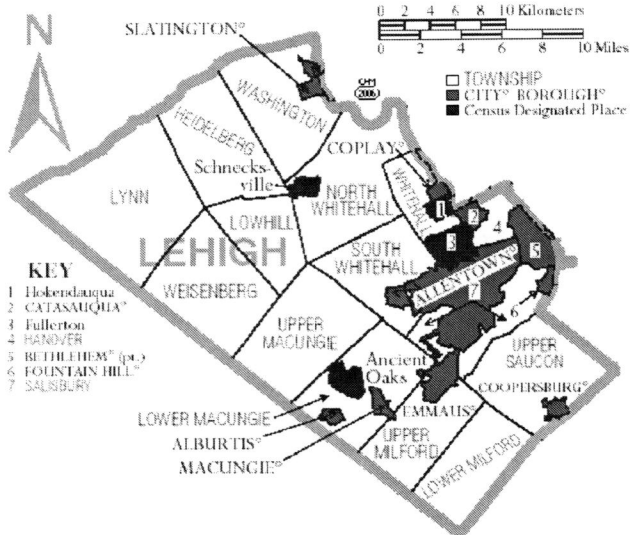

Map of Lehigh County, Pennsylvania with Municipal Labels showing Cities and Boroughs (red), Townships (white), and Census-designated places (blue).

- Allentown
- Bethlehem (situated in both Lehigh and Northampton counties)

Boroughs

- Alburtis
- Catasauqua
- Coopersburg
- Coplay
- Emmaus
- Fountain Hill
- Macungie
- Slatington

Townships

- Hanover Township
- Heidelberg Township
- Lower Macungie Township
- Lower Milford Township
- Lowhill Township
- Lynn Township
- North Whitehall Township
- Salisbury Township
- South Whitehall Township
- Upper Macungie Township
- Upper Milford Township
- Upper Saucon Township
- Washington Township
- Weisenberg Township
- Whitehall Township

Census-designated places

Census-designated places are geographical areas designated by the U.S. Census Bureau for the purposes of compiling demographic data. They are not actual jurisdictions under Pennsylvania law. Other unincorporated communities, such as villages, may be listed here as well.

- Ancient Oaks
- Fullerton
- Hokendauqua
- Schnecksville

Notable villages

- Breinigsville
- Cementon
- Center Valley
- Cetronia
- Dorneyville
- East Texas
- Egypt
- Fogelsville
- Germansville
- Guthsville
- Ironton
- Kuhnsville
- Lanark
- Laurys Station
- Limeport
- Lynnport
- Mechanicsville
- Meyersville
- Neffs
- New Tripoli
- Orefield
- Pleasant Corners
- Sherersville
- Shimerville
- Slatedale
- Summit Lawn
- Trexlertown
- Vera Cruz
- Walbert
- Wescosville

Education

4-Year Colleges and Universities

- Cedar Crest College, Allentown
- DeSales University, Center Valley
- Muhlenberg College, Allentown
- Penn State Lehigh Valley, Center Valley

2-Year Colleges and Technical institutes

- Baum School of Art, Allentown
- Lehigh Carbon Community College - Main Campus, Schnecksville, and Donley Center, Allentown
- Lehigh Valley College, Center Valley
- Lincoln Technical Institute, Allentown

Public school districts and schools

- Allentown School District

  - William Allen High School, Allentown
  - Louis E. Dieruff High School, Allentown
  - Francis D. Raub Middle School
  - Harrison-Morton Middle School
  - South Mountain Middle School
  - Trexler Middle School
- Catasauqua Area School District

  - Catasauqua High School, Northampton
  - Catasauqua Middle School
- East Penn School District

  - Emmaus High School, Emmaus
  - Eyer Middle School, Macungie
  - Lower Macungie Middle School, Macungie
- Northern Lehigh School District

  - Northern Lehigh High School, Slatington
  - Northern Lehigh Middle School, Slatington
- Northwestern Lehigh School District

  - Northwestern Lehigh High School, New Tripoli
- Parkland School District

  - Parkland High School, South Whitehall Township
  - Orefield Middle School, Orefield
  - Springhouse Middle School, Allentown
- Salisbury Township School District

  - Salisbury High School, Salisbury Township
  - Salisbury Middle School

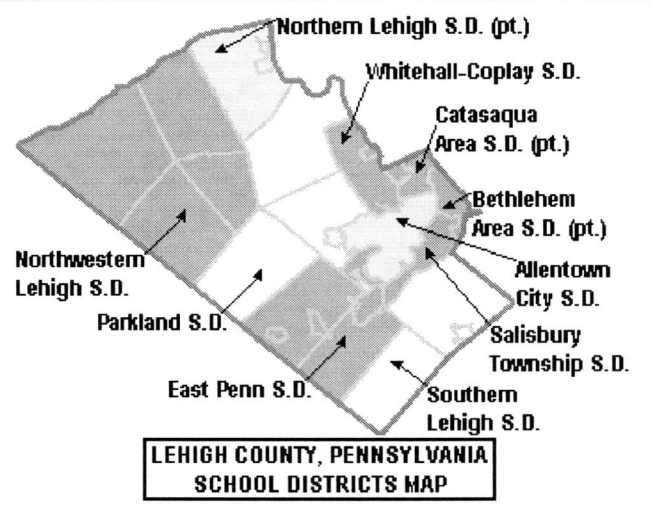

Map of Lehigh County, Pennsylvania School Districts

- Southern Lehigh School District
  - Southern Lehigh High School, Center Valley
- Whitehall-Coplay School District
  - Whitehall High School, Whitehall Township
  - Whitehall-Coplay Middle School

Non-public high schools and charter schools

- Allentown Central Catholic High School, Allentown
- Lehigh Career and Technical Institute, Schnecksville
- Lehigh Valley Christian High School, Allentown
- Roberto Clemente Charter School, Allentown
- Salem Christian School, Macungie
- Seven Generations Charter School, Emmaus

Transportation

Main article: Transportation in the Lehigh Valley

Air transportation

Lehigh County's primary airport, Lehigh Valley International Airport (IATA: **ABE**, ICAO: **KABE**), is located three miles (5 km) northeast of Allentown in Hanover Township.

The county is also served by Allentown Queen City Municipal Airport, a two-runway general aviation facility located off of Allentown's Lehigh Street. Queen City is used predominantly by private aviation that was awarded General Aviation Airport of the year by the Eastern Region of the Federal Aviation Administration in 2006.

Bus transportation

Public bus service in Lehigh County is available through the Lehigh and Northampton Transportation Authority, known as LANTA. Several private bus lines, including Bieber Tourways, Susquehanna Trailways and Trans-Bridge Lines, provide bus service from Allentown to New York City's Port Authority Bus Terminal, Philadelphia's Greyhound Terminal, Atlantic City's Bus Terminal, and other regional locations.

Road transportation

Interstates

- I-78
- I-476 -Northeast Extension of the Pennsylvania Turnpike

US Highway System

- Route 22
- Route 222

Pennsylvania Highway System

- Route 29 South
- Route 100
- Route 143
- Route 145
- Route 309
- Route 329
- Route 378
- Route 863
- Route 873
- Route 987

Other roads

- Cedar Crest Boulevard
- Lehigh Street

Media

Main article: Media in the Lehigh Valley

The Lehigh County is part of the Philadelphia broadcast media market, though numerous New York City radio and television stations also are available in Allentown and its suburbs. Lehigh County-based media include *The Morning Call*, a daily newspaper in Allentown, and two Allentown-based television stations: WLVT Channel 39 (a PBS affiliate) and WFMZ Channel 69 (an unaffiliated, independent television station).

Television

The four major Philadelphia-based network stations serving Lehigh County include: KYW-TV (CBS), WCAU (NBC), WPVI (ABC) and WTXF (Fox).

Print

The primary newspaper for the county is *The Morning Call*, based in Allentown.

Radio

Lehigh County-area radio stations include WAEB-AM, a news, talk and sports station (in Allentown), WAEB-FM (known as B104), a Top 40 music station (in Allentown), WZZO, a hard rock music station (in Whitehall Township), and others. Some major New York City stations and every major Philadelphia station also can be heard in the county.

Telecommunications

Lehigh County was once served only by the 215 area code from 1947 (when the North American Numbering Plan of the Bell System went into effect) until 1994. With the county's growing population, however, Lehigh County areas were afforded area code 610 in 1994. Today, Lehigh County is covered by 610. An overlay area code, 484, was added to the 610 service area in 1999. A plan to introduce area code 835 as an additional overlay was rescinded in 2001.

Public parks and recreation

See also: List of sites of interest in Allentown, Pennsylvania

Most municipalities in the county have set aside at least some land for public recreation, from neighborhood parks and playgrounds to the more expansive parkways developed by the county, city and several townships. Following are the public parks within the county of more than of 25 acres, including listings of their primary activities:

- **Cedar Creek Parkway**, Allentown, 127 acres. City-owned park along Cedar Creek that includes Lake Muhlenberg and Malcolm W. Gross Rose Gardens. Activities: hiking/walking, jogging, basketball, fishing, swimming and picnicking. Mayfair, an annual arts festival, is held in the Parkway each May.
- **Cedar Creek Parkway East**, South Whitehall Township, 37.5 acres. County-owned park along Cedar Creek that includes Haines Mill Museum. Activities: hiking/walking, soccer, fishing, nature study and picnicking.
- **Cedar Creek Parkway West**, South Whitehall Township, 261 acres. County-owned park along Cedar Creek. Activities: hiking/walking, jogging, baseball, softball, soccer, tennis, basketball, swimming, nature study and picnicking.

- **Covered Bridge Park**, South Whitehall Township, 165 acres. Township-owned park along Jordan Creek that includes two historic covered bridges. Activities: hiking/walking, jogging, football, soccer fields, volleyball, handball, fishing, disc golf, playground and nature study.
- **Jordan Creek Parkway**, Whitehall & South Whitehall Townships, 296.1 acres. County-owned park along Jordan Creek. Activities: hiking/walking, jogging, bicycling, softball, baseball, soccer, tennis, fishing, cross country skiing and nature study.
- **Leaser Lake**, Lynn Township, 540.5 acres. County-owned park (227.6 acres) and Pennsylvania Fish Commission-owned (312.9 acres) recreation area that includes a 117-acre lake. Activities: hiking/walking, fishing, hunting, boating (sail, other non-motor and small electric motor), cross country skiing, ice-skating, nature study and picnicking.
- **Lehigh Canal Park**, Allentown, 55 acres. City-owned park along the Lehigh River. Activities: hiking/walking, fishing and non-motor boating.
- **Lehigh Parkway**, Allentown, 999 acres. City-owned park along Little Lehigh Creek that also includes the Lil-Le-Hi Trout Nursery. Activities: hiking/walking, bicycling, fishing, disc golf, nature study and picnicking.
- **Lock Ridge Park**, Alburtis, 59.2 acres. County-owned park along Swabia Creek that includes the Lock Ridge Furnace Museum. Activities: hiking/walking, baseball, bicycling, fishing, cross country skiing, nature study and picnicking.
- **Lower Macungie Township Community Park**, Lower Macungie township, 56. acres. Township-owned park along Spring Creek. Activities: hiking/walking, jogging, soccer and picnicking.
- **Bob Rodale Cycling and Fitness Park**, Upper Macungie Township, 103.4 acres. County-owned bicycle track and fitness area. Activities: Hiking/walking, bicycling, softball, cricket, soccer, basketball, cross country skiing, roller blading, jogging, nature study, playground and picnicking.
- **South Mountain Big Rock Park**, Upper Saucon and Salisbury Townships, 57.1 acres. County-owned park. Activities: hiking/walking, picnicking and nature study.
- **Trexler Memorial Park**, Allentown, 134 acres. City-owned park along Cedar Creek. Activities: hiking/walking, jogging and nature study.
- **Trexler Nature Preserve**, 1108 acres. County-owned park along Jordan Creek, formerly Trexler-Lehigh County Game Preserve, which includes the Lehigh Valley Zoo and is adding 18 miles of trails in 2010. Activities: hiking/walking, mountain biking, jogging, fishing, hunting, nature study and picnicking.
- **Upper Macungie Park**, Upper Macungie Township, 156.2 acres. Township-owned park with nature trail. Activities: hiking/walking, baseball, softball, sand volleyball, horse shoes, playground, jogging, nature study and picnicking.
- **Whitehall Parkway**, Whitehall Township, 110 acres. Township-owned park connected to the nine-mile Ironton Rail-Trail. Activities: hiking/walking, bicycling, jogging and nature study.

Famous people from Lehigh County

See also: List of people from the Lehigh Valley

Lehigh County is the birthplace of, or home to, several notable Americans, including:

- Chuck Bednarik, former professional football player, Philadelphia Eagles, and member of Pro Football Hall of Fame.
- Stephen Vincent Benét, author.
- Michaela Conlin, stage and television actress, *Bones*.
- Don Cunningham, politician who has been elected mayor of Bethlehem and Executive of Lehigh County.
- Charlie Dent, Member of Congress.
- H.D., writer.
- Peter Gruner, professional wrestler.
- Lee Iacocca, former chairman of Chrysler Corporation.
- Keith Jarrett, jazz musician.
- Michael Johns, health care executive and former White House speechwriter.
- Carson Kressley, fashion consultant on Bravo's *Queer Eye for the Straight Guy*.
- Matt Millen, former professional football player, Oakland Raiders, San Francisco 49ers and Washington Redskins, and former President and General Manager, Detroit Lions.
- Andre Reed, former professional football player, Buffalo Bills and Washington Redskins.
- Amanda Seyfried, model and actress, The CW's *Veronica Mars* and HBO's *Big Love*.
- Curt Simmons, former professional baseball player, California Angels, Chicago Cubs, Philadelphia Phillies and St. Louis Cardinals.
- Dana Snyder, voice actor, Cartoon Network's *Aqua Teen Hunger Force*.
- Christine Taylor, actress and wife of actor Ben Stiller.
- Lauren Weisberger, author of *The Devil Wears Prada*.

See also

- Allentown Parking Authority
- List of municipal authorities in Lehigh County, Pennsylvania

External links

- Lehigh County travel guide from Wikitravel.
- Lehigh County Government Official Web Site [4].
- "Living in the Greater Lehigh Valley," by *The Allentown Morning Call* [5].

Geographical coordinates: 40°37′N 75°35′W

Northampton County, Pennsylvania

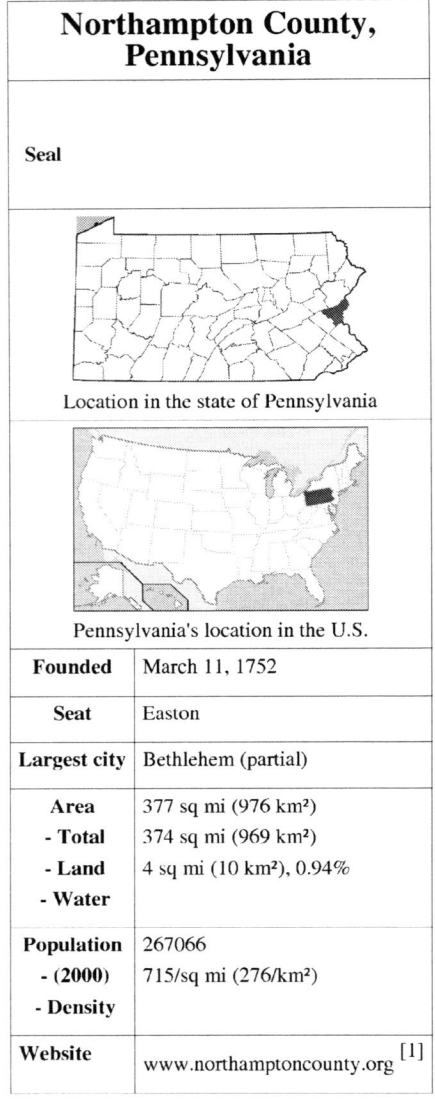

Northampton County, Pennsylvania	
Seal	
Location in the state of Pennsylvania	
Pennsylvania's location in the U.S.	
Founded	March 11, 1752
Seat	Easton
Largest city	Bethlehem (partial)
Area	
- Total	377 sq mi (976 km²)
- Land	374 sq mi (969 km²)
- Water	4 sq mi (10 km²), 0.94%
Population	267066
- (2000)	715/sq mi (276/km²)
- Density	
Website	www.northamptoncounty.org [1]

Northampton County is a county located in the U.S. state of Pennsylvania. It was formed in 1752 from parts of Bucks County. As of 2000, the population was 267,066, (2008 estimate 294,787). Its county seat is Easton.

Northampton County is located in Pennsylvania's Lehigh Valley. Its northern edge borders The Poconos. The eastern section of the county borders the Delaware River, which divides Pennsylvania and New Jersey. It is bordered on the west by Lehigh County, Pennsylvania, the Lehigh Valley's more highly populated county.

The county is industrially-oriented, producing anthracite coal, cement, and other industrial products. Bethlehem Steel, once one of the world's largest manufacturers of steel, was located there prior to its closing in 2003.

Geography

According to the U.S. Census Bureau, the county has a total area of 377 square miles (977 km²), of which 374 square miles (968 km²) is land and 4 square miles (9 km²) (0.94%) is water.

Adjacent counties

- Monroe County (north)
- Warren County, New Jersey (east)
- Bucks County (south)
- Lehigh County (west)
- Carbon County (northwest)

National protected areas

- Delaware Water Gap National Recreation Area (part)
- Middle Delaware National Scenic River (part)

Government

Northampton is one of the six counties in Pennsylvania which has adopted a home rule charter. Instead of being run by a Board of Commissioners and several Row Officers, voters elect an Executive, a nine-person Council, a Controller, and a District Attorney. The Executive, Controller and District Attorney are elected by all voters in the County, as are five members of the Council. The other four Councilmen are elected by districts.

Elected Officials[2]

- County Executive:
  - John Stoffa, Democrat
- County Council:
  - Ron Angle, Republican
  - John Cusick, Republican
  - Thomas H Dietrich, Republican
  - J. Michael Dowd, Republican
  - Margaret (Peg) Ferraro, Republican

- Bruce A Gilbert, Republican
- Lamont G. McClure Jr., Democrat
- Ann McHale, Democrat
- Barbara A. Thierry, Republican
- Clerk of Courts:
  - Leigh Ann Fisher, Democrat
- County Controller:
  - Stephen Barron, Jr. , Democrat
- District Attorney:
  - John Morganelli, Democrat
- Prothonotary:
  - Holly Ruggiero, Democrat
- Register of Wills:
  - Dorothy Cole, Democrat
- Sheriff:
  - Randall Miller

Demographics

Historical populations		
Census	Pop.	%±
1900	99687	—
1910	127667	28.1%
1920	153506	20.2%
1930	169304	10.3%
1940	168959	–0.2%
1950	185243	9.6%
1960	201412	8.7%
1970	214368	6.4%
1980	225418	5.2%
1990	247105	9.6%
2000	267066	8.1%

Est. 2009	298990		12.0%

As of the census of 2000, there were 267,066 people, 101,541 households, and 71,078 families residing in the county. The population density was 714 people per square mile (276/km²). There were 106,710 housing units at an average density of 286 per square mile (110/km²). The racial makeup of the county was 91.23% White, 2.77% Black or African American, 0.15% Native American, 1.37% Asian, 0.03% Pacific Islander, 3.06% from other races, and 1.39% from two or more races. 6.69% of the population were Hispanic or Latino of any race. 24.0% were of German, 14.0% Italian, 8.8% Irish, 5.1% English and 5.1% American ancestry according to Census 2000. 89.3% spoke English and 5.5% Spanish as their first language.

There were 101,541 households out of which 31.20% had children under the age of 18 living with them, 56.40% were married couples living together, 9.80% had a female householder with no husband present, and 30.00% were non-families. 24.70% of all households were made up of individuals and 11.20% had someone living alone who was 65 years of age or older. The average household size was 2.53 and the average family size was 3.02.

In the county, the population was spread out with 23.30% under the age of 18, 9.20% from 18 to 24, 28.30% from 25 to 44, 23.40% from 45 to 64, and 15.70% who were 65 years of age or older. The median age was 38 years. For every 100 females there were 94.80 males. For every 100 females age 18 and over, there were 91.70 males.

Politics

As of January 2010, there are 196,862 registered voters in Northampton County.

- Democratic: 98,451 (50.00%)
- Republican: 65,975 (33.51%)
- Other Parties: 32,436 (16.48%)

In recent decades, Northampton has been identified as one of Pennsylvania's "swing counties," with statewide winners carrying it in most cases. All five statewide winners carried it in November 2004 and all four statewide Democratic candidates carried it in November 2008, with its DA John Morganelli doing well there despite losing statewide to incumbent Attorney General Tom Corbett. The Democratic Party has been dominant most of the time in county-level politics in recent decades, County Executive John Stoffa, and most of the row offices. However with only two out of nine current county council seats.

County Council Members

- Ron Angle, President,Republican, District 4
- John Cusick, Vice President, Republican, (At-Large)
- Thomas H Dietrich, Republican, (At-Large)
- J. Michael Dowd, Republican, District 2
- Margaret (Peg) Ferraro, Republican, (At-Large)
- Bruce A Gilbert, Republican, (At-Large)
- Lamont G. McClure Jr., Democrat, District 3
- Ann McHale, Democrat, District 1
- Barbara A. Thierry, Republican, (At-Large)

State Representatives

- Karen D. Beyer, Republican, 131st district
- Joseph F. Brennan, Democrat, 133rd district
- Steve Samuelson, Democrat, 135th district
- Robert L. Freeman, Democrat, 136th district
- Richard Grucela, Democrat, 137th district
- Marcia Hahn, Republican, 138th district
- Julie Harhart, Republican, 183rd district

State Senators

- Pat Browne, Republican, 16th district
- Lisa Boscola, Democrat, 18th district
- Bob Mensch, Republican, 24th district
- Dave Argall, Republican, 29th district

US Representative

- Charlie Dent, Republican, 15th district

Famous people from Northampton County

Main article: List of people from the Lehigh Valley

- Marco Andretti, professional race car driver.
- Mario Andretti, former professional race car driver.
- Michael Andretti, professional racing team owner, former professional race car driver.
- Jonathan Frakes, director and actor.
- Larry Holmes, boxing's former heavyweight champion of the world.

- Daniel Dae Kim, actor.
- Samuel Henry Kress, founder of S. H. Kress & Co. and noted art collector.
- Kristen Maloney, gymnast and former Olympian.
- Bob Parsons, former professional football player, Chicago Bears.
- Aldo Ray, actor.
- Daniel Roebuck, actor.
- Brian Schneider, professional baseball player, Philadelphia Phillies.
- Tighe Scott, NASCAR and modified driver.
- Jonathan Taylor Thomas, actor.
- George Wolf, Governor of Pennsylvania 1829-1835

Municipalities

Under Pennsylvania law, there are four types of incorporated municipalities: cities, boroughs, townships, and two towns. The following cities, boroughs and townships are located in Northampton County:

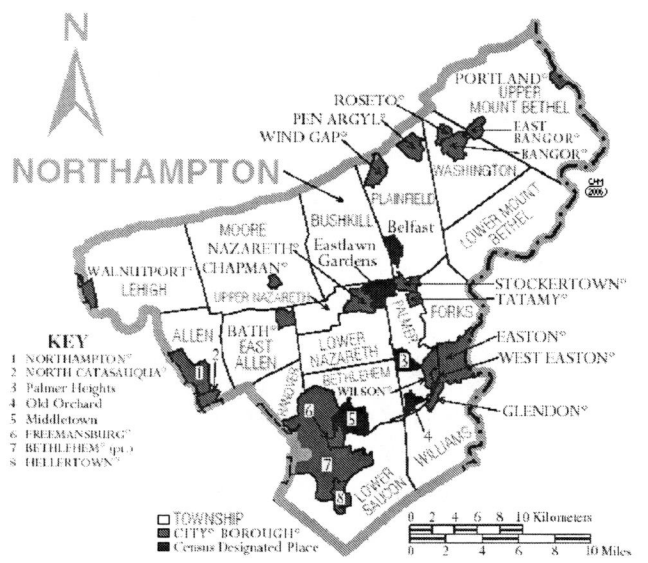

Map of Northampton County, Pennsylvania with Municipal Labels showing Cities and Boroughs (red), Townships (white), and Census-designated places (blue).

Cities

- Bethlehem
- Easton

Boroughs

- Bangor
- Bath
- Chapman
- East Bangor
- Freemansburg
- Glendon
- Hellertown
- Nazareth
- North Catasauqua
- Northampton
- Pen Argyl
- Portland
- Roseto
- Stockertown
- Tatamy
- Walnutport
- West Easton
- Wilson
- Wind Gap

Townships

- Allen Township
- Bethlehem Township
- Bushkill Township
- East Allen Township
- Forks Township
- Hanover Township
- Lehigh Township
- Lower Mount Bethel Township
- Lower Nazareth Township
- Lower Saucon Township
- Moore Township
- Palmer Township
- Plainfield Township
- Upper Mount Bethel Township
- Upper Nazareth Township
- Washington Township
- Williams Township

Census-designated places

Census-designated places are geographical areas designated by the U.S. Census Bureau for the purposes of compiling demographic data. They are not actual jurisdictions under Pennsylvania law. Other unincorporated communities, such as villages, may be listed here as well.

- Belfast
- Eastlawn Gardens
- Middletown
- Old Orchard
- Palmer Heights

Education

Colleges & Universities

- Lafayette College, Easton.
- Lehigh University, Bethlehem.
- Moravian College, Bethlehem.
- Northampton County Area Community College, Bethlehem Township.

Public school districts & schools

- Bangor Area School District
  - Bangor Area High School, Upper Mount Bethel Township
- Bethlehem Area School District
  - Freedom High School, Bethlehem
  - Liberty High School, Bethlehem
- Catasauqua Area School District
  - Catasauqua High School, Northampton
- Easton Area School District
  - Easton Area High School, Palmer Township
- Nazareth Area School District
  - Nazareth Area High School, Nazareth
- Northampton Area School District
  - Northampton Area High School, Northampton
- Pen Argyl Area School District
  - Pen Argyl Area High School, Pen Argyl
- Saucon Valley School District
  - Saucon Valley High School, Hellertown
- Wilson Area School District
  - Wilson Area High School, Wilson

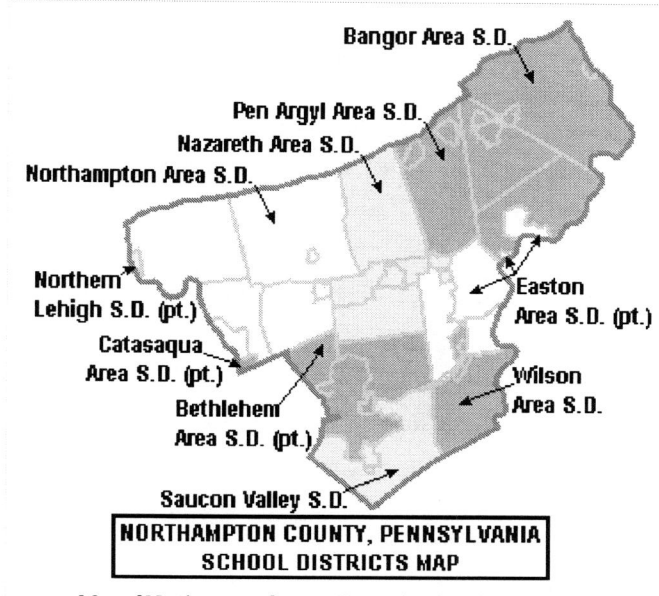

Map of Northampton County, Pennsylvania School Districts

Public Charter High Schools

The Lehigh Valley Charter High School for the Performing Arts, Bethlehem

Non-public high schools

- Bethlehem Catholic High School, Bethlehem
- Holy Family School, Nazareth
- Moravian Academy, Bethlehem
- Notre Dame High School, Bethlehem Township
- Pius X High School, Bangor

Transportation

See also: Transportation in the Lehigh Valley

Air transportation

Air transport to and from Northampton County is available through Lehigh Valley International Airport (IATA: **ABE**, ICAO: **KABE**).

Bus transportation

Public bus service in Northampton County is available through the Lehigh and Northampton Transportation Authority, known as LANTA.

Expressways

- Interstate 78
- Pennsylvania Route 33
- U.S. Route 22

Telecommunications

Northampton County was once served only by the 215 area code from 1947 (when the North American Numbering Plan of the Bell System went into effect) until 1994. With the county's growing population, however, Northampton County was afforded area code 610 in 1994. Today, Northampton County is covered by 610. An overlay area code, 484, was added to the 610 service area in 1999. A plan to introduce area code 835 as an additional overlay was rescinded in 2001.

Recreation

There are 2 Pennsylvania state parks in Northampton County.

- Delaware Canal State Park follows the course of the old Delaware Canal along the Delaware River from Easton in Northampton County to Bristol in Bucks County.
- Jacobsburg Environmental Education Center

See also

- Lehigh Valley Conference
- List of municipal authorities in Northampton County, Pennsylvania
- List of shopping malls in the Lehigh Valley
- Media in the Lehigh Valley

External links

- Northampton County travel guide from Wikitravel.
- Northampton County news at Lehigh Valley Live [3].
- Northampton County Official Web Site [4].
- "Living in the Greater Lehigh Valley," by *The Allentown Morning Call* [5].

Geographical coordinates: 40°45′N 75°19′W

Center Valley, Pennsylvania

Center Valley is an unincorporated village one mile north of Coopersburg, Pennsylvania, at the intersection of Pennsylvania Route 309 and Pennsylvania Route 378 in Upper Saucon Township, Lehigh County, Pennsylvania, in the United States.

In 1990, Center Valley had a population of 900.

Commerce

The Stabler Center, one of the largest areas of land being developed in the Lehigh Valley, is located in Center Valley. In October 2006, The Promenade Shops at Saucon Valley, the Lehigh Valley's highest-end mall, opened for business.

Center Valley also is the location for the headquarters of Olympus Corporation for the Americas and the headquarters of the Patriot League college athletic conference, which has 23 sports (men's: 11; women's: 12), including NCAA Division I FCS football.

Education

Three campuses of higher education are located in Center Valley:

- DeSales University (formerly Allentown College of St. Francis de Sales)
- Penn State Lehigh Valley
- Strayer University (Allentown campus)

Hanover Township, Pennsylvania

Hanover Township is the name of some places in the U.S. state of Pennsylvania:

- Hanover Township, Beaver County, Pennsylvania
- Hanover Township, Lehigh County, Pennsylvania
- Hanover Township, Luzerne County, Pennsylvania
- Hanover Township, Northampton County, Pennsylvania
- Hanover Township, Washington County, Pennsylvania

See also:

- East Hanover Township, Pennsylvania
- South Hanover Township, Pennsylvania
- West Hanover Township, Pennsylvania

Things to Do and See

Musikfest

	Official Poster for Musikfest 2010
Location(s)	Bethlehem, Pennsylvania
Years active	1984 - Present
Founded by	Jeff Parks
Date(s)	Begins on the Friday before the first Saturday in August and ends on the Sunday ten days later
Genre	Classic Rock, Rock and Roll, Alternative Rock, Hard Rock, Grunge, Southern Rock, Soft Rock, Indie, Country, Progressive Rock, New Wave, Americana, R&B, Soul, Rockabilly, Funk, Bluegrass, Pop, Polka, Fusion, Jazz, Jam, Blues, Classical, Folk, Latin, Celtic, World
Website	www.musikfest.org [1]

Musikfest is a music festival that has been held each August in Bethlehem, Pennsylvania, USA since 1984. The festival begins on the first Friday in August and ends on Sunday ten days later.

Each year, thousands of visitors and residents of Pennsylvania make the trip to Bethlehem to participate in a celebration that weaves through a Moravian community that dates back to 1741. Festival visitors are treated to hundreds of free shows over the course of the event. Each night, the festival's premium stage, RiverPlace, hosts a nationally-known recording artist. These premium concerts, along with select shows at other stages, require paid tickets to gain admission.

Past headlining shows have included Stone Temple Pilots, Clay Aiken, Air Supply, Alice in Chains, Boston, The Beach Boys, Tony Bennett, Boyz II Men, Carrie Underwood, Collective Soul, Ray Charles, George Clinton, Dixie Chicks, Dr. Demento, Weird Al Yankovic, Poison, Duran Duran, Earth, Wind & Fire, Fuel, Ludacris, Hootie & the Blowfish, Kool & The Gang, Jethro Tull, Jonny Lang, Lynyrd Skynyrd, Martina McBride, Steve Miller Band, Live, REO Speedwagon, Staind & George Thorogood.

Local German roots are the foundation of the celebration, and most of the festival's venues use the German word for place, "platz", at the ends of their names. A popular place for eating and listening to music, for example, is the large "Festplatz", which includes 300 dining tables and usually features a polka band each night. Beyond that, however, Musikfest's music, food and other attractions represent a broad range of ethnicities.

Musikfest is presented by ArtsQuest, a nonprofit arts organization founded to "celebrate arts and culture" in the Lehigh Valley and beyond. Proceeds from the event benefit ArtsQuest ventures such as the Banana Factory community arts center in South Bethlehem, as well as other nonprofit groups throughout the region.[2]

2010 Performers

Musikfest 2010, which is presented by ArtsQuest, will take place 5-11 p.m. Aug. 6 and noon-11 p.m. Aug. 7-15. The festival will include some 500 musical performances on 14 indoor and outdoor stages throughout Bethlehem's historic, 18th-century downtown. In addition, the event will showcase delicious food and desserts by more than 60 vendors, a variety of children's activities, visual arts and crafts and a closing-night fireworks display. The official theme of this year's festival is Transformation, and to show this a new stage will be added to the festival known as the Transformation Series Stage, which is to be located at Moravian College. [3] [4]

Sands RiverPlace Stage

- August 6, 2010 - **Counting Crows with Augustana** - Sponsored by: The Morning Call, 100.7 WLEV, and 69-WFMZ-TV

- August 7, 2010 - **Norah Jones with Elvis Perkins** - Sponsored by: The Harold S. Campbell Foundation, Lafayette Ambassador Bank, and 100.7 WLEV

- August 8, 2010 - **Martina McBride** - Sponsored by: PenTeleData, Cat Country 96, and The Express-Times

- August 9, 2010 - **Lynyrd Skynyrd** - Sponsored by: Independence IT, Bank of America and 99.9 The Hawk

- August 10, 2010 - **Heart** - Sponsored by: Lehigh Valley Health Network, B.Braun Medical/Aesculap, and 99.9 The Hawk

- August 11, 2010 - **The Doobie Brothers** - Sponsored by: Highmark Blue Shield and 99.9 The Hawk

- August 12, 2010 - **Styx and Blue Öyster Cult** - Sponsored by: Edwards Business Systems, AD Computer, and 99.9 The Hawk

- August 13, 2010 - **Adam Lambert with Orianthi and Allison Iraheta** - Sponsored by: B104 and Pottstown Mercury

- August 14, 2010 - **Selena Gomez & The Scene with JLS and Hot Chelle Rae** - Sponsored by: B104, MacIntosh Linens, and 69-WFMZ-TV

- August 15, 2010 - **Sublime With Rome and special guests The Dirty Heads and The Movement** - Sponsored by: WZZO

Musikfest Performing Arts Series

Dark Star Orchestra, and The Avett Brothers

PNC Bank Candlelight Concert Series

The Music of Simon & Garfunkel Performed by A.J. Swearingen & Jonathan Beedle, Joe Lovano & John Scofield Quartet, Richie Havens, Cherish the Ladies, Dave Mason, and Suzy Bogguss

Amped Up!

Similar to Musikfest 2009's Mid-Atlantic Band Competition, Musikfest 2010 features a competition for various bands to compete for spots at Musikfest. This year's competition is going to be called "Amped Up!". Beginning in April 2010 and ending later that month, bands interested in competing are to enter on the festival's official website.[5] 10 bands will be chosen out of the multitude that will enter. Of those 10, the top 3 with the most votes will earn a concert at Musikfest as well as a monetary prize.

Amped Up! Finalists

Blue Wave Theory, BoomBoxRepairKit, Chewsen, Downtown Harvest, Open Till Midnight, **Panic Years**, Revolution I Love You, **The Atomic Square**, **The Hide and Seek Effect**, and The Ugly Club

- **Bold** denotes that the band was one of the three winners of the contest.

The Platzes

Eleven of Musikfest's 14 stages, including the new Transformation stage, feature free concerts [6].

Americaplatz: Trombone Shorty & Orleans Avenue, Rod Piazza & The Mighty Flyers, Chris Duarte, The Commander Cody Band, The Dirty Guv'nahs, Shane Dwight, Ana Popović, Sarah Borges & The Broken Singles, Wailing Waters, Philadelphia Funk Authority, Grayson Capps & The Stumpknockers, Craig Thatcher Band, Eric Steckel, Westside Winders, The Headers, Bronze Radio Return, Mike Dugan and The Blues Mission, The Mike Montrey Band, Meeting in the Aisle - A Tribute to Radiohead, James Supra Blues Band, BC Combo, Start Making Sense - Talking Heads Tribute, The Blues Brotherhood, Friar's Point, She Said Sunday, Lou Franco Project, FortyGrand, The Difference, and Peripheral Vision.

Fowler & Peña Banana Island: Mingo Fishtrap, Lipbone Redding & The Lipbone Orchestra, Missy Raines & The New Hip, Elvis Bossa Nova, Zen For Primates, Craig Kastelnik & Friends, Bill Warfield Octet, Shelly Clark & Friends, The Gas House Gorillas, Jenny Dee & The Deelinquents, Babatunde Lea, Eric Mintel Quintet, Dueling Pianos, Big Bang Boom, The Cat's Pajamas, boyintheshade, Dave

Fry, Frank Gisaullo Quartet, Kira Willey, The Riffters, The Shalitas, Tommy Zito, Uproar of the 70's, Tony & The Tonics, Steve Pullara & His Cool Beans Band, Large Flowerheads, Butterjive, Dan DeChillis Trio, Fusion Jazz Trio, Lachi, Miss Amy & Her Big Kids Band, Yosi & The Superdads, Alex & The Kaleidoscope Band, Hot Peas 'N Butter, Baze & His Silly Friends, Key Wilde & Mr. Clarke, Starfish, Peanut Butter Jellyfish, B.D. Lenz, Uncle Rock, Ernie & Neal, Nina Music, and Guitar Students with BASD.

Chamber Series: Satori, Carpe Diem String Quartet, Denis Azabagic, and Silver & Brass.

SuperGuarantee Festplatz: George Gee Swing Orchestra, The Fabulous Greaseband, Mingo Fishtrap, Sensational Soul Cruisers, Rob Stonebeck Big Band, The Flamin' Caucasians, Spitze!, Jimmy Sturr & His Orchestra, Main Street Cruisers, Lucky 7, M-80, CrazyHeart, Kickin' Polkas, John Stevens' Doubleshot, Dennis Polisky & The Maestro's Men, The Adlers, O.L.B. Part Power, Polka Country Musicians, Walt Groller Orchestra, Henry & The Versa J's, Lenny Gomulka & The Coalminers, The Alex Meixner Band, Joe Weber, Joe Kroboth, Jolly Joe Timmer, Eddie Forman Orchestra, and Lindyhop Swing Dancers.

Handwerkplatz: Cast in Bronze.

Liederplatz: Hoots & Hellmouth, Christine Havrilla, Edie Carey, Pamela Means, Bronze Radio Return, The Arrogant Worms, The Guggenheim Grotto, Three Legged Fox, Sweetback Sisters, Eric Steckel, Cabinet, The Bruce Katz Band, Cathie Ryan, The Headers, Todd Wolfe, Tin Bird Choir, Two Man Gentleman Band, Billy Bauer Band, Donovan Roberts, Scott Marshall & Marshall's Highway, Mike Cross, The Rosie Burgess Trio, Lindsay Mac, Dina Hall, Acoustic Roadshow, The Best of Godfrey Daniels' Open Mic Show, The Lehigh Valley Folk Music Society, and The Bucks County Folk Song Society.

Martin Guitar Lyrikplatz: Jennie Arnau, Lachi, Bud Buckley, Mishal Moore, Scott McKenna, Shoulders of Giants, Jacob Vanags, Brosky 'N Meyer, Anna Rose, BC Combo, John Conahan, Lizanne Knott, Ben Arthur (musician), Michael Berkowitz, Dave Fry, Grace McLean, Quincy Mumford, Mr. Chris, Marnee, Daryl Shawn, ilyAIMY, Shannon & Natalie, The Philly Songwriters Showcase, Slate Belt Idol, Wild Flower Cafe Showcase, Barnaby Bright, Sarah Donner, Annie Simoni, Tim Butler, Ashley Lennon Thomas, Brian Mackey, Andrew Portz, Maura Jensen, Olivier Nataf-NO, Chris Bruni, Pat Guadagno, Craig Bickhardt, Ellen Woloshin, Pete Hanks, and Carlos Barata.

Main Street: Overlook, Oso, The Greatest Funeral Ever, Elvis Bossa Nova, My Cousin the Emperor, Andy Suzuki & The Method, Amplify This, The Great Unknown, The Almighty Terribles, Grey Sky Turn, Steve Brosky 'N Jimmy Meyer, Two Man Gentleman Band, Little Buddy, Mark Zaleski, Abrams Brothers, Fellswoop, Loretta Hagen, Kinobe & Soul Beat Africa, Banjo Dan and the Mid-nite Plowboys, Parkington Sisters, The Hillbilly Souls, Joe White, Marnee, The Rosie Burgess Trio, The Wallace Brothers, Wineskin, Hogmaw, Ben Mauger's Dixieland Jazz Band, The Syncopatin' Six, and Audio Dynamikz Presents Vibrations On Main.

The Morning Call Plaza Tropical: LaExcelencia, The Clarks, Splintered Sunlight, Los Straitjackets, The Arrogant Worms, Celtic Cross, Munelly, Jimmy & The Parrots, Papote Jimenez & Lower East Salsa, Luisto Rosario & Orquestra, Willie Colón, Santa Mamba, The Big Dirty, The Insidious Rays, Orchestra Herencia de Sonoros, CHEMBO and Grupo CHAWORD, Karen Rodriguez Latin Jazz Ensemble, ReggaeInfinity, David Cedeno & His Orchestra, Tieweb, Los Pocos Locos, The Hooligans, Davey & The Waverunners, Inner Visions, Freddie Long Band, Pete Francis, The B-Attitudes, b9 Fate, Five Mile Fall, The Mango Men, Ricky Smith & The Crush, School of Rock - Bank Street Band, Sabroso Video Showcase, Traditions of Hanover, Sumer Bleu's Violin Studio, LV Community Music School, The Doug Hawk Proposition, AMLA, SUYA, HALA - Salseros 2010, Lehigh Valley Piano Teachers Association, The Lesson Center, Bethlehem Music Settlement, and Lehigh Valley Community Music School.

Transformation Series: John Scofield & Joe Lovano, Babatunde Lea, Cherish the Ladies, The Philadelphia Handbell Ensemble, and Elaine & Susan Hoffman-Watts.

Vesper Series: Philadelphia Handbell Ensemble, Georgia Guitar Quartet, Innovata, The Altino Brothers, and The Dali Quartet.

Pennsylvania Lottery Volksplatz: Trombone Shorty & Orleans Avenue, Igor & The Red Elvises, Scythian, Los Straitjackets, Rosie Ledet & The Zydeco Playboys, Mama Jama, Enter The Haggis, Diego's Umbrella, Red Baraat, Brother Josephus & The Love Revival Revolution Orchestra, Spiritual Rez, RubbieBucket, 2U - U2 Tribute, Zen for Primates, Sweetback Sisters, Seamus Kennedy, Philly Bloco, Barleyjuice, Daisy Jug Band, Kagero, River City Slim & The Zydeco Hogs, Malinky, Burning Bridget Cleary, Balla Kouyate & World Vision, The Fabulous Shpielkehs, Kinobe & Soul Beat Africa, Satabdi Express, Abrams Brothers, Alex Meixner, The Alex Meixner Band, Rosie Burgess Trio, Great White Caps, Blackwater, Steppin' Razor, Brown Penny, Limpopo International Band, Jamani Drummers, Barynya Balalaika Duo, O'Grady Quinlan Academy, Sharon Plessl School of Dance, Allegro Dance Studio, Monarch Dance Company, Blue Ribbon Cloggers, Lehigh Valley Cloggers, and The Irish Stars.

2009 Performers

Sands RiverPlace Stage

The Commodores, The Wallflowers and Chris Isaak, Yes and Asia, David Cook with Green River Ordinance, Third Eye Blind with Matt Nathanson, The B-52's and Joan Jett & The Blackhearts, Puddle of Mudd and Trapt with Stasis, Pat Benatar and Blondie with The Donnas, George Thorogood & The Destroyers with Jonny Lang, and Crosby, Stills & Nash.

- Panic! at the Disco and Owl City were originally on the lineup, but had to cancel due to scheduling conflict. They have since been replaced by The Commodores.[1]

Independence IT Performing Arts Series

Ladysmith Black Mambazo, Gordon Lightfoot, and Rufus Wainright.

PNC Bank Candlelight Concert Series

Martin Sexton, Al Stewart, Leon Redbone, Dar Williams, The Broadway Boys, and Simone.

Northampton Community College Mid-Atlantic Band Competition

A first for 2009, Musikfest is holding a web-based competition for any band in the mid-Atlantic region of the United States to win a gig at this year's Musikfest. Twenty bands are slated to be chosen by online voting, out of the estimated hundreds that will most likely enter the competition. Of those twenty, 4 will be chosen after competitions between the bands, and those 4 bands will get performances at Musikfest 2009, as well as monetary prizes. Of those 4 bands, one will have their performance filmed and be guaranteed a booking at Musikfest 2010.[7]

Entrance for the bands has since ended and the voting process will begin soon.

Northampton Community College Mid-Atlantic Band Competition Winners

The following 4 bands have been chosen out of the original Top 10 and have won the Mid-Atlantic Band Competition.

Dephonic, Jaded Son, Parkwright, and Reilly.[8]

- The Gary Bonnett Band had originally been one of the four finalists, but had to cancel their performance for personal reasons. The band Reilly has since been given the honor of becoming one of the finalists.

The Platze

Eleven of Musikfest's 14 stages, located at platze (places) throughout the festival area, feature free concerts.

Americaplatz: Sarah Ayers Band, The Craig Thatcher Band, HER & King's Country, Cooper Boone, Antsy McClain & The Trailer Park Troubadors, Eric Steckel, Larry Holmes & Marmalade, Rosie Flores, Peripheral Vision, Frog Holler, Dr. Dog, Deb Callahan Band, BC & Company, Ronnie Baker Brooks, Don Cunningham and His Cabinet, Steve Brosky & His Big Lil' Band, Stars of Bethlehem, Friar's Point, Todd Wolfe, Davy Knowles & Back Door Slam, The Doughboys, The Difference, Marcia Ball, Mike Dugan & The Blues Mission, Grayson Capps & The Stumpknockers, John Lee Hooker Junior, Scott Marshall & Marshall's Highway, Guitardogs, and The Philadelphia Funk Authority.

Fowler & Peña Banana Island: The Trophy Husbands, The Uptown Band, Steve Pullara, Thaddeus Rex, The McKrells, Alison Brown Quartet, David Fry, The Dirty Sock Funtime Band, Nancy Coletti, Magnum, Trombosis, Ray Owen, The Cat's Pajamas, Tommy Zito, The Large Flowerheads, Kira

Willey, BASD Guitar Camp, Fusion Jazz Trio, Big City Music Band, Project, Baze & His Silly Friends, Hot Peas 'N Butter, Women's Blues Alliance, Mingo Fishtrap, Two-of-a-Kind, Big Bang Boom, Shelly Clark, Craig Kastelnik, Miss Amy & Her Big Kids Band, BoyintheShade, Dan DeChellis Trio, Dueling Pianos, Suzi Shelton, Princess Katie & Racer Steve, Brad Litwin, John Németh, Missy Raines & The New Hip, Uncle Rock, Yosi & The Superdads, Marlene Gilley Swingtet, and Lucy Bonilla.

Chamber Series: City Winds Trio, The Mascaro-Newman Duo, Innovata, Gabriel Chamber Ensemble, and The Sybarite Five.

Evolution Music Series: Latin Fiesta: The Evolution of Latin Music, David Leonhardt: The Evolution of Jazz, Brad Litwin: The Evolution of Blues, Barry Hannigan: The Evolution of the Piano, and Dave Fry - Rock Roots: The Evolution of Rock 'n' Roll.

The Morning Call Festplatz: Jolly Joe Timmer, Lenny Gomulka & The Chicago Push, Dennis Polisky & The Maestro's Men, Jump City Jazz, Walt Groller Orchestra, Jimmy Sturr & His Orchestra, Main Street Cruisers, Joe Weber, Polka Family Band, Crazy Heart, Joe Lastovica & The Polka Punch, Jon Stevens' Doubleshot, The Sensational Soul Cruisers, Die Fahrenbacher, The Slicked Up 9's, City Rhythm Orchestra, The Polka Quads, The Fabulous Greaseband, Josef Kroboth, The Steve Meisner Band, Lucky 7, Henry & The Versa J's, UUU, The Flamin' Caucasians, The Adlers, Brave Combo, and Alex Meixner & Bubba Hernandez.

Handwerkplatz: Cast in Bronze

Liederplatz: Scott Paul, Donovan-Roberts, Zen For Primates, Bronze Radio Return, Lili Añel, The Headers, The Dan May Band, Webb Wilder & The Beatnicks, Eric Steckel, Lehigh Valley Folk Music Society, Catie Curtis, Digney Fignus, Antsy McClain & The Trailer Park Troubadours, Andrew Portz, Justin Solonyka, Emerald City, Burning Bridget Cleary, The Tartan Terrors, Seamus Kennedy, Acoustic Roadshow, Project, Lovell sisters, Natural Breakdown, Jack Murray, Paul Rishell and Annie Raines, Godfrey Daniels, Hoots & Hellmouth, The Chandler Travis Philharmonic, Chris Smither, Philadelphia Songwriters, David Jacobs-Strain, The Youngers, Carrie Rodriguez, Oakhurst, Matt Watroba, Andy Cohen, Robin Greenstein, Peter Siegel, Annie Hills with Jay Ansill & Strings, Bob Carlin & Cheick Hamala Diabaté, Beaucoup Blue, Radio Free Earth, Women in Docs, The Duhks, The Arrogant Worms, Lisa Bodnar Band, Fellswoop, Girls, Guns & Glory, and Chuck Mead.

Martin Guitar Lyrikplatz: Jennie Arnau, Lachi, Bud Buckley, Mishal Moore, Scott McKenna, Shoulders of Giants, Jacob Vanags, Brosky 'N Meyer, Anna Rose, BC Combo, John Conahan, Lizanne Knott, Ben Arthur, Michael Berkowitz, Dave Fry, Grace McLean, Quincy Mumford, Mr. Chris, Marnee, Daryl Shawn, ilyAIMY, Shannon & Natalie, The Philly Songwriters Showcase, Slate Belt Idol, Wild Flower Cafe Showcase, Barnaby Bright, Sarah Donner, Annie Simoni, Tim Butler, Ashley Lennon Thomas, Brian Mackey, Andrew Portz, Maura Jensen, Olivier Nataf-NO, Chris Bruni, Pat Guadagno, Craig Bickhardt, Ellen Woloshin, Pete Hanks, and Carlos Barata.

Plaza Tropical: Ogans, Luisito Rosario & Orquetra, PhillyBloco, Latin Fiesta, Chino Nunez, AMLA Showcase, The Young Werewolves, The Coffin Daggers, Los Straitjackets, HALA Solseros 2009, Lehigh Valley Pennsylvania Music Teachers Association, Bethlehem Music Settlement, Go Trio, Sandlot Heroes, Dephonic, Jaded Son, Paul Green School of Rock Music, Community Music School, Irish Stars Parker School of Irish Dance, Monarch Dance Company, Talking Heads Tribute: Start Making Sense, Parkwright, Reilly, The Oasis Band, SWiM, Beyond Barriers, Butterjive, KEF, Splintered Sunlight, The Mango Men, Parrot Beach, The Toga Party Band, Jimmy & The Parrots [9], Lehigh Valley Charter High School for the Performing Arts, The Lesson Center, 3D Ritmo de Vida, Santa Mamba, Sergio Rivera & Friends Salsa, SUYA, Frankie Morales & the Mambo of the Times Orchestra, Pablo Mayor & Folklore Urbano, Sabroso Video Showcase, and Hector Rosado y su Orchestra Aché.

Pennsylvania Lottery Volksplatz: George Hrab & the Geologic Orchestra, Brother, Auerhahn Schuhplattler Verein, Li'l Anne & Hot Cayenne, Trouble City All Stars, Trombone Shorty & Orleans Avenue, Blue Ribbon Cloggers, C'est Si Bon, Jamnazi Africa Band, Daisy Jug Band, The Tartan Terrors, Alô Brasil, Seamus Kennedy, Digney Fignus, Lovell sisters, Zydeco-A-Go-Go, Los Straitjackets, Allegro Dance Company, The Jamani Drummers, Bearfoot, Salsa Celtica, Mingo Fishtrap, Mama Jama, Music From China, Blackwater, Oakhurst, Scythian, O'Grady-Quinlan Academy, Barynya Russian Balalaika Duo, The Doc Marshalls, Spiritual Rez, Tempest, Brownpenny, The Martin Family Band, Super Haki Haki with Dola Kabarry, West Philadelphia Orchestra, The Red Elvises, Lehigh Valley Cloggers, I Paesani, The Afromotive, Witches in Bikinis, Sharon Plessl/Excel Dance Company, Catfish and The Crawdaddies, and The Blues Brotherhood.

Vesper Series: The Colorado Quartet, Bay Street Brassworks, The Ravel Trio, All4One Piano Duo, and Barry Hannigan.

2008 Performers

Straub Dodge Chrysler Jeep RiverPlace Stage

Avril Lavigne, Live and Collective Soul, Kool & The Gang, Boston, Poison, Earth, Wind & Fire, Jethro Tull, Lonestar and Diamond Rio, and John Fogerty.

MRK Hostwindow Performing Arts Series

Lez Zeppelin, Dennis DeYoung, .38 Special, Phil Vassar, Citizen Cope, and Rosanne Cash

PNC Bank Candlelight Concert Series

John Gorka, Eileen Ivers, Over the Rhine, Edwin McCain, The Dixie Hummingbirds, and Christian McBride.

The Platze

Americaplatz: Sarah Ayers, Tommy Castro, Collins Brothers Band, Mother Truckers, Matt Jenkins, The Rob Stoneback Big Band, Antsy McClain & The Trailer Park Troubadours, West Side Winders, The Mayor & His Cabinet, The Craig Thatcher Band, Roomful of Blues, Peripheral Vision, Deb Callahan, Lil' Ed & The Blue Imperials, Leslie, Webb Wilder, Matt Zeiner, The Last Waltz Ensemble, Ryan Shaw, Eric Steckel, Todd Wolfe, Blue Wild Gypsy, and The Sensational Soul Cruisers.

Banana Island: Joe Baione, Zen for Primates, Steve Pullara & The Cool Beans Band, Yosi & The Superdads, BC & The Blues Crew, Geoff Achinson & The Souldiggers, Thaddeus Rex, The Cat's Pajamas, Dan DeChellis, Craig Kastelnik, Ray Owen, The Jimmies, Dave Fry, Tommy Zito, Triple Play, Uproar of 1968, Mister Ray, Moove & Groove, Lauren Musurneci & Joe Musurneci, Kind of Blue, Dueling Pianos, Starfish, David Joel, The Element, Big Jeff & His Mid-Sized Band, Miss Amy, Tim Marchetto, Lao Tizer, Mingo Fishtrap, and Marlene Giley.

Festplatz: Eddie Forman, Jolly Joe Timmer, Dennis Polisky & The Maestro's Men, Big Tubba Mista, Jump City Jazz, Steve Meisner, Walt Groller, Jimmy Sturr, Josef Kroboth, Polka Family Band, The Farmer's Daughter, Crazy Heart, Lucky 7, Die Mariazeller, Joe Grikman, Lebanon Big Swing Band, City Rhythm Orchestra, Doubleshoot, Fabulous Greaseband, Adam Barthalt, Shama Lama, UUU, The Flamin' Caucasians, Joe Weber, The Adlers, Lyn Marie & The Boxhounds, and Alex Meixner.

Main Street: Religion & Cash, Jackie Tice, Kane & Beatty, Straight Drive, Tavern Tan Band, Not Quite Sure, Beaucoup Blue, The Syncopatin' Six, Mad Sweet Pangs, Scott Marshall, Jackknife Betty, Mount Laurel Bluegrass Band, My Better Half, Russ Rentler, Erick Macek, Marc Silver, Tin Kettle, Jay Smar, Run Mountain, The Big Dirty, Doug Smith, Two Man Gentlemen Band, Wahoo Skiffle Crazies, and Quick Step John.

Liederplatz: Women In Docs, Cadillac Sky, Straight Drive, Ernie Hawkins, Paul & Storm, Chestnut Brass Company, J.B. Kline, Frank Bey & The Swing City Blues Band, Alathea, Emerald City, Kennedy's Kitchen, Sligo Rags, The Lovell Sisters, Jason Spooner, Janis Ian, Toby Walker, Godfrey Daniels, The McKrells, Susan Werner, The Electric Farm, The Philadelphia Songwriters, Tommy Womack, The Doc Marshalls, The Section Quartet, Cathy & Marcy, Radio Free Earth, Dan May, The Daisy Jug Band, The DoughBoys, Jann Klose, Vanida Gai, Craig Bickhardt, Lizanne Knot, and Peter Karp.

Lyrikplatz: Jerry Haines, Lester Hersch, Lisa Bodnar, Sara Cox, Gillian Grassie, Brian Thomas Jackson, Kendra Ross, Tim Miller, Arlon Bennett, Lili Anel, Steve Mahoney, Donovan Roberts, Tim Marchetto, Andrew Portz, David LaFleur, Skip Denenberg, Shawn Z., HelenMaria, Joey Mutis, Jeff Umbehauer, Christy Jefferson, Steve Brosky & Jimmy Meyer, Laura Warshauer, Ken Waldman, Eric Macek, Sarah Donner, George Hrab, Casey Desmond, Phoebe Henry, Ange & Ris, John Conahan, Susie Keynes, Jann Klose, Vanida Gail, and Alfred James.

Plaza Tropical: 3D Ritmo De Vida, Santa Mamba, D'La Kalle, Chino Nunez & Friends, Frankie Morales & The Mambo of the Time Band, AMLA, The Coffin Daggers, The Atomic Mosquitoes, Diamond Head, The Salseros, Beyond Barriers, SWiM, Cubana Tres, Butterjive, Project 222, Splintered Sunlight, The John Frizi Band, Jimmy & The Parrots, 1910 Fruitgum Company, Manuel Quintana, Larry Hoppen, Robbie Dupree, Mama Jama, Sabroso, and Luisito Rosario.

Volksplatz: Sharon Plessel, Zydeco-A-Go-Go, Alex Meixner, Finn's Fury, Yo Mama's Big Fat Booty Band, Blue Ribbon Cloggers, Resonance Percussion, Terrance Simien, Barynaya Russian Balalaika Duo, The Lovell Sisters, Dixie Power, Entrain, Seamus Kennedy, O'Grady Quinlan School of Irish Dance, The Martin Family Band, Paul Cebar, Post Junction, Tempest, Flamenco Tabla, Ansambl Mastika, The Chicago Afro-Beat Project, Scythian, Kazka, The VooDudes, Red Elvises, Animus Mediterranean World Fusion & Dance, River City Slim, Raposo, and The Blues Brotherhood.

2007 Performers

Straub Dodge Chrysler Jeep RiverPlace Stage

The Black Crowes, B. B. King, Etta James, Meat Loaf, The Moody Blues, Patti LaBelle, Deep Purple, John Kay & Steppenwolf, Ludacris, Joe Walsh, Big & Rich with Cowboy Troy and Stone Sour.

MRK Hostwindow Performing Arts Series

The Yellowjackets, Joan Osborne, Dark Star Orchestra, The Manhattan Transfer, The Yardbirds and Petula Clark.

PNC Bank Candlelight Concert Series

Amos Lee, Jonatha Brooke, Tom Rush, Kim Richey, Cornell Gunter's Coasters and David Bromberg.

Performances by

Bang Camaro, Tea Leaf Green, Rod Piazza & the Mighty Flyers, Watermelon Slim & the Workers, Babatundae Lea, Stanton Moore, Entrain, Zydepunks, Yo Mama's Big Fat Booty Band, The Fabulous Greaseband, Jimmy Sturr & His Orchestra, Enter the Haggis, Scythian, Brother, Shafatullah Khan, Mingo Fishtrap, GrooveLily, The Arrogant Worms and literally hundreds more performers of countless different genres.

1984 Performers

1984 marked the first year for the annual festival. There were far fewer acts then there are currently, and the size of the festival was much smaller than it is right now. 182,000 people attended the very first festival, and since then that number has greatly increased. [10]

Performers included Don McLean, Louis Armstrong All-Stars, The Rob Stonebeck Big Band, Park Frankenfield & The Dixieland All-Stars, The Lehigh Valley Chamber Orchestra, The Polish-American String Band of Philadelphia, Johnson Mountain Boys, Stadkappelle Berching, John Gorka, Mary Faith Rhodes, John Pearse, Claudia Schmidt, and Touchstone.[11]

External links

- Musikfest Official Web Site [1].
- Fest.org [12].
- ArtsQuest - Musikfest's parent organization [13].
- Official Musikfest page at MySpace [14].
- Official Musikfest Twitter Page [15].
- Complete Musikfest coverage with The Express-Times [16].

Zoellner Arts Center

Zoellner Arts Center is an arts center located on the campus of Lehigh University in Bethlehem, Pennsylvania, in the United States. It opened in 1997, and houses the following facilities:

- **Baker Hall** - a 946-seat auditorium with multi-purpose proscenium stage, suited for concerts, stage productions, ceremonies and lectures.
- **Diamond Theater** - a small 309-seat 3/4 thrust theater with steeply raked stadium seating suited for theatrical and small music groups.
- **Black Box Theater** - a smaller 125-seat theater
- A two-story art gallery
- Additional facilities including several rehearsal rooms, recording studio, dance studio, practice rooms, scene shop, costume shop, dressing rooms and green room, classrooms, music library, box office, faculty and staff offices, and three large lobbies and a 345-car parking deck attached to the building.

The venue has had a wide array of performers, including: the New York Philharmonic and Itzhak Perlman, the Tuvan throat singers Huun-Huur-Tu and Laurie Anderson, Hubbard Street Dance Chicago, MOMIX, the Aquila Theatre Company, Lily Tomlin, Bernadette Peters and Queen Latifah.

The Progressive Rock music festival NEARFest is held each summer at the arts center as well, though it is not affiliated with the University.

The building was designed by Dagit Saylor Architects in Philadelphia.

See also

- List of concert halls

External links

- Zoellner Arts Center Web Site [1].

Sands Casino Resort Bethlehem

Sands Casino Resort Bethlehem	
Facts and statistics	
Location	Bethlehem, PA (USA)
Address	77 Sands Blvd. Bethlehem, PA 18015
Opening date	May 22, 2009
Theme	Industrial
No. of rooms	300 (when completed)
Total gaming space	139000 sq ft (12900 m^2)
Signature attractions	The Shoppes at Sands (when completed)
Notable restaurants	Emeril's Chop House St. James Gate Irish Pub and Carvery The Market Gourmet Express Cobalt Café International Food Buffet Coil Molten
Casino type	Land-Based Riverfront
Owner	**Direct:** Sands Bethworks Gaming, LLC **Indirect:** Las Vegas Sands Corporation
Previous names	Sands BethWorks (while in planning)
Years renovated	Casino floor expansion (late 2009-2010)
Coordinates	40°36′54″N 75°21′24″W
Website	PaSands.com [1]

Sands Casino Resort Bethlehem is a casino in Bethlehem, Pennsylvania in the Lehigh Valley region of eastern Pennsylvania, in the United States.

The casino is owned, operated, and constructed by the Las Vegas Sands corporation. It is one of five stand-alone casinos that was awarded a slots license by the Pennsylvania Gaming Control Board on December 20, 2006. The casino was slated to open in July 2008, but demolition took longer than expected due to the heavy concrete foundations of the old Steel building. Its opening was delayed until the second quarter of 2009. The first concrete for the complex, which is located on the former Bethlehem Steel land on the south side of the city, was poured on November 15, 2007 at a ceremony attended by the President of Las Vegas Sands Corp.

Construction of the casino at the defunct Bethlehem Steel site, with an original ore crane pictured

The casino opened May 22, 2009. In the winter of 2009-2010, the Casino was granted a license for table games which will allow the casino to expand its games to include poker, blackjack and craps. Table games began operation on July 18, 2010.

Overview

Since the expansion in November 2009, Sands Casino Resort Bethlehem features 3,250 slot machines and electronic table games. Self parking and valet parking are available. It is the only casino in the United States to carry the Sands brand (Las Vegas Sands demolished Sands Resorts in Las Vegas and created The Venetian and sale and demolished of Sands Atlantic City).

Hotel amenities

In May 2011, the hotel will open. It will feature 300 rooms, 22 suites, 8,000 sq.ft. of meeting space, an indoor pool and a fitness center.

Dining

- Burgers And More by Emeril (BAM)
- Carnegie Deli
- Cobalt Café
- Emeril's Chop House
- St. James Gate Irish Pub and Carvery
- The Market Gourmet Express: Bananas, Green Leaf's, South Philly Steaks & Fries, Villa Fresh Italian Kitchen, Mo' Burger, Far East, Casa Java

Nightlife

Four nightclubs are planned and will be housed on the property, including:

- Coil bar
- Infusion
- Molten Lounge
- St. James Gate

Other nightlife includes:

- The Blues Brotherhood: A Tribute To The "Blues Brothers"
- DJ Cap Cee of B104
- Live Band Karaoke
- R.e.M.I.X.T.D.
- Football at the Sands

Shopping

Over 40 stores will be built in a shopping mall, **The Shoppes at Sands**, connecting the casino with the hotel. The shopping mall is being built under the Minsi Trail Bridge. The casino will have 200000 sq ft (19000 m^2) of retail space. The Sands & Co. gift shop is open and is located just off the casino floor in the casino lobby.

Parking and Transportation

The casino's parking garage has 3300 spaces. There are also 1400 parking spaces available in lots near the uncompleted hotel tower. The Bethlehem Loop also shuttles guests from Bethlehem's public parking garages. LANTA buses also have stops at the casino. Trans-Bridge Lines and other motorcoaches also connect to New York City and Philadelphia. The bus bay has room for up to 13 buses.

Players Club

Sands Bethlehem has a players club, **My Sands Rewards**, for players to earn and redeem comps. The card has the following levels:

- **My Sands Card**: Free to gamblers 21 and older.
- **My Sands Preferred**: Invited high rollers only.

Gaming Tables

Sands spent $26 million to add these 89 games: 41 blackjack tables, four craps, four roulette, four three-card poker, five mini-baccarat, four midi-baccarat, four pai gow, one Big Six, two Let It Ride, two Caribbean stud, four Texas Hold'em Bonus, one Casino War, one sic bo and 12 poker tables. Table games began operation on July 18, 2010.

See also

- Las Vegas Sands
- List of casinos in Pennsylvania
- Pennsylvania Gaming Control Board

External links

- Official Site [2]
- Las Vegas Sands [3]

NEARfest

The **North East Art Rock Festival**, or **NEARfest** for short, is a two-day event celebrating the resurgence of progressive and eclectic music in the United States and around the world. The event is held annually in early summer in Bethlehem, Pennsylvania, approximately one hour north of Philadelphia and less than two hours west of New York City. The festival was founded in the spring of 1998 by Robert LaDuca and Chad Hutchinson, with the first event occurring in 1999. NEARfest has quickly grown to become "the most prestigious progressive music festival in the world."[citation needed]

The May 2008 issue of SPIN Magazine listed NEARfest as one of the top 72 festivals in the United States.

Venues

NEARfest is held in Baker Hall, at the Zoellner Arts Center which is located on the campus of Lehigh University in Bethlehem, Pennsylvania (2000-2001, 2004-present). Baker Hall has a capacity of 1,002 seats. However, in its inaugural year, NEARfest was held in Foy Hall at Moravian College in Bethlehem, Pennsylvania which has a capacity of 428 seats. In 2002 and 2003, NEARfest was held in Trenton, New Jersey at the Patriots Theater in the Trenton War Memorial, which has a capacity of 1,850 seats. All NEARfests have been complete sellouts to date.

Future

In 2008, the festival celebrated its 10th anniversary with NEARfest X and marked the last event organized by Hutchinson and LaDuca. NEARfest and New Jersey ProgHouse veterans Jim Robinson, Ray Loboda and Kevin Feeley are their successors. NEARfest is a registered 501(c)(3) non-profit organization. The name "NEARfest" is a registered trademark of Progressive Arts, Inc.

Recordings

NEARfest Records was launched in 2003 to release select live performances from NEARfest. The first compilation DVD, "NEARfest 2005: Rising to the Surface," was released on April 10, 2007. Other releases includes live CDs of Steve Hackett, Djam Karet, Nathan Mahl, Thinking Plague, Birdsongs of the Mesozoic, Glass Hammer, Steve Roach, Pure Reason Revolution (out of print) and Hidria Spacefolk (out of print).

List of all festivals and performers

NEARfest 2010

Steve Hackett, Eddie Jobson's Ultimate Zero Project, Three Friends, The Enid, Riverside, Pineapple Thief, Iona, Forgas Band Phenomena, Astra, and Moraine

NEARfest '09 (June 19, 20 & 21, 2009)

PFM, Gong, Van der Graaf Generator, Steve Hillage Band, Trettioåriga Kriget, Beardfish, DFA, Cabezas de Cera, Oblivion Sun, Quantum Fantay

NEARfest X (2008)

Banco del Mutuo Soccorso, Liquid Tension Experiment, Fish, Peter Hammill, Synergy, echolyn, Discipline, Radio Massacre International, Mörglbl, and Koenji Hyakkei

NEARfest 2007

Magma, Hawkwind, Pure Reason Revolution, Magenta, La Maschera di Cera, NeBeLNeST, Indukti, IZZ, Robert Rich, and Bob Drake
(Progressive Arts Preshow: Allan Holdsworth, Secret Oyster and One Shot)

NEARfest 2006

Keith Emerson, Ozric Tentacles, Ange, FM, Michael Manring, Richard Leo Johnson, Niacin, Riverside, Guapo, and KBB
(Progressive Arts Preshow: Hatfield and the North and The Tony Levin Band)

NEARfest 2005

Le Orme, IQ, Present, Kenso, Steve Roach, Matthew Parmenter, The Muffins, Frogg Cafe, Wobbler, and Knight Area

(Progressive Arts Preshow: PFM and Proto-Kaw)

NEARfest 2004

Strawbs, Univers Zero, Mike Keneally Band, Planet X, Richard Pinhas, Sean Malone, Metamorfosi, Pallas, Yezda Urfa, and Hidria Spacefolk

(Progressive Arts Preshow: The Musical Box)

NEARfest 2003

Camel, Magma, The Flower Kings, Änglagård, Kraan, Tunnels, Glass Hammer, Alamaailman Vasarat, High Wheel, and Sleepytime Gorilla Museum

(The Laser's Edge/Cuneiform Records Preshow: Miriodor, Woodenhead, and IZZ)

NEARfest 2002

Steve Hackett, Nektar, echolyn, Caravan, Isildurs Bane, Enchant, Miriodor, Gerard, La Torre dell'Alchimista, and Spaced Out

(The Laser's Edge/Cuneiform Records Preshow: McGill/Manring/Stevens, Dr. Nerve, and Dysrythmia)

NEARfest 2001

Banco del Mutuo Soccorso, Porcupine Tree, Deus Ex Machina, After Crying, White Willow, California Guitar Trio with Tony Levin, Djam Karet, Birdsongs of the Mesozoic, The Underground Railroad, and Under the Sun

(Independently organized preshow: Land of Chocolate, The Red Masque, Electric Sheepdog and Wine of Nails)

NEARfest 2000

Transatlantic, Happy the Man, Anekdoten, Pär Lindh Project, Iluvatar, Il Balletto di Bronzo, DFA, Thinking Plague, North Star, and Nexus

(Official Preshow: echolyn and Priam)

NEARfest 1999

Spock's Beard, IQ, Solaris, Mastermind, Larry Fast, Crucible, Scott McGill's Hand Farm, Ice Age, Alaska, and Nathan Mahl

Logo

Since 2001, the ever-changing festival logo has been designed by British artist Roger Dean, famous for his work with Yes and Asia. The NEARfest 2000 logo was designed by Paul Whitehead, who is known for his album artwork for Van der Graaf Generator, Genesis, and Italian prog-rock band Le Orme. In addition to Roger Dean, Mark Wilkinson (Marillion and Fish album covers) displayed his art at NEARfest 2006. Annie Haslam of Renaissance attended NEARfest 2004, 2005, 2007 and 2009 to host a display of her oil paintings.

External links

- NEARfest Official Site [1]
- NEARfest Records [2]
- Progressive World NEARfest Overview [3]

SouthSide Film Festival

The **SouthSide Film Festival** is an annual non-competitive, not-for-profit film festival that takes place each June in Bethlehem, Pennsylvania, USA. The first festival took place in 2004.

The "SouthSide" refers to the area of the city on the south side of the Lehigh River which was home to Bethlehem Steel and is currently undergoing redevelopment.

The festival's logo pays homage to that industrial heritage by including a representation of a blast furnace,still highly visible in Bethlehem. Film screenings take place on the campus of Lehigh University and in alternative venues such as Godfrey Daniels [1] Listening Club and Deja Brew Coffeehouse.

From its inception through 2008, the festival has screened films from 54 countries and 31 states of the U.S. The festival focuses on independent filmmaking and features Invitational Films and Juried Selections, a highlighted genre, and a highlighted cultural region. Also included in the annual festival are filmmaking workshops to teach techniques and concepts to accomplished and aspiring filmmakers. Returning teachers include Mel Halbach and Clayton Farr of FilmTreks [2], Shanti Thakur [3] of Hofstra University, and Pawel Partyka of Se-Ma-For animation studio.

The SouthSide Film Festival and its host organization, The SouthSide Film Institute, have received numerous grants and awards including a Bethlehem Fine Arts Commission Organization of the Year award which noted "By providing access to independent films for the public, creating a venue for film enthusiasts and filmmakers to come together, and mounting a children's film series, (the SouthSide Film Festival is) developing an appreciation for film as an art form and contributing to a thriving arts scene in Bethlehem that benefits the Lehigh Valley"

External links

- SouthSide Film Festival site [4]
- SouthSide Film Festival Online Film Channel via Haydenfilms [5]
- VisitPA.com [6]
- Lehigh University 6/19/08 news article [7]

Attractions

Lehigh Canal

Lehigh Canal	
U.S. National Register of Historic Places	
U.S. Historic District	

The Lehigh Canal as seen from Guard Lock 8 & Lockhouse, Island Park Road, Glendon, Northampton County, PA.	
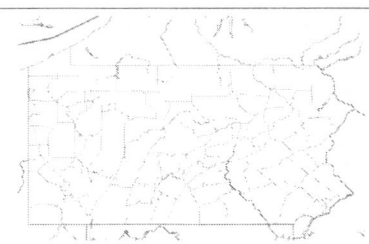	
Location:	Lehigh River
Coordinates:	40°46′09″N 75°36′13″W
Built/Founded:	1819
Architect:	Canvass White, Josiah White
Governing body:	Local
Added to NRHP:	Earliest October 2, 1978
NRHP Reference#:	78002437, 78002439, 79002179, 79002307, 80003553

The **Lehigh Canal** was constructed to carry anthracite from the upper Lehigh Valley to the urban markets of the northeast, especially Philadelphia. With the discovery of large deposits of anthracite coal, the Lehigh Coal Mine Company was formed to transport the coal down the Lehigh River to the Delaware River and on to the growing consumer markets in Philadelphia via a connection with the Pennsylvania Canal (Delaware Division) in Easton.

History

The Lehigh Canal, designed by Canvass White, an engineer of New York's Erie Canal, was constructed between 1827 and 1829. The enlarged Lehigh Navigation extended 46 miles (74 km) between Mauch Chunk, Pennsylvania (present-day Jim Thorpe) and Easton with 52 locks, eight guard locks, eight dams and six aqueducts, allowing the waterway to overcome a difference in elevation of over 350 feet (107 m). A weigh lock determined canal boat fees a half mile (1 km) south of Mauch Chunk. A connection across the Delaware River to the Morris Canal through New Jersey allowed the coal from the Lehigh Canal to be shipped more directly to New York City.

During the 1830s, an extension of 26 miles (42 km) to White Haven, Pennsylvania, which included 20 dams and 29 locks, was constructed, covering a difference in elevation of over 600 feet (183 m) to Mauch Chunk.

In 1855, the canal reached its peak of more than one million tons of cargo. However, competition from railroads and the catastrophic flood of June 4, 1862, were all steps towards the canal's demise. The canal was used as a means of transportation until the 1940s (about a decade after other similar canals ceased operations), making it the last fully functioning towpath canal in North America. In 1962, most of it was sold to private and public organizations for recreational use.

Several segments of the canal are listed on the National Register of Historic Places. An 8-mile (13 km) segment of the canal towpath has been converted into a multi-use trail that runs from Freemansburg through Bethlehem to Allentown. The trail runs along the river and active railroad tracks. A section near Jim Thorpe is accessible to recreational users. The final section in Easton is maintained and operated by the National Canal Museum. Other short sections are accessible, but there are parts of the canal towpath that have been worn by the elements and are not safe to access.

Pictures

Loading coal at the Mauch Chunk chutes, 1873

The canal passing through Bethlehem, 1907

Remains of Lock 25, 2006

See also

- Pennsylvania Canal (Delaware Division) - A sister canal along the Delaware River that provided a connection to the Philadelphia markets via a link up in Easton.
- Morris Canal - A New Jersey canal that provided direct access to the New York City markets via a cross-Delaware River connection in Phillipsburg, New Jersey.
- List of canals in the United States

External links

- National Canal Museum: Lehigh Navigation [1]
- Historic photos of the Lehigh Coal and Navigation Canal [2]
- Delaware & Lehigh Canal State Heritage Corridor [3]
- Lehigh Canal History [4]

Lehigh River

Geographical coordinates: 40°41′20″N 75°12′17″W

Lehigh River	
River	
 Lehigh River near Jim Thorpe, Pennsylvania	
Country	▦ United States
State	▦ Pennsylvania
Counties	Wayne, Lackawanna, Monroe, Luzerne, Carbon, Lehigh, Northampton
Tributaries	
- left	Tobyhanna Creek, Pohopoco Creek, Aquashicola Creek, Hokendauqua Creek, Monocacy Creek
- right	North Bear Creek, Nesquehoning Creek, Mauch Chuck Creek, Mahoning Creek, Lizard Creek, Jordan Creek, Saucon Creek
Cities	Lehighton, Allentown, Bethlehem, Easton
Source	Pocono Peak Lake
- location	Lehigh Township, Wayne County, Pennsylvania, USA
- elevation	2056 ft (627 m)
- coordinates	41°16′42″N 75°24′22″W
Mouth	Delaware River
- location	Easton, Northampton County, Pennsylvania, USA
- elevation	160 ft (49 m)
- coordinates	40°41′20″N 75°12′17″W
Length	103 mi (166 km)
Basin	1345 sq mi (3484 km²)

Discharge	for Glendon
- average	3740 cu ft/s (106 m³/s)
- max	11700 cu ft/s (331 m³/s)
- min	1160 cu ft/s (33 m³/s)
Discharge elsewhere (average)	
- Stoddartsville	280 cu ft/s (8 m³/s)

Lehigh River watershed

The **Lehigh River**, a tributary of the Delaware River, is a 103-mile (166-km) long river located in eastern Pennsylvania, in the United States. Part of the Lehigh, along with a number of its tributaries, is designated a Pennsylvania Scenic River by the state's Department of Conservation and Natural Resources. "Lehigh" is an Anglicization of the Lenape name for the river, "Lechewuekink," meaning "where there are forks."

The river flows in a highly winding course through valleys between ridges of the Appalachian Mountains. Its upper course is characterized by numerous whitewater rapids and supports a broad range of recreational pursuits including whitewater rafting, kayaking and canoeing. Its lower course forms the heart of the Lehigh Valley, an historically important anthracite coal and steel-producing region of Pennsylvania.

The river rises in the Pocono Mountains of northeastern Pennsylvania, in several ponds in southwestern Wayne County, approximately 15 miles (24 km) southeast of Scranton. It flows initially southwest, through southern Lackawanna County, through Francis E. Walter Reservoir. Near White Haven, Middleburg, it turns south, following a zigzag whitewater course through Lehigh Gorge State Park to Jim Thorpe, then southeast, past Lehighton. Southeast of Lehighton, it passes through Blue Mountain in a narrow opening called the Lehigh Gap.

From the Lehigh Gap, the river flows southeast to Allentown, where it is joined by the Little Lehigh Creek, then northeast past Bethlehem, where it joins the Delaware River in Easton, along Pennsylvania's border with New Jersey.

See also

- Lehigh Canal
- List of Pennsylvania rivers
- Pennsylvania Real Time River Flows from the USGS [1]
- Rafting

External links

- U.S. Geological Survey: PA stream gauging stations [2]
- Water Flow at Francis E Walter Reservoir outlet [3]
- Lehigh River Watershed Conservation Management Plan [4]
- Lehigh River and Canal at Jim Thorpe [5].
- Lehigh River Whitewater Rafting [6]
- Lehigh River Fly Fishing Adventures [7].
- Lehigh River Sojourn [8].
- Lehigh River Watershed Association [9].
- Lehigh River Water Trail [10].
- Lehigh River Whitewater [11].
- Lehigh River Whitewater Rafting [12].
- Lehigh River Scenic River Corridor [13].

The Lehigh River near Slatington at the Lehigh County–Northampton County line.

References

"Fast Facts About Lehigh River" [14]. *Lehigh Earth Observatory's Envirosci Inquiry*. Retrieved 2008-05-05.

Bethlehem Steel F.C.

Bethlehem Steel Football Club (1911-1930) was one of the most successful early American soccer clubs. Known as the Bethlehem Football Club from 1911 until 1915 when it became the Bethlehem Steel Football Club, the team was sponsored by the Bethlehem Steel corporation and played their home games first at East End Field in Bethlehem, Pennsylvania, in the Lehigh Valley.

History

The first soccer ball came to Bethlehem in 1904, according to a June 2, 1925, article in the *Bethlehem Globe*. The sport took hold of the town and local steel workers formed a recreational team. On November 17, 1907, the Bethlehem Football Club played its first official match, an 11-2 loss to West Hudson A.A., at the time one of the top professional teams in the country. In 1913 the steel company created Bethlehem Steel Athletic Field, the country's first soccer field with stadium-seating. In 1914 Charles Schwab, owner of the Steel Company, took the team professional, using his wealth to induce several top players to move to Bethlehem Steel and changing the team name to the Bethlehem Steel Football Club. Schwab would eventually begin importing players from Scotland and England. From 1911 to 1915, the club was a member of the amateur Allied American Foot Ball Association before moving to the American Soccer League of Philadelphia, another amateur league, for the 1915-1916 season. Bethlehem Steel was not associated with a league from 1916 to 1917, playing only exhibition or cup games. In 1917, it joined the professional National Association Foot Ball League. In 1921, several teams from the NAFBL and other regional leagues joined together to form the American Soccer League. Although one of the strongest teams of the time, the owners decided to disband the club, moving the players and management to Philadelphia where it competed as the Philadelphia Field Club.

Although Philadelphia won the first ASL championship, the team was in financial trouble and lacked fan support. The ownership moved it back to Bethlehem the next year taking back their old name. In 1925, Bethlehem, and the rest of the ASL, boycotted the National Challenge Cup. While this created some animosity with the United States Football Association, no serious ramification resulted. However, in 1928, the ASL again boycotted the Challenge Cup. When Bethlehem Steel chose to ignore the boycott, the league expelled them. Under the leadership of the USFA, Bethlehem Steel and two other expelled teams joined with teams from the Southern New York State Soccer Association to create the Eastern Soccer League. These actions, part of the 1928-1929 "Soccer Wars", along with the Great Depression, financially devastated the ASL, ESL and Bethlehem Steel. While Bethlehem Steel rejoined the ASL in 1929, the damage was done and the team folded after the spring 1930 season.

Year-by-year

Year	Division	League	Reg. Season	Playoffs	Challenge Cup	American Cup
1911/12	*N/A*	AAFBA	*N/A*	Final	*N/A*	*Did not enter*
1912/13	*N/A*	AAFBA	1st	Champion (no playoff)	*N/A*	*Did not enter*
1913/14	*N/A*	AAFBA	1st	Champion (no playoff)	Third round	Champion
1914/15	*N/A*	ALAFC	1st	Champion (no playoff)	Champion	Semifinal
1915/16	*N/A*	ALP	2nd	*No playoff*	Champion	Champion
1916/17	*N/A*	*N/A*	*N/A*	*N/A*	Final	Champion
1917/18	*N/A*	NAFBL	2nd	*No playoff*	Champion	Champion
1918/19	*N/A*	NAFBL	1st	Champion (no playoff)	Champion	Champion
1919/20	*N/A*	NAFBL	1st	Champion (no playoff)	Quarterfinal	Final
1920/21	*N/A*	NAFBL	1st	Champion (no playoff)	Second round	Semifinal
1921/22	see Philadelphia Field Club					
1922/23	1	ASL	2nd	*No playoff*	Third round	Second round
1923/24	1	ASL	2nd	*No playoff*	Semifinals	Champion
1924/25	1	ASL	2nd	*No playoff*	*Did not enter*	*N/A*
1925/26	1	ASL	4th	*No playoff*	Champion	*N/A*
1926/27	1	ASL	1st	Champion (no playoff)	Semifinals	*N/A*
1927/28	1	ASL	2nd (1st half); 4th (2nd half)	Semifinals	First Round	*N/A*
1928/29	1	ASL	*withdrew after 6 games*	*N/A*	*N/A*	*N/A*
1928-29	*N/A*	ESL	1st	Champion (no playoff)	Quarterfinal	*N/A*
1929	*N/A*	ESL	1st	Champion (no playoff)	*N/A*	*N/A*
1930	1	ACL (ASL)	7th (Spring)	*No playoff*	Semifinals	*N/A*

Honors

- **League Champion**
  - **Winner (9):** 1913, 1914, 1915, 1919, 1920, 1921, 1927, 1929, Fall 1929
  - **Runner Up (5):** 1916, 1918, 1923, 1924, 1925
- **National Challenge Cup**
  - **Winner (5):** 1915, 1916, 1918, 1919, 1926
  - **Runner Up (1):** 1917
- **American Cup**
  - **Winner (6):** 1914, 1916, 1917, 1918, 1919, 1924
  - **Runner Up (1):** 1920
- **Lewis Cup**
  - **Winner (1):** 1928
- **Allied Amateur Cup**
  - **Winner (1):** 1914
  - **Runner Up (1):** 1912

Coaches

- Harry Trend: 1909
- Carpenter: 1913
- William Sheridan: -1924
- Jimmy Easton: 1924-
- William Sheridan: 1930

Notable players

- Tommy Fleming
- Findlay Kerr
- Alex Massie
- Robert Millar
- Harry Ratican
- Archie Stark

External links

- History of Bethlehem Steel [1] by Dan Morrison.

John Andretti

Born	March 12, 1963
Hometown	Bethlehem, Pennsylvania, U.S.
NASCAR Sprint Cup Series statistics	
Car #, team	1. 38/#34 - Front Row Motorsports
2009 Sprint Cup position	36th
Best cup position	11th - 1998
First race	1993 Tyson/Holly Farms 400 (North Wilkesboro
Last race	2010 Daytona 500 (Daytona)
First win	1997 Pepsi 400 (Daytona)
Last win	1999 Goody's Body Pain 500 (Martinsville)

Wins	Top tens	Poles
2	37	4

NASCAR Nationwide Series statistics	
2007 NNS position	147th
Best NNS position	12th - 2006
First race	1998 Goody's 300 (Daytona)
Last race	2007 Orbitz 300 (Daytona)

Wins	Top tens	Poles
0	4	0

NASCAR Camping World Truck Series statistics	
6 races run over 2 years	
First race	2005 O'Reilly Auto Parts 250 (Kansas)
Last race	2008 Mountain Dew 250 Fueled by Winn-Dixie (Talladega)

Wins	Top tens	Poles
0	3	0

Statistics current as of March 27, 2009.

John Andretti	
CART Championship Car	
Years active	1987-1994
Teams	Curb Motorsports Vince Granatelli Racing Porsche Motorsports Hall-VDS Racing A. J. Foyt Enterprises
Starts	73
Wins	1
Poles	0
Best finish	8th in 1991 & 1992
Previous series	
1984-1987, 1989	IMSA Camel GT
1984	USAC Sprint Car
1983	USAC Midgets

John Andretti (born March 12, 1963 in Bethlehem, Pennsylvania), is an American race car driver. He currently drives the #38/#34 Chevrolet Impala in the NASCAR Sprint Cup Series for Front Row Motorsports out of Statesville NC. He has won in CART, NHRA Top Fuel Dragsters, endurance racing and NASCAR stock car racing. He was the last NASCAR driver to win a Cup Race for the famous

Petty Enterprises team.

Andretti family

Andretti's father, Aldo Andretti, had his racing career cut short due to a racing accident. He also has a younger brother named Adam Andretti who has also competed in several racing series; they are both nephews of IndyCar racing legend Mario Andretti (Aldo's twin), cousin of Mario's sons Michael and Jeff. Andretti is the godson of four-time Indianapolis 500 winner A. J. Foyt. The Andretti family became the first family to have four relatives (Michael, Mario, Jeff, and John) compete in the same series (CART). In 1990, 1991 and 1992, they had four family members competing in the Indy 500.

CART

Andretti has one win (Australia, '91) and 61 top-10s in 74 career races in CART. He joined the PPG Indy Car World Series (CART) in 1987, winning the Rookie of the Year award. In 1988, Andretti made his debut at the Indianapolis Motor Speedway, racing as high as seventh before mechanical problems forced him to finish 21st.

In 1991 he won the only race of his CART career, winning the Gold Coast Grand Prix in Surfer's Paradise, Australia. That same year he finished a career-best fifth in the Indianapolis 500. A week later at the Milwaukee Mile, Michael, John and Mario became the only known family in motorsports history to finish first, second and third respectively in a major auto race. In 1994, he became the first driver to attempt the "double," racing in the Indy 500 and NASCAR's Coca-Cola 600 in Charlotte, N.C., on the same day. The 1994 Indy 500 would be his last Indy 500 effort until 2007.

IMSA GTP & Rolex Sports Car Series

In 1986 Andretti drove a BMW M12 March along with co-driver Davy Jones in the IMSA Camel GT Series. While the BMWs had limited success in IMSA competition, Andretti and Jones won the Kodak Copier 500 at Watkins Glen on September 21, 1986.

In 1989, Andretti drove the Miller High Life/BFGoodrich Porsche 962 to victory in the Rolex 24 Hours at Daytona (called the *Sunbank 24 at Daytona* at the time) along with co-drivers Bob Wollek and Derek Bell. Andretti and Wollek went on to win another race on the 1989 IMSA circuit at the Pontiac Grand Prix of Palm Beach, driving the same Porsche 962. Andretti finished 5th in points (112) after the 1989 IMSA season and first among Porsche drivers.

In 2001 Andretti teamed up with Kyle Petty to win a 6 hour sportscar race at Watkins Glen.

Andretti returned to the 24 Hours of Daytona in the Rolex Sports Car Series in 2008. Team drivers for the Vision Racing #03 Porsche Crawford Prototype included Ed Carpenter, A. J. Foyt IV, and Vitor Meira. The Porsche Crawford Prototype entry in the 24 Hours of Daytona marked the first attempt for this team which resulted in 25th overall finish in the race.

NHRA Full Throttle Drag Racing

In 1993, John Andretti drove the Taco Bell Express Top Fuel Dragster for owner Jack Clark, reaching the semi-finals in his first national event at Atlanta during the FRAM Southern Nationals and clocking a career best speed of 299 mph (481 km/h). In that race he bet 1992 T/F Champion Joe Amato in Round 1 and Mopar Express Lube driver Tommy Johnson Jr. in Round 2 only to lose to Mike Dunn in Darrell Gwynn's La Victoria Salsa Car in the semi-finals. That race was won by Eddie Hill in the Pennzoil car over Dunn.

NASCAR

1993-1999

Andretti made his Winston Cup debut in 1993 driving the #72 Tex Racing Chevy for Tex Powell at North Wilkesboro Speedway, starting 31st and finishing 24th. After running three more races in 1993, he began the 1994 season driving the #14 Financial World Chevy for Billy Hagan. On May 29, he became the first driver in history to race in both the Indianapolis 500 and the Coca-Cola 600 on the same day, finishing tenth at Indy and thirty-sixth in the Coca-Cola 600 after suffering mechanical failures. In the middle of the season he switched to the #43 STP Pontiac for Petty Enterprises finishing a best 11th at Richmond International Raceway. He ended the season 32nd in points and fifth in the Rookie of the Year battle.

1997 racecar

In 1995, he began driving for Michael Kranefuss in #37 Kmart/Little Caesars Ford Thunderbird. He won his first career pole at the Southern 500 and finished in the top-ten five times, and ended the season eighteenth in points. During the 1996 season, he switched to the #98 RCA Ford owned by Cale Yarborough (while Jeremy Mayfield, the previous driver of the #98 car, moved to Kranefuss' team) and responded with a fifth-place finish at the Hanes 500. He finished in the top ten twice more. In 1997, he scored his first career win at the Pepsi 400 and finished 23rd in points. He returned to the #43 Petty car in 1998 and despite not winning another race, he had ten top-tens and finished a career-best 11th in points. He won his second career race in 1999 at Martinsville Speedway, making up a lost lap and taking the lead with four laps to go, as well as winning the pole at Phoenix International Raceway.

2000-2005

Midway through the 2000 season, Cheerios became Andretti's primary sponsor, but he fell to 23rd in points after finishing in the top-ten twice. Over the next two seasons, Andretti posted three top-ten finishes, before he was released midway through the 2003 season. He originally ran a couple of races for Haas CNC Racing and Richard Childress Racing before running a majority of the remainder of the season in the #1 Pennzoil Chevy for Dale Earnhardt, Inc., his best finish was a 12th at New Hampshire International Speedway.

Andretti opened the 2004 season driving the #1 part-time for DEI, but departed midway through the season. He ended the year driving the #14 Victory Brand Ford Taurus for ppc Racing, finishing 22nd at Charlotte Motor Speedway. Andretti started 2005 with ppc before the team was forced to dissolve due to a lack of funding. He drove four races in the Craftsman Truck Series for Billy Ballew Motorsports, finishing eighth at Memphis Motorsports Park. He also attempted a handful of Cup races for Morgan-McClure Motorsports' #4 Lucas Oil entry, finishing 28th at Michigan International Speedway.

2006- Present

In 2006, Andretti returned to ppc to drive their #10 car. Before the season, his only Busch start came in 1998 at Daytona, where he finished 13th in the #96 Chevy fielded by the Curb Agajanian Performance Group. Despite having made over three hundred Cup starts with two victories, Andretti applied for and was accepted as a contender for Rookie of the Year. He finished runner-up to Danny O'Quinn for the award.

In 2007, Andretti's plans were to drive a in the Busch Series for Braun Racing. Andretti drove the #10 FreedomRoads/Camping World/RVs.com [1] Car for Braun Racing at Daytona through their affiliation with his former team ppc Racing. When funding for the team became questionable, Andretti left Braun Racing with the team using various drivers in 2007 in any attempt to maintain a two car team. Andretti drove four races for Petty Enterprises in the #45 car, filling in for Kyle Petty in when Petty was working as a broadcaster for TNT's race coverage, as well as driving part-time briefly for Front Row Motorsports. He finished the season in the #49 Paralyzed Veterans of America Dodge for BAM Racing.

2008 Sprint Cup car at Daytona

Andretti drove for Front Row Motorsports in 2008 by driving the car number #34 Chevrolet Impala SS in the Sprint Cup Series. He raced his way into the 2008 Daytona 500 in the second Gatorade Duel race. He drove in the first ten races of the season in the 34 before leaving to focus on his IndyCar team.

Andretti returned to the 34 in 2009 full-time, driving with a partnership between Front Row and Earnhardt Ganassi Racing. The 34 has had sponsorship from Window World, myAutoloan.com, and Taco Bell. He does not have a full-time ride for 2010, but will drive the #34 Front Row Motorsports entry in the Daytona 500. He also plans to compete in Charlotte and at the Indy 500.

IRL IndyCar Series

On May 16, 2007, it was officially announced that Andretti would return to the Indianapolis 500 for the first time since 1994 when he pulled the double (competed in the Indy 500 and the Coca-Cola 600 in the same day). He drove the third entry from Panther Racing, with Camping World as the sponsor. On May 19, he qualified for the 91st Indianapolis 500 with an average speed for the four lap qualifying run of 221.756 mph (356.882 km/h). He started in 24th on the eighth row, but crashed on lap 95, and finished 30th.

Andretti driving the Roth Racing #24 car in practice for the 2008 Indianapolis 500

It was announced on May 10, 2008 that John Andretti would replace Jay Howard in the Roth Racing #24 Dallara-Honda. John qualified for his 9th Indy 500 on Saturday, May 17, 2008 with a 4-lap average of 221.550 mph (356.550 km/h) that put him 21st on the grid and finished on the lead lap in 16th place. On May 30 it was announced that Andretti would continue in the #24 car in the Milwaukee Mile and Texas Motor Speedway races. On June 6 Andretti was offered a deal that would keep him in the car the rest of the season which he ultimately did not accept.

Andretti's run with Roth Racing produced some notable results for the team. He managed to qualify 7th at the Texas Motor Speedway race. Although a great start, he would ultimately wind up finishing 16th. He began his trip to Iowa Speedway with a rough 23rd position start, but steadily worked his way through the field to capture an 11th place finish. His 11th place finish was the best for a Roth Racing machine. His last start for the team was at Richmond International Raceway the next week where he was knocked out by a crash. Roth Racing contracted to a single car for the

Andretti with uncle Mario at the 2007 Indy 500

rest of the season and ceased operations at the end of the season. Andretti finished 30th in the 2008 IndyCar points standings.

In April 2009 Andretti and NASCAR car owner Richard Petty announced a joint venture with Dreyer & Reinbold Racing where Andretti would return to Indianapolis to drive the #43 car in the 93rd Indianapolis 500. As in his previous two trips to Indianapolis, Andretti did not race the Indy/Charlotte double in the same day, and also missed the Southern 500 as well as the Coca-Cola 600 to prepare for the race. Andretti qualified for the race on bump day in 28th, and finished the race in 19th, the final car on the lead lap. Andretti returned to drive the #34 at Front Row Motorsports immediately following the Indianapolis 500, returning for the Dover 400 in June.

On March 31, 2010, Andretti announced that he would join forces with both Richard Petty and Window World again, but this time by running in two events instead of just one. The #43 returns to the entry, which this year will be backed Andretti Autosport, owned by John's cousin Michael. The team's first race was the RoadRunner Turbo Indy 300 at Kansas Speedway on May 1. Andretti qualified 15th but worked his way up to finish in 9th, one lap down. They also competed 94th Indianapolis 500 on May 30. After failing to qualify on pole day, Andretti made the race on bump day qualifying 28th for the second consecutive year. Andretti crashed out of the race on lap 65, and was credited with a 30th place finish.

Off the Track

Andretti is active in the Central Indiana community. Each year during the Brickyard 400 week, John teams up with 93.1 WIBC, and Dave "The King" Wilson, and General Mills to hold the Race for Riley, benefiting James Whitcomb Riley Hospital for Children. It takes place at the Mark Dismore Karting Center in New Castle, Indiana. Graduated from Moravian College with degree in business management and believes he would've been an investment banker or stock broker if he hadn't started racing. Enjoys Joe Pesci and Nicolas Cage movies. Favorite movie is raucous comedy "Animal House." Favorite band is hard-rock group AC/DC. In December 2004, spent seven days in the Middle East visiting service personnel in the U.S. Navy and U.S. Marine Corps.

As of 2007, John can be heard as the part-time co-host of The Driver's Seat with John Kernan on Sirius Satellite Radio's NASCAR channel 128.

Career history

American open–wheel results

(key) (Races in **bold** indicate pole position)

CART

Year	Team	1	2	3	4	5	6	7	8	9	10	11	12	13	14	15	16	17	Rank	Points
1987	Curb	LBG	PHO	IND	MIL	POR	MEA	CLE	TOR	MCH	POC	ROA 6	MDO 10	NAZ 11	LAG 7	MIA 8			17th	23
1988	Curb	PHO Ret	LBG Ret	IND Ret	MIL Ret	POR Ret	CLE 8	TOR Ret	MEA Ret	MCH Ret	POC Ret	MDO	ROA	NAZ Ret	LAG	MIA			31st	5
1989	Granatelli	PHO	LBG	IND Ret	MIL	DET	POR	CLE	MEA	TOR Ret	MCH Ret	POC 17	MDO	ROA	NAZ Ret	LAG 12			31st	1
1990	Porsche	PHO Ret	LBG Ret	IND Ret	MIL 7	DET Ret	POR Ret	CLE 5	MEA Ret	TOR 13	MCH 7	DEN 6	VAN 5	MDO 13	ROA Ret	NAZ Ret	LAG Ret		10th	51
1991	Hall/VDS	SUR 1	LBG Ret	PHO 11	IND 5	MIL 2	DET 6	POR Ret	CLE Ret	MEA 4	TOR 5	MCH 6	DEN 7	VAN 7	MDO 10	ROA Ret	NAZ 9	LAG 19	8th	105
1992	Hall/VDS	SUR 6	PHO 6	LBG Ret	IND 8	DET Ret	POR 5	MIL 9	NHA 5	TOR 5	MCH 6	CLE 12	ROA 6	VAN Ret	MDO 4	NAZ Ret	LAG 5		7th	99
1993	Foyt	SUR	PHO	LBG	IND 10	MIL	DET	POR	CLE	TOR	MCH	LOU	ROA	VAN	MDO	NAZ	LAG		28th	3
1994	Foyt	SUR	PHX	LGB	IND 10	MIL	DET	POR	CLE	TOR	MIS	MDO	NHA	VAN	ROA	NAZ	LAG		29th	3

IndyCar Series

Year	Team	1	2	3	4	5	6	7	8	9	10	11	12	13	14	15	16	17	18	Rank	Points
2007	Panther	HMS	STP	MOT	KAN	INDY 30	MIL	TXS	IOW	RIR	WGL	NSH	MDO	MIS	KTY	SNM	DET	CHI		35th	10
2008	Roth	HMS	STP	MOT[1]	LBH[1]	KAN	INDY 16	MIL 19	TXS 16	IOW 11	RIR 21	WGL	NSH	MDO	KTY	SNM	DET	CHI	SRF[2]	30th	71
2009	D & R/Petty	STP	LBH	KAN	INDY 19	MIL	TXS	IOW	RIR	WGL	TOR	EDM	KTY	MDO	SNM	CHI	MOT	HMS		37th	12
2010	Andretti/Petty	BRA	STP	ALA	LBH	KAN 9	INDY 30	TXS	IOW	WGL	TOR	EDM	MDO	SNM	CHI	KTY	MOT	HMS		32nd	35

[1] *Run on same day.*

[2] *Non-points race.*

Years	Teams	Races	Poles	Wins	Podiums (Non-win)	Top 10s (Non-podium)	Indianapolis 500 Wins	Championships
4	4	9	0	0	0	1	0	0

Indy 500 results

Year	Chassis	Engine	Start	Finish	Team
1988	Lola	Cosworth	27	21	Curb
1989	Lola	Buick	12	25	Granatelli
1990	March	Porsche	10	21	Porsche
1991	Lola	Chevrolet	7	5	Hall/VDS
1992	Lola	Chevrolet	14	8	Hall/VDS
1993	Lola	Ford-Cosworth	24	10	Foyt
1994	Lola	Ford-Cosworth	10	10	Foyt
2007	Dallara	Honda	24	30	Panther

2008	Dallara	Honda	21	16	Roth
2009	Dallara	Honda	28	19	Richard Petty
2010	Dallara	Honda	28	30	Richard Petty

References

- John Andretti at Daytona 500 Racing [1]
- NASCAR drivers statistics at racing-reference.info [2]

External links

- The Official Andretti Family Website [3]
- Front Row Motorsports Website [4]
- Race 4 Riley Hospital for Children [5]
- John Andretti Fan Page [6]
- John's window to Indy 2009 [7]

Michael Andretti

Michael Mario Andretti	
Michael Andretti at Michigan International Speedway in 2007.	
Nationality	American
Date of birth	October 5, 1962
Place of birth	Bethlehem, Pennsylvania
Related to	Mario Andretti (father) Jeff Andretti (brother) Marco Andretti (son) Aldo Andretti (uncle) John Andretti (cousin) Adam Andretti (cousin)
2011 IRL IndyCar Series	
Debut season	1983
Current team	Andretti Autosport

Former teams	Kraco Racing Target Chip Ganassi Racing Newman/Haas Racing
Starts	317
Wins	42
Poles	32
Best finish	1st in 1991
Previous series	
1983-1992 **1993** **1994-2002**	CART IndyCar World Series Formula One CART IndyCar World Series
Championship titles	
1991	1
Awards	
1991	CART IndyCar World Series Champion

Date of birth	October 5, 1962
Formula One World Championship career	
Active years	1993
Teams	McLaren
Races	13
Championships	0
Wins	0
Podiums	1
Career points	7
Pole positions	0
Fastest laps	0
First race	1993 South African Grand Prix
Last race	1993 Italian Grand Prix

Michael Mario Andretti (born October 5, 1962 in Bethlehem, Pennsylvania) is an American retired CART and Formula One driver. He now owns the Andretti Autosport team in the Indy Racing League. Andretti is the son of Mario Andretti, one of the most successful auto racing drivers of all time. His son is IndyCar Series driver Marco Andretti.

Andretti racing at Monterey, California, October 1991

Racing career

Early career

Andretti started racing in 1980, driving a Formula Vee car in Local SCCA events. In 1981 he won six of the 11 Super Vee races and won the championship. He moved on to drive in Formula Atlantic, and won the Championship in 1983. In the same year he joined his father and Philippe Alliot in the Porsche Kremer Racing Team, taking third place in the Le Mans 24 Hours, driving a Porsche 956.

Michael (right) practicing against Marco at Indy

CART

He made his CART debut in 1984, racing for the Kraco team. He managed five third place finishes and ended the season in seventh overall. In the Indianapolis 500, he finished fifth and shared the Rookie of the Year award with Roberto Guerrero. He went on to win his first IndyCar race in 1986 at Long Beach, finishing that year as championship runner-up after collecting other wins at Milwaukee and Phoenix.

Andretti achieved major title success by winning the 1991 CART/PPG IndyCar World Series for Newman/Haas Racing. He won 8 of 17 races; Milwaukee, Toronto, Vancouver, the Marlboro Challenge, and all 5 permanent road course events (Portland, Cleveland, Mid-Ohio, Road America, and Laguna Seca).

Andretti at the Indianapolis Motor Speedway in May 2008.

Futility at Indianapolis

The Andretti family's bad luck at the Indianapolis Motor Speedway is known as the Andretti Curse. As a driver, he is largely remembered for being unlucky at the Indianapolis 500. In 1991, he led with twelve laps remaining, but finished second to Rick Mears after battling the multiple Indy 500 winner. In 1992, he dominated the race, leading a full four-fifths of the laps, but, with eleven laps remaining, his fuel pump failed, and his car coasted to a stop. He finished in 13th place. He also dropped out while leading the Indy 500 in 1989, 1995 and 2003. Michael holds the record for most laps led in the Indy 500 without having achieved a victory.

Formula One

After his 1991 CART title win, Andretti joined the McLaren Formula One team for 1993, alongside the triple World Champion Ayrton Senna. Unfortunately, the season was not a success. A string of collisions meant that he only completed three laps in his first three races, and he never fully got to grips with Formula One cars. Highly technical aspects which he was not used to in the technologically simpler IndyCars such as active suspension and traction control hampered Andretti's chances for the 1993 F1 season. This combined with the fact that he commuted to races and test sessions from the USA, rather than re-locating full-time to Europe were also contributing factors to his lack of success in Formula One. Three points-scoring finishes, including a third place at Monza, were perceived as too little, too late, and he left the team and the series by mutual agreement after that race.

However, according to son Marco, the McLaren team Andretti drove for "sabotaged" his chances at being competitive in order to replace him with Finnish driver Mika Häkkinen, who would require a smaller salary. "The reality of it was, they had Mika Häkkinen ready to come in for a lot less than what my dad was getting paid, and that's all it was. Right then and there, they had to make him look [bad]," claimed Marco in 2008. "They would make the car do weird things in the corner electronically, stuff out of his control.'" However, Andretti still had problems in practice at Monza, and both he and Senna spun off with brake balance problems early in the race. Andretti was able to continue and fought back up to third, holding off Karl Wendlinger. Throughout the season, Senna experienced similar reliability problems to Andretti, mainly electronic gremlins, particularly in San Marino, Canada, Hungary and Belgium. After Andretti's departure, both Senna and Häkkinen continued to have reliability issues, although Häkkinen equalled Andretti's third place Monza finish in Japan.

At the start of the 1993 season, Ron Dennis signed Häkkinen as a backup to Senna, who was initially reluctant to commit to the team for the whole season. The *F1 Rejects* website states that this created a difficult atmosphere for Andretti, who would be in the shadow of the three-time F1 champion Senna, and also faced the threat of being replaced by Häkkinen.

After Andretti's unsuccessful Formula 1 season, he never returned to the cockpit in that series.

Return to CART

After McLaren replaced Andretti with Häkkinen, Michael returned to the CART series for 1994 and drove for Chip Ganassi, where he once again proved very successful. He went on to win in his very first race back in the series at the Surfers Paradise event in Australia, having led every lap along the way. That win also got Reynard's first win in CART in their debut. In 1995 he returned to Newman/Haas Racing. He finished as runner-up to Jimmy Vasser in 1996 and more race wins followed in the years to come, but his 1991 championship success remained his only title in CART/IndyCar racing.

His career in CART ended in 2002, in which he took his 42nd and final career victory at the Long Beach Grand Prix - placing him in third place for all-time victories in championship car racing behind his father, Mario Andretti (52 wins) and A.J. Foyt (67 wins).

Michael Andretti is also tied with Al Unser, Jr. for the most wins in a CART/IndyCar season with eight victories. He achieved this during his championship-winning season of 1991.

Sports cars

Michael has driven in numerous sports car races at different times in his career. Many were Andretti family efforts, especially with his father Mario.

Michael and Mario's 1989 Porsche 962 driven in the 24 Hours of Daytona.

Semi-retirement and team owner

After competing in the 2003 Indianapolis 500, Andretti retired from full-time IndyCar racing. He led the race for 28 of the opening 94 laps before a throttle linkage failure put him out of contention once again. That year he bought into the "Team Green" squad run by brothers Kim and Barry Green in CART. It became Andretti Green Racing and for 2003 the team moved to the Indy Racing League IndyCar Series.

That year, Tony Kanaan won the 2004 IndyCar Series Championship for Andretti Green Racing. In 2005, Britain's Dan Wheldon won the Indy 500, and the Championship for the team. In 2007, Scotland's Dario Franchitti won the Indianapolis 500 and the IndyCar Series title for AGR.

Return to racing at Indy

Andretti returned to the driver's seat for the 2006 Indianapolis 500 in a one-time effort to assist the development of his son, Marco, an IndyCar rookie for the '06 season. Michael led the race with four laps to go, before falling to second behind his son a lap later. He went on to finish third, while Marco only just missed out on the 500 victory after he was passed just before the start/finish line on the last lap by three-time Indycar champion Sam Hornish, Jr.

After qualifying his car in 11th place for the 2007 Indianapolis 500, Andretti went on to finish 13th. He then announced that this would be his last Indy 500 as a driver.

Andretti leaves driving competition at Indy with a frustrating distinction - the driver who's led the most laps (431) without winning the race. He competed in 16 Indy 500s, with a top finish of second in 1991, but led the race nine times.

As a car owner, however, he has far more success. In 2005, only three years after Andretti acquired primary ownership of the team, Andretti-Green Racing (AGR) saw its first 500 triumph come from Dan Wheldon in the #26 Klein Tools Special entry, and in 2007 an even stronger second victory, from Scottish driver Dario Franchitti in the #27 Canadian Club-sponsored car, who won the rain-shortened event at the completion of 166 of the scheduled 200 laps, but after another AGR team driver, Tony Kanaan, had himself led half of the eventual laps, and showed potential of renewing his challenge for supremacy after a fourth turn late-race incident.

Personal life

Andretti was married to Sandra Spinozzi from November 1985 to 1996 and they had two children, son Marco (born March 13, 1987) and daughter Marissa (born October 31, 1990). He remarried on December 24, 1997 to Leslie Wood. They had a son, Lucca, born September 16, 1999. On September 7, 2004 Andretti filed for divorce. Two years later on July 15, 2006 Andretti announced his engagement to former Miss Oregon Teen USA 1994, model, actress and 2000 *Playboy* Playmate of the Year Jodi Ann Paterson. The couple were married on October 7, 2006 at the Andretti Winery in Napa Valley, California.

Andretti family

Michael is from the famous Andretti racing family. His brother Jeff Andretti competed in IndyCar. Michael's uncle Aldo Andretti was an open wheel racer until an accident ended his racing career. Aldo's son John Andretti (Michael's cousin) raced in IndyCar before he became a NASCAR regular. He returned to IndyCar in 2007 and 2008 to race the Indy 500, and will race in the 2009 edition too. Aldo's other son, Adam also is a racecar driver. The Andretti family became the first family to have four relatives (Michael, Mario, Jeff, and John) compete in the same series (CART).

Michael Andretti has an estate upon an adjacent tract of land to his father's mansion of "Montona" in Nazareth, Pennsylvania, where he grew up. However that property was listed for sale in January 2008 for $3.4 million. His sister Barbara is the listing agent and said Michael has several other homes and will always have a Nazareth connection. Michael's other homes include a property in downtown Indianapolis where his son lives (near his championship race team headquarters), a residence in Miami Beach, and several other properties for investment purposes.

Motorsports career results

American Open Wheel racing (1983-1992)

(key)

Year	Team	Series	1	2	3	4	5	6	7	8	9	10	11	12	13	14	15	16	17	18	Rank	Points
1983	Kraco	CART	ATL	INDY	MIL	CLE	MIS1	ROA	POC	RIV	MDO	MIS2	LVG Ret	LS Ret	PHX 9						T-26th	4
1984	Kraco	CART	LBH 10	PHX1 3	INDY 5	MIL 4	POR 12	MEA Ret	CLE 3	MIS1 Ret	ROA 16	POC Ret	MDO Ret	SAN 3	MIS2 7	PHX2 3	LS 3	LVG Ret			7th	102
1985	Kraco	CART	LBH Ret	INDY 8	MIL Ret	POR Ret	MEA 4	CLE 7	MIS1 Ret	ROA 2	POC Ret	MDO Ret	SAN Ret	MIS2 Ret	LS 9	PHX 5	MIA Ret				9th	53
1986	Kraco	CART	PHX1 Ret	LBH 1	INDY 6	MIL 1	POR 2	MEA Ret	CLE 2	TOR Ret	MIS1 Ret	POC Ret	MDO 10	SAN 6	MIS2 2	ROA 2	LS 3	PHX2 1	MIA Ret		2nd	171
1987	Kraco	CART	LBH 4	PHX 4	INDY Ret	MIL 1	POR 2	MEA 5	CLE 6	TOR 5	MIS 1	POC 8	ROA Ret	MDO Ret	NAZ 1	LS Ret	MIA1 Ret	MIA 1			2nd	158
1988	Kraco	CART	PHX 3	LBH 7	INDY 4	MIL 7	POR 11	CLE Ret	TOR 3	MEA 6	MIS 3	POC Ret	MDO Ret	ROA 5	NAZ 2	LS 2	MIA1 1	MIA Ret			6th	119
1989	Newman Haas	CART	PHX 4	LBH 2	INDY Ret	MIL 2	DET Ret	POR 6	CLE Ret	MEA Ret	TOR 1	MIS 1	POC 3	MDO 3	ROA Ret	NAZ 5	LS1 7	LS 7			3rd	150
1990	Newman Haas	CART	PHX Ret	LBH 4	INDY Ret	MIL 5	DET 1	POR 1	CLE Ret	MEA 1	TOR 2	MIS Ret	DEN 5	VAN Ret	MDO 1	ROA 1	NAZ1 6	NAZ 5	LS 3		2nd	181
1991	Newman Haas	CART	SRF Ret	LBH Ret	PHX 4	INDY 2	MIL 1	DET Ret	POR 1	CLE 1	MEA Ret	TOR 1	MIS Ret	DEN 3	VAN 1	MDO 1	ROA 1	NAZ 3	LS1 1	LS 1	1st	234
1992	Newman Haas	CART	SRF Ret	PHX 10	LBH Ret	INDY Ret	DET 4	POR 1	MIL 1	NHM 2	TOR 1	MIS Ret	CLE 2	ROA 4	VAN 1	MDO Ret	NAZ1 2	NAZ 2	LS 1		2nd	192

(Event)[1] : non-championship, exhibition race held day preceding next championship race.

Formula One

(key)

Year	Entrant	Chassis Engine	1	2	3	4	5	6	7	8	9	10	11	12	13	14	15	16	WDC	Points
1993	Marlboro McLaren	McLaren MP4/8 Ford V8	RSA Ret	BRA Ret	EUR Ret	SMR Ret	ESP 5	MON 8	CAN 14	FRA 6	GBR Ret	GER Ret	HUN Ret	BEL 8	ITA 3	POR	JPN	AUS	11th	7

American Open Wheel racing (1994-2007)

(key)

Year	Team	Series	1	2	3	4	5	6	7	8	9	10	11	12	13	14	15	16	17	18	19	20	21	Rank	Points
1994	Ganassi	CART	SRF 1	PHX Ret	LBH 6	INDY 6	MIL 4	DET 5	POR Ret	CLE Ret	TOR 1	MIS Ret	MDO 5	NHM 5	VAN 3	ROA Ret	NZR 9	LS Ret						4th	118
1995	Newman Haas	CART	MIA Ret	SRF Ret	PHX 2	LBH 9	NZR Ret	INDY Ret	MIL 3	DET 4	POR 4	ROA Ret	TOR 1	CLE 7	MIS Ret	MDO Ret	NHM 2	VAN Ret	LS 4					4th	123
1996	Newman Haas	CART	HMS 9	RIO Ret	SRF Ret	LBH 7	NZR 1	MIS1 Ret	MIL 1	DET 1	POR 11	CLE Ret	TOR Ret	MIS2 Ret	MDO 3	ROA 1	VAN 1	LS 9						2nd	132
1997	Newman Haas	CART	HMS 1	SRF 2	LBH Ret	NZR 2	RIO Ret	STL 11	MIL 2	DET 2	POR 8	CLE Ret	TOR 4	MIS Ret	MDO 8	ROA Ret	VAN Ret	LS Ret	FON Ret					8th	108
1998	Newman Haas	CART	HMS 1	MOT 14	LBH Ret	NZR Ret	RIO 5	STL 2	MIL Ret	DET 10	POR 17	CLE 2	TOR 2	MIS 6	MDO Ret	ROA Ret	VAN 2	LS 10	HOU Ret	SRF Ret	FON Ret			8th	108
1999	Newman Haas	CART	HMS 2	MOT 5	LBH 7	NZR 6	RIO Ret	STL 1	MIL 15	POR 10	CLE 3	ROA 2	TOR Ret	MIS 4	DET 4	MDO 8	CHI Ret	VAN 14	LS 10	HOU 3	SRF 5	FON Ret		4th	151
2000	Newman Haas	CART	HMS Ret	LBH Ret	RIO 9	MOT 1	NZR 6	MIL 2	DET Ret	POR 4	CLE 4	TOR 1	MIS 2	CHI 2	MDO 8	ROA Ret	VAN Ret	LS 14	STL Ret	HOU 13	SRF Ret	FON Ret		8th	127

2001 — Team Motorola

CART — 3rd, 147

MTY	LBH	TXS	NAZ	MOT	MIL	DET	POR	CLE	TOR	MIS	CHI	MDO	ROA	VAN	LAU	ROC	HOU	LS	SRF	FON
4	Ret	NH	6	Ret	2	4	8	15	1	Ret	Ret	Ret	2	3	4	5	Ret	14	2	7

IndyCar — 34th, 35

PHX	HMS	ATL	INDY	TXS	PPIR	RIR	KAN	NSH	KTY	STL	CHI	TX2
			3									

2002 — Team Motorola

CART — 9th, 110

MTY	LBH	MOT	MIL	LS	POR	CHI	TOR	CLE	VAN	MDO	ROA	MTL	DEN	ROC	MIA	SRF	FON	MEX
12	1*	16	7	11	9	15	11	2	6	3	10	8	13	10	8	9	2	17

IndyCar — 38th, 26

HMS	PHX	FON	NZR	INDY	TXS	PPIR	RIR	KAN	NSH	MIS	KTY	STL	CHI	TX2
				7										

2003 — Andretti Green

IndyCar — 24th, 80

HMS	PHX	MOT	INDY	TXS	PPIR	RIR	KAN	NSH	MIS	STL	KTY	NZR	CHI	FON	TX2
6	Ret	4	Ret												

2006 — Andretti Green

IndyCar — 24th, 35

HMS	STP	MOT	INDY	WGL	TXS	RIR	KAN	NSH	MIL	MIS	KTY	SNM	CHI
			3										

2007 — Andretti Green

IndyCar — 27th, 17

HMS	STP	MOT	KAN	INDY	MIL	TXS	IOW	RIR	WGL	NSH	MDO	MIS	KTY	SNM	DET	CHI
				13												

Indianapolis 500 results

Year	Chassis	Engine	Start	Finish	Team
1984	March	Cosworth	4	5	Kraco
1985	Lola	Cosworth	15	8	Kraco
1986	March	Cosworth	3	6	Kraco
1987	March	Cosworth	9	29	Kraco
1988	March	Cosworth	10	4	Kraco
1989	Lola	Chevrolet	21	17	Newman/Haas
1990	Lola	Chevrolet	5	20	Newman/Haas
1991	Lola	Chevrolet	5	2	Newman/Haas
1992	Lola	Ford-Cosworth	6	13	Newman/Haas
1994	Reynard	Ford-Cosworth	5	6	Ganassi
1995	Lola	Ford-Cosworth	4	25	Newman/Haas

2001	Dallara	Oldsmobile	21	3	Team Green
2002	Dallara	Chevrolet	25	7	Team Green
2003	Dallara	Honda	13	27	Andretti Green
2006	Dallara	Honda	13	3	Andretti Green
2007	Dallara	Honda	11	13	Andretti Green

See also

- Michael Andretti's World GP, a video game that licensed his name

External links

- The Official Andretti Family Website [3]
- Article on Andretti's F1 career [1]

Dwayne Johnson

Dwayne Johnson

Johnson at the 2009 Tribeca Film Festival

Born	Dwayne Douglas Johnson May 2, 1972 Hayward, California, U.S.
Other names	The Rock, Rocky Maivia
Occupation	Actor/Wrestler

Years active	1990–2004 (wrestler)
	2001–present (actor)
Spouse	Dany Garcia
	(1997–2007)

Dwayne Douglas Johnson (born May 2, 1972) is an American actor and former professional wrestler. He is also known by his former ring name **The Rock** and is occasionally credited as **Dwayne "The Rock" Johnson**.

Johnson was a collegiate football player and, in 1991, he was part of the University of Miami's national championship team. He later played for the Calgary Stampeders in the Canadian Football League, but was cut two months into the season. This led to his decision to become a professional wrestler like his grandfather, Peter Maivia, and his father, Rocky Johnson. He gained mainstream fame as a wrestler in World Wrestling Entertainment (WWE), originally known as the World Wrestling Federation (WWF), from 1996 to 2004, and was the first third-generation superstar in the company's history. Johnson was quickly given a push in the WWF, first as "Rocky Maivia", and then as "The Rock", a member of the Nation of Domination. Two years after he joined the WWF, Johnson won the WWF Championship, and became one of the most popular wrestlers within the company's history for his engaging interviews and promos. In 2001, he began acting and occasionally returned to the ring. His primary focus, as of 2010, is his acting career.

In WWE, Johnson was a nine-time world champion, having won the WWF/E Championship seven times (with his last reign being as the WWE Undisputed Champion) and the WCW/World Championship two times. In addition to these championships, Johnson has also won the WWF Intercontinental Championship two times and the WWF Tag Team Championship five times. He is also the sixth WWF/E Triple Crown champion and was the winner of the 2000 Royal Rumble.

In 2000, Johnson made his literary debut by publishing his autobiography, *The Rock Says*. It debuted at number one on The New York Times Best Seller list and remained on the list for several weeks. Johnson is also an actor, and his first leading role, in 2002, was in *The Scorpion King*. For this film, he received the highest salary for an actor in his first starring role, earning $5.5 million[citation needed]. He has since appeared in movies such as *The Rundown, Be Cool, Walking Tall, Gridiron Gang, The Game Plan, Get Smart, Race to Witch Mountain, Planet 51, Tooth Fairy, Doom, Why Did I Get Married Too?* and *The Other Guys*.

Early life

Dwayne Johnson, the son of Ata Johnson (*née* Maivia) and professional wrestler "Soulman" Rocky Johnson, was born in Hayward, California. His maternal grandfather, "High Chief" Peter Maivia, was also a professional wrestler. His maternal grandmother, Lia Maivia, ran Polynesian Pacific Pro Wrestling from 1982 until 1988 following her husband's death, becoming one of wrestling's few female professional promoters. His father is of Black Nova Scotian (Canadian) origin and his mother is of Samoan heritage. For a brief period, Johnson lived in Auckland, New Zealand, with his mother's family. During this time his mother Ata ensured Johnson was exposed to one of the urban Polynesian cultural strongholds of the Southern Hemisphere. Johnson attended Richmond Road Primary School before returning to the United States with his parents.

He spent 10th grade at President William McKinley High School in Honolulu, Hawaii. As he entered 11th grade, Johnson's father's job required his relocation to Bethlehem, Pennsylvania, in the state's Lehigh Valley region. He began playing football at Bethlehem's Freedom High School in the highly competitive Lehigh Valley Conference. In addition to playing football at Freedom High School, he also was a member of the high school's track and field and wrestling teams.

Education and football

Johnson was heavily recruited by many Division I collegiate programs but ultimately accepted a full scholarship from the University of Miami to play defensive tackle. In 1991, he was part of the Miami Hurricanes' national championship team. After an injury kept him sidelined, Johnson was replaced by fellow Hurricane and future National Football League (NFL) star Warren Sapp.

While attending Miami, Johnson met his future wife, Dany Garcia. Garcia, who graduated from the university in 1992, is a member of its Board of Trustees, and the founder of a Miami-based wealth management firm. The two have remained close to their alma mater, giving a $2-million donation in 2006 to build a living room at the university's alumni center. Johnson graduated from Miami in 1995 with a Bachelor of Science degree in criminology and physiology.

Dwayne Johnson greeting fans in 2006

On November 10, 2007 he returned to the Orange Bowl in Miami to participate in the festivities surrounding the University of Miami's last home football game at the stadium.

Johnson continued his football career in 1995, joining the Calgary Stampeders of the Canadian Football League after being passed over by the NFL, but he was cut two months into the season.

Johnson has two nephews who play football. Kaluka Maiava played football at USC and was drafted by the Cleveland Browns in 2009, while Kaluka's brother Kai Maiava currently plays at UCLA.

Professional wrestling career

Training and Rocky Maivia (1996)

Dwayne Johnson	
Ring name(s)	Flex Kavana Rocky Maivia The Rock
Height	6 ft 4 in (1.93 m)
Weight	250 lb (110 kg)
Billed height	6 ft 5 in (1.96 m)
Billed weight	275 lb (125 kg)
Born	May 2, 1972 Hayward, California
Resides	Fort Lauderdale, Florida
Billed from	Miami, Florida
Trained by	Rocky Johnson Pat Patterson
Debut	1995
Retired	March 14, 2004

Along with his father and grandfather, several members of Johnson's family are current and former professional wrestlers, including his uncles, the Wild Samoans (Afa and Sika Anoa'i) and cousins, such as Manu, Yokozuna, Rikishi, Rosey, and Umaga. When he declared his intention to join the family business, his father resisted, but agreed to train his son himself, warning him that he would not go easy on him. With help from veteran wrestler Pat Patterson, Johnson had several tryout matches with WWE in 1996; he defeated The Brooklyn Brawler at a house show under his real name, Dwayne Johnson, and lost the others to Chris Candido and Owen Hart. Impressed by his talent and charisma, Johnson was signed to a contract after wrestling at Jerry Lawler's United States Wrestling Association, where he wrestled under the ring name "Flex Kavana". While there, he won the USWA World Tag Team Championship twice with Bart Sawyer in the summer of 1996.

World Wrestling Federation / Entertainment (1995–2004)

Johnson made his WWF debut as Rocky Maivia, which combined his father and grandfather's ring names; Johnson was initially reluctant to the idea, but was persuaded to go ahead with the name by Vince McMahon and Jim Ross. In addition to taking on the nickname "The Blue Chipper," the WWF played up his connection to his father and grandfather, calling him the company's first third-generation wrestler.

Johnson, who was first portrayed as a clean-cut face character (fan favorite), was pushed heavily from the start despite his lack of in-ring experience. He debuted at Survivor Series in November 1996 and was the sole survivor, and he won the WWF Intercontinental Championship from Hunter Hearst Helmsley on *Raw* on February 13, 1997, after only three months in the company. Fans, however, quickly grew sick of the one-dimensional good guy character, thanks in part to the increasing popularity of Stone Cold Steve Austin. As a result, a regular occurrence during Johnson's matches was the fans' angry chants of *"Die Rocky Die!"* and *"Rocky Sucks!"*

Nation of Domination and feuding with DX (1997–1998)

Main article: Nation of Domination

After losing the Intercontinental Championship to Owen Hart on the April 28, 1997 edition of *Raw is War*, and returning from an injury, Johnson turned into a heel character (villain). He joined the Nation of Domination with Faarooq, D'Lo Brown, and Kama, using the ring name "The Rock" Rocky Maivia, which was quickly shortened to simply "The Rock". During that time, Johnson attacked and insulted the fans in his promos. In sharp contrast to the overly positive persona of Rocky Maivia, The Rock was a charismatic bully, eventually driving out the group leader, Faarooq in March 1998. The Rock also referred to himself in the third person, starting many sentences with *"The Rock says..."*

Johnson was soon recognized for cutting arguably the best promos in the industry. In his 2000 autobiography, Johnson attributed this skill to his exceptional performance in speech communications classes at Miami, in which he earned "A" grades. At In Your House: D-Generation X, Austin defeated The Rock in less than six minutes to retain the Intercontinental Championship. The following night on *Raw is War*, Austin was ordered by Mr. McMahon to defend the Intercontinental Championship in a rematch, but Austin decided to forfeit it instead, and handed the championship over to The Rock before performing the Stone Cold Stunner on him. Rock spent the end of 1997 and the beginning of 1998 feuding with both Austin and Ken Shamrock.

The Rock next feuded with Faarooq, who was angry at the Rock for usurping his position. The two had a title match at Over the Edge, where Rock retained the Intercontinental Championship. The Rock then moved into a feud with Triple H and D-Generation X. Nation members fought DX while The Rock fought Triple H over the Intercontinental Championship. They first had a two out of three falls match at Fully Loaded for Rock's title, where the Rock retained the title in controversial fashion. This led to a ladder match at SummerSlam where Rock lost the belt. At Breakdown, the Rock defeated Ken Shamrock and Mankind in a triple threat steel cage match to become the number one contender to the WWF Championship before feuding with fellow Nation member Mark Henry, effectively disbanding the Nation.

The Corporation (1998–1999)

Main article: The Corporation

Johnson's popularity as The Rock propelled him to the WWF Championship. The Rock began to conduct many entertaining interviews, and thus he got over with the fans. Fan reaction effectively turned him into a face character, and he began to feud with Mr. McMahon, who said he has a *"problem with the people"* and thus he should target the "People's Champion" (as The Rock claimed himself to be). A double turn occurred at Survivor Series, when The Rock defeated the then-villain Mankind in the finals of the "Deadly Game" tournament for the vacant WWF Championship. At the end of the match, The Rock applied a Sharpshooter on Mankind. As he did this, McMahon called for the bell to be rung and then ordered for The Rock to be declared the winner. This was a parody of the Montreal Screwjob, which happened one year earlier at Survivor Series.

With the plan coming to fruition, The Rock turned into a villain again and sided with Vince and Shane McMahon as the crown jewel of The Corporation stable. This was also a start of a double turn, as Mankind was kicked out of The Corporation and became a fan favorite. Later, The Rock had his own pay-per view, Rock Bottom: In Your House, where he had a rematch against Mankind for the WWF Championship. Mankind won the match by knocking the Rock out with Mr. Socko and the mandible claw, but Mr. McMahon said that The Rock did not tap out and therefore The Rock would retain his title. The Rock began a feud with Mankind over the WWF Championship, during which the title changed hands back and forth between the two, first during the main event of the January 4, 1999 edition of *Raw is War*, when Mankind defeated The Rock with the help of Stone Cold Steve Austin. The Rock captured his second WWF Championship in an "I Quit" match at Royal Rumble in early 1999, when a pre-recorded sample of Mankind saying *"I quit"* from an interview segment was played over the sound system. This latest reign did not last long, however. In a match that counter-programmed the Super Bowl halftime show on January 31, 1999, Mankind pinned The Rock using a forklift truck in an Empty Arena Match where the competitors used everything from bags of popcorn to garbage to punish each other. This feud lasted until February 15 edition of *Raw is War*, where The Rock won his third WWF Championship in a ladder match after The Big Show chokeslammed Mankind off a ladder.

With Mankind out of the way, The Rock had to defend his WWF Championship at WrestleMania XV, but lost the belt to Austin. Rock lost the title rematch to Austin at Backlash: In Your House. WWF fans began to cheer The Rock despite him being a villain, due to his comedic interviews, promos and segments which mocked wrestlers and announcers and made him popular to the fans. Rock eventually transitioned into a face character again after being betrayed by Shane McMahon and established a feud with The Undertaker, Triple H and the Corporate Ministry. During this feud, he sometimes found himself fighting alongside Steve Austin. Rock defeated Triple H at Over the Edge before losing to WWF Champion The Undertaker at King of the Ring. He continued his rivalry with Triple H, after losing to him in a number one contender's match due to interference from Mr. Ass at Fully Loaded.

The Rock 'n' Sock Connection (1999)

Main article: Rock 'n' Sock Connection

Later on, besides feuding with Triple H, The Rock also feuded with Mr. Ass throughout the summer of 1999, including a "Kiss My Ass" match at SummerSlam. In the fall of the same year, The Rock found himself in several singles and tag team championship opportunities. He teamed with former enemy Mankind to create the Rock 'n' Sock Connection, after The Rock challenged the team of The Undertaker and The Big Show, which led to Mankind offering his help. The Rock accepted, and they went on to win the WWF Tag Team Championship three times. Aside from the championships, the team was regarded as one of the most entertaining teams in history, as Mankind imitated The Rock, who ignored Mankind, with both wrestlers having support from the crowd. The team was also involved in a segment which occurred on *Raw is War* called *"This Is Your Life"*, in which Mankind brought out people from The Rock's past, such as his high school girlfriend and gym teacher. The segment earned an 8.4 Nielsen rating and is, to this day, one of the single highest rated segments in terms of viewership in Raw history.

Feuds for the WWF Championship (2000–2001)

At Royal Rumble in early 2000, The Rock entered in the Royal Rumble match and lasted until he and The Big Show were the final two men. In the final moment of the match, The Big Show was seemingly going to throw The Rock over the top rope in a running powerslam-like position, but when they got to the apron The Rock reversed the throw, sending The Big Show to the outside floor and then came back up. The Rock's feet, however, hit the floor first, although those watching the event did not see that. The Big Show attempted to prove that The Rock's feet, not his, touched the ground first. He provided video footage showing that he was the

The Rock making his entrance at WrestleMania X-Seven, Houston.

rightful winner. Despite that, the decision that The Rock had won the Rumble match could not be reversed, so a number one contender's match for the WWF Championship at No Way Out was held, which saw The Big Show come out on top after Shane McMahon interfered, knocking The Rock in the head with a steel chair as he attempted to finish off his opponent with a People's Elbow. The Rock later defeated The Big Show on March 13, 2000 edition of *Raw is War* to regain the right to face the WWF Champion, Triple H, at WrestleMania 2000 in a Fatal Four-Way Elimination match where The Big Show and Mick Foley competed, as well. Each competitor had a McMahon in their corner; for Triple H, his on-screen wife and then off-screen girlfriend Stephanie McMahon; for Mick Foley, the matriarch Linda McMahon; for The Rock, Vince McMahon; and in Big Show's corner, Shane McMahon. Triple H retained the title when Vince betrayed The Rock, hitting him with a chair, allowing Triple H to pin The Rock for the three-count.

The Rock taunts Rob Van Dam at ringside.

Over the next couple of months The Rock feuded with Triple H over the WWF Championship. A month after the match at WrestleMania 2000, The Rock had a rematch with Triple H at Backlash in which The Rock won his fourth WWF Championship, after Stone Cold Steve Austin made a brief return and intervened on The Rock's behalf. Later, at Judgment Day, the two had an Iron Man match with Shawn Michaels as the special guest referee, that saw The Undertaker return. The Rock got disqualified and lost the title, as a result of The Undertaker attacking Triple H. The following night on *Raw is War*, The Rock got his revenge, taking out the entire McMahon-Helmsley Faction with the help of The Undertaker. He later won his fifth WWF Championship at King of the Ring in a tag team match, which saw him team up with Kane and The Undertaker to fight Vince McMahon, Shane McMahon and Triple H. He successfully defended the championship against superstars such as Chris Benoit, Kurt Angle, Triple H, Kane, The Undertaker, and Shane McMahon.

The Rock later lost the WWF Championship to Angle at No Mercy in October. During this time, he feuded with Rikishi and defeated him at Survivor Series. He also participated in a six-man Hell in a Cell match at Armageddon for the WWF Championship, in which Kurt Angle retained the title. Around that same time, Rock held the WWF Tag Team Championship with The Undertaker and the duo exchanged the titles with Edge and Christian.

In 2001, The Rock continued his feud with Angle over the WWF Championship, which they eventually settled at No Way Out. After a battle that saw both wrestlers kick out of each other's finishers, The Rock finally came out on top and won the WWF Championship for the sixth time. Afterwards, he feuded with the Royal Rumble winner, Stone Cold Steve Austin. The Rock went into WrestleMania X-Seven as the WWF Champion, but he was defeated after Austin used Mr. McMahon to win the title. During a Steel Cage match with Austin in a rematch for the WWF Championship on the following night's *Raw is War*, Triple H came down to the ring with a sledgehammer. Many thought he was coming to aid The Rock, due to the hatred between Austin and Triple H (and an argument with Vince earlier in the night), but it transpired that he had joined the Austin/McMahon partnership by hitting The Rock instead. Austin and Triple H became a tag team and called themselves "The Two-Man Power Trip". Rock went on to film the movie "*The Mummy Returns*" after a storyline suspension.

The Invasion and final storylines (2001–2003)

Main article: The Invasion

He returned in late July 2001 and had to decide if he wanted to join the WWF or The Alliance during The Invasion, eventually siding with the WWF. At SummerSlam, The Rock defeated Booker T to win the WCW Championship. He lost the WCW Championship to Chris Jericho, with whom he won the WWF Tag Team Championship around the same time, at No Mercy.

Rock defeated Jericho on November 5 edition of *Raw* for his second WCW Championship. The Rock ultimately decided to join the WWF in its battle against The Alliance and was involved in a "Winner Takes All" match at Survivor Series, which saw him end up one on one with Steve Austin. The Rock seemed to be superior to Austin, until Chris Jericho, who was also a member of team WWF and was eliminated a few minutes before that point, came inside the ring and attacked The Rock. Austin took advantage of that and tried to defeat The Rock, but Kurt Angle, a supposed teammate of Austin, proved out to be a mole planted by Vince McMahon and hit Austin in the head with a title belt, allowing The Rock to eliminate him, destroying The Alliance once and for all. The Rock closed out the year losing the WCW Championship to Chris Jericho at Vengeance as Jericho became the first Undisputed WWF Champion.

In early 2002, Rock feuded with Jericho and challenged him for the Undisputed Championship at Royal Rumble, but lost the match. After losing to Jericho, Rock engaged in feuds and wrestled the likes of The Undertaker at No Way Out and Hollywood Hulk Hogan at WrestleMania X8. On July 21, The Rock won his record-breaking seventh and final WWE Championship, which was known as the WWE Undisputed Championship at the time. He defeated Kurt Angle and The Undertaker in a match at Vengeance, after he hit the Rock Bottom on Angle. The Rock successfully defended the title at *Global Warning* against Triple H and Brock Lesnar by pinning Triple H, who then saved The Rock after Lesnar tried to ambush him after the match. Johnson finally dropped the WWE Undisputed Championship to Lesnar at SummerSlam, ending his final championship reign, and making Lesnar the youngest WWE Champion in history, a record previously held by The Rock. The Rock then went on a six month hiatus from WWE.

He returned in January 2003, and began his last villainous turn on *SmackDown!*, publicly criticizing Hulk Hogan. Their WrestleMania X8 rematch at No Way Out ended with The Rock claiming victory again, with assistance from Vince McMahon and the referee, Sylvain Grenier. The Rock later drafted himself to the Raw brand and started a feud with The Hurricane and other fan favorites. He also had a comical gimmick, where he played the guitar and sang songs mocking the host city for the event, which culminated in a "Rock concert" that took place during the main event of the March 24, 2003 edition of *Raw*, where The Rock mocked the host city, Sacramento, California, because of the Sacramento Kings' inability to beat the Los Angeles Lakers.

When Stone Cold Steve Austin returned, they once again feuded, and The Rock defeated Austin at WrestleMania XIX, which was Austin's last major appearance in a wrestling role. The Rock then had a feud with Bill Goldberg, to whom Rock lost at Backlash. The Rock then turned into a fan favorite once more by engaging in a one night feud against Chris Jericho and Christian (who was a heel during that time). During his previous villainous turn, he had declared Christian as his favorite wrestler, leading Christian to begin calling himself the "new people's champion" and referring to his fans as "his peeps."

Retirement and part–time WWE appearances (2004–present)

The Rock made occasional wrestling appearances up to 2004's WrestleMania XX, when the storyline revolving around Mick Foley had him brought back to help in his feud with Evolution (Ric Flair, Randy Orton, Triple H and Batista). One humorous in-ring segment involved The Rock hosting his own version of "This Is Your Life" for Foley on the March 8, 2004 edition of *Raw*. Rock reunited with Foley after five years, as the Rock 'n' Sock Connection. The duo went on to lose to Orton, Flair and Batista at WrestleMania XX in a handicap match when Orton pinned Foley with an RKO. As of 2010, this was Rock's last match.

He made sporadic appearances in WWE following WrestleMania, including standing up for Eugene, making a cameo appearance in his hometown of Miami and helping Foley turn back La Résistance. In 2004, he hosted a "Pie-Eating Contest" during the WWE Diva Search and ended the segment by giving Jonathan Coachman a Rock Bottom and a People's Elbow. After this appearance, Johnson reported in several interviews that he was no longer under contract with WWE. He also reported that the reason he was able to continue using the name "The Rock" was part of a dual ownership between him and WWE.

On March 12, 2007, The Rock made an appearance on WWE after a near three year absence, appearing on *Raw* via a pre-taped segment on the titantron. He correctly "predicted" that Bobby Lashley would defeat Umaga at WrestleMania 23 in Donald Trump and Vince McMahon's "Battle of the Billionaires" match.

On March 29, 2008, The Rock inducted his father, Rocky Johnson, and his grandfather, Peter Maivia into the WWE Hall of Fame. During his induction speech he roasted WWE superstars such as John Cena, Santino Marella, Chris Jericho, Mick Foley, Shawn Michaels, and Steve Austin. In September 2009, Johnson appeared at a World Xtreme Wrestling show in order to support longtime friend and mentor Jimmy Snuka's daughter's debut in professional wrestling.

On October 2, 2009, on the 10th anniversary of *SmackDown*, The Rock made a special appearance in a pre-recorded video where he talked about *SmackDown*'s anniversary. He also hinted about "guest hosting" *Raw* in the near future. In an interview with *Sports Illustrated* to promote his new film, *Tooth Fairy*, The Rock mentioned that he was supposed to host *Raw* in January 2010, but had to be in Mexico to promote the movie so he had to cancel. He however announced that he plans to come back sometime in 2010 and guest host Raw. He said he does not just want to come back and guest host but he wants to entertain the fans in a way they haven't been entertained in years. The Rock claimed in an interview to Boston Mix's 104 that he had plans of returning but not for a wrestling match. When asked if he plans on wrestling a match, The Rock said: "How I would come back is a different capacity than what Hulk

Hogan did or I believe Ric Flair is doing. Those guys are coming back to actually wrestle. I don't want to wrestle; I have no intention of wrestling a match." However, The Rock later stated that wrestling a match was something that he wouldn't put out of his mind yet.

Television and film career

The success of Johnson's in-ring character allowed him to cross over into mainstream popularity, and he appeared on Wyclef Jean's 2000 single "It Doesn't Matter" and the accompanying video. That same year, he hosted *Saturday Night Live*. Fellow wrestlers Triple H, The Big Show, and Mick Foley appeared on the show. According to Johnson, it was due to the success of that episode that he began receiving offers from Hollywood studios.

Johnson filmed guest roles on *Star Trek: Voyager* and *That '70s Show*, where he played his father, Rocky Johnson. His motion picture debut was a brief appearance as The Scorpion King in the opening sequence of *The Mummy Returns*. His character later appears in the climax as a CGI Character. The film's financial success led to his first leading role starring in the follow-up, *The Scorpion King*. He was considered for the lead in a feature-length *Johnny Bravo* film, but it was canceled during production.

Dwayne Johnson photographed by Jerry Avenaim for *Vanity Fair* in 2001.

Since his last WWE match in 2004, he has quit wrestling and focused solely on acting. He also continued to make television appearances, including Disney Channel's hit show *Cory in the House*, in the episode entitled "Never the Dwayne Shall Meet." Though Johnson is no longer active with WWE, the company continues to sell "The Rock" merchandise, and Johnson continues to be featured prominently in the opening montages of their television programming. The Rock has continued to show a multitude of his acting/talent skills including film roles like the cocky famous football player Joe Kingman in *The Game Plan*, and in *Get Smart* where he played Agent 23.

Johnson was featured in the 2007 *Guinness Book of World Records* for having the highest salary as an actor in his first starring role, receiving $5.5 million. He appeared at the 80th Academy Awards on February 24, 2008 as a presenter for the Academy Award for Best Visual Effects. He was nominated for Favorite Movie Actor at the 2008 Nickelodeon Kids' Choice Awards for his role in *The Game Plan*, but lost out to Johnny Depp, who won for his performance in *Pirates of the Caribbean: At World's End*.

On March 20, 2009, Johnson appeared on The Tonight Show with Jay Leno. Johnson hosted the 2009 Nickelodeon Kids' Choice Awards on March 28. Johnson also appeared on the *Wizards of Waverly*

Place episode "Art Teacher" as part of his stint with The Walt Disney Company.

Johnson has made various guest appearances on Saturday Night Live, reviving his character of The Rock Obama, a parody of The Hulk. When you make Barack Obama angry, he turns into The Rock Obama.

Johnson also made an uncredited cameo in the 2010 film *Tyler Perry's Why Did I Get Married Too?* as a handsome psychiatrist who asks out the recently widowed Patricia Agnew (Janet Jackson).

On April 29, 2010, it was announced he will join the cast of Simon West's new film, currently titled *Protection*. The film is slated for a 2012 release and is scheduled to shoot this fall in New Mexico. The screenplay is by Brandon Noonan.

Filmography and TV roles

Film			
Year	Film	Role	Notes
1999	*Beyond the Mat*	Himself	Documentary
2000	*Longshot*	The Mugger	
2001	*The Mummy Returns*	The Scorpion King	
2002	*The Scorpion King*	Mathayus the Scorpion King	
2003	*The Rundown*	Beck	"Welcome to the Jungle (UK title)"
2004	*Walking Tall*	Chris Vaughn	
2005	*Be Cool*	Elliot Wilhelm	
	Doom	Sarge	
2006	*Gridiron Gang*	Sean Porter	
2007	*Reno 911!: Miami*	Agent Rick Smith	Cameo
	Southland Tales	Boxer Santaros	
	The Game Plan	Joe Kingman	Last movie to use ring name "The Rock" 2007
2008	*Get Smart*	Agent 23	
2009	*Race to Witch Mountain*	Jack Bruno	
	Planet 51	Capt. Charles 'Chuck' Baker	Voice

2010	*Tooth Fairy*	Derek Thompson / Tooth Fairy	
	Tyler Perry's Why Did I Get Married Too?	Daniel Franklin (Patricia's new boyfriend)	Uncredited
	Faster	Driver	
	The Other Guys	Detective Christopher Danson	
	You Again	Air Marshall	Uncredited
2011	*Fast Five*	Hobbs	*Post Production*
	Journey 2: The Mysterious Island	TBA	*Announced*
2012	*Protection*	TBA	*In production*

Television			
Year	**Title**	**Role**	**Notes**
2010-TBA	*Transformers: Prime*	Cliffjumper	Voice, Post Production

Television guest appearances			
Year	**Title**	**Role**	**Notes**
1999	*That '70s Show*	Rocky Johnson	Episode: "That Wrestling Show"
	The Net	Brody	Episode: "Last Man Standing"
2000	*Star Trek: Voyager*	The Champion	Episode: "Tsunkatse"
2007	*Cory in the House*	Himself	1 episode
2008	*Hannah Montana*		
2009	*Wizards of Waverly Place*		
2010	*Family Guy*		

Personal life, public activities, and philanthropy

Johnson married Dany Garcia on May 3, 1997, a day after his 25th birthday. Johnson and his wife have a daughter, Simone Alexandra, born August 14, 2001. On June 1, 2007, Johnson and Garcia announced that they would be splitting up after 10 years of marriage. They indicated that their parting was amicable and that they would spend the rest of their lives together as best friends.

Dany Garcia and Johnson at the 2009 Tribeca Film Festival.

In 2006, Johnson began "The Dwayne Johnson Rock Foundation", which is known for its charitable work with at-risk and terminally ill children. On October 2, 2007, Johnson and his wife donated an additional $1 million to the University of Miami to support the renovation of its football facilities; it was noted as the largest donation ever given to the university's athletics department by former students. The University of Miami renamed the Hurricanes' locker room in Johnson's honor.

In 2000, Johnson attended both the 2000 Republican National Convention and the 2000 Democratic National Convention, giving a speech at the former. Both appearances were part of the WWE's non-partisan "Smackdown your Vote" campaign which aims to increase voting among young people without endorsing any candidate or party.

Because his mother, Ata Fitisemanu Maivia, had royal blood, Samoan King Malietoa Tanumafili II bestowed Johnson with the noble title of *Seiuli* during his visit to Samoa in July 2004 in recognition of his service to the Samoan people. He is therefore known in Samoan circles as *Seiuli Dwayne Johnson*. He is a supporter of the Samoa national rugby union team, as the team's website during the run-up to the 2007 Rugby World Cup showed him holding a personalized Manu Samoa jersey with "The Rock" emblazoned on the back. He also acknowledges his heritage through a pe'a tattoo he got in 2003.

Johnson is good friends with current California Governor Arnold Schwarzenegger, and X-Men star, Hugh Jackman. Michael Clarke Duncan and Johnson are also very close.

Johnson published his autobiography, *The Rock Says...*, in 1999, with Joe Layden.

Johnson is related to the famed Anoa'i family.

In wrestling

- **Finishing moves**
  - Diving crossbody − 1996–1997
  - *People's Elbow / Corporate Elbow* (Feint leg drop transitioned into a high impact elbow drop to the opponent's chest, with theatrics)
  - *Rock Bottom* (Lifting side slam)
  - Running shoulderbreaker − 1996–1997; used as a regular move from 1997–2003

- **Signature moves**
  - Double leg takedown spinebuster
  - Float-over DDT
  - Flowing snap DDT, sometimes followed by a kip up
  - Running swinging neckbreaker
  - Running thrust lariat
  - Samoan drop
  - Sharpshooter
  - Snap overhead belly to belly suplex, sometimes to an oncoming opponent

- **Managers**
  - Debra
  - Vince McMahon
  - Shane McMahon

- **Nicknames**
  - "The People's Champion"
  - "The Brahma Bull"
  - "The Corporate Champion"
  - "The Great One"
  - "The Most Electrifying Man in Sports Entertainment"
  - "Rocky"

- **Entrance themes**
  - "Destiny" by Jim Johnston (1996–1997)
  - "Do You Smell It" by Jim Johnston (1998–1999)
  - "Know Your Role" by Method Man (2000)
  - "Know Your Role" by Jim Johnston (1999–2001, 2004–)
  - "If You Smell..." by Jim Johnston (2001–2003)
  - "Is Cookin'" by Jim Johnston (2003)

Relatives in wrestling

Main article: Anoa'i family

Championships and accomplishments

- **Pro Wrestling Illustrated**

  - PWI Match of the Year (1999) vs. Mankind in an "I Quit" match at Royal Rumble
  - PWI Match of the Year (2002) vs. Hulk Hogan at WrestleMania X8
  - PWI Most Popular Wrestler of the Year (1999, 2000)
  - PWI Wrestler of the Year (2000)
  - PWI ranked him **#2** of the 500 best singles wrestlers of the year in the PWI 500 in 2000

- **United States Wrestling Association**

  - USWA World Tag Team Championship (2 times) – with Bart Sawyer

- **World Wrestling Federation / World Wrestling Entertainment**

  - WCW World Heavyweight Championship (2 times)[1]
  - WWF/E Championship (7 times)[2]
  - WWF Intercontinental Championship (2 times)
  - WWF Tag Team Championship (5 times) – with Mankind (3), The Undertaker (1), and Chris Jericho (1)
  - Royal Rumble (2000)
  - Slammy Award for New Sensation (1997)
  - Sixth Triple Crown Champion

- **Wrestling Observer Newsletter**

  - Best Box Office Draw (2000)
  - Best Gimmick (1999)
  - Best on Interviews (1999, 2000)
  - Most Charismatic (1999–2002)
  - Most Improved (1998)
  - Wrestling Observer Newsletter Hall of Fame (Class of 2007)

[1]Won during The Invasion.

[2]Final reign was as WWE Undisputed Champion.

External links

- WWE Alumni Profile [1]
- Dwayne Johnson [2] at the Internet Movie Database
- Dwayne "The Rock" Johnson profile at NNDB [3]
- Online World of Wrestling's Profile [4]

- Dwayne Johnson [5] at Memory Alpha (a Star Trek wiki)
- Q&A: Dwayne "The Rock" Johnson at Sports Illustrated [6]
- Professional wrestling record for The Rock from The Internet Wrestling Database [7]

Transport

Transportation in the Lehigh Valley

The Lehigh Valley is served by air, car, bus, and taxi, with rail service being investigated. A growing population has called for the many types of transportation.

Transportation to the Lehigh Valley

Airports

Lehigh Valley International Airport (IATA: **ABE**, ICAO: **KABE**) serves the Lehigh Valley for major flights. It is located just north of the Allentown city line. The airlines serving Lehigh Valley International Airport are Air Canada, AirTran Airways, Allegiant Air, Continental Airlines, Delta Air Lines, Direct Air, United Airlines, and US Airways.

One of the Lehigh Valley's other airports, Allentown Queen City Municipal Airport (IATA: **XLL**, ICAO: **KXLL**), is used mostly for private aviation. It is located near Interstate 78 in Southwest Allentown.

Braden Airpark is located in Easton, Pennsylvania and is used for private aviation and flight lessons.

Buses

Trans-Bridge Lines runs daily buses to and from New York City and Philadelphia. Other motorcoaches run from New York and Philadelphia to the Sands Casino Resort Bethlehem. Bieber Tourways also offers service from Philadelphia and Reading.

Roads

The easiest and most widely used way to get into the Lehigh Valley is to drive. Interstate 78 connects the Lehigh Valley with Harrisburg and New York City. Interstate 476 is a toll road that connects the Lehigh Valley with Scranton and Philadelphia. US Route 22 is an expressway that runs through the Lehigh Valley, but it is often congested on weekdays and at rush hour. PA Route 309 connects the Lehigh Valley with Quakertown and the Coal Region. PA Route 33 is an expressway that connects the Valley with the Poconos. PA Route 378 is an expressway that runs through Bethlehem. US Route 222 is a bypass highway around Hamilton Boulevard and later connects with Reading and Lancaster.

Transportation around the Lehigh Valley

Buses

LANTA provides extensive bus service across the Lehigh Valley area. The Bethlehem Loop is a bus service running around Bethlehem to the Sands Casino. LANTA also operates shuttles in addition to its regular routes.[1]

Easton Coach provides motorcoach and local transit services including buses and trolleys.[2]

Car

Driving the Lehigh Valley is the easiest way to get around. Interstate 78 runs to the south of the Lehigh Valley, while US Route 22 connects the northern areas. City streets can be busy at times and are not always comfortable for an unexperienced driver.

Highways

Several highways/expressways serve the Lehigh Valley.

- I-78 serves as a bypass just to the south of Allentown.
- US 22 (Lehigh Valley Thruway) is an east-west highway just north of the three cities. It turns to an at-grade roadway through Phillipsburg.
- I-476/Pennsylvania Turnpike runs from Philadelphia to Scranton and is part of the PA Turnpike's Northeast Extension.
- PA 309 is a highway beginning at US 22, meeting and staying concurrent with I-78, and then turning off to Quakertown.
- PA 33 begins at I-78 near Easton and continues as a highway north into The Poconos.
- PA 378 is a spur route connecting US 22 with Center City and South Side Bethlehem.
- US 222/PA 100 (Jaindl Highway) is an expressway bypassing Trexlertown and the surrounding area.

Rental Cars

A number of rental car companies can be found at Lehigh Valley International Airport, such as Alamo, Avis, Budget, Dollar, Enterprise, Hertz, and National.

Parking

Allentown and Bethlehem both have many parking lots, garages, and meters. There are 5 public parking decks in Allentown and 3 public parking decks in Bethlehem. Most charge $1.00 per hour with a $6.00 maximum.

Taxicab

Several cab companies offer taxi service around the Lehigh Valley. Some of these are:

* **Lehigh Valley Taxicab Co.**
* **Quick Service Taxi Co.**
* **Yellow Cab of Easton**

Limousine

* **A&A Limousine, Inc.** has a smaller fleet specializing in casino trips, weddings, and proms.[3]
* **ABE Limousine** offers service to any special events.[4]
* **Adamo Limo**[5]
* **All American Limo**
* **Car One Limousine**[6] is the corporate transportation specialist and can handle last minute requests.
* **Champagne Limousine** specializes in weddings, airport transportation, and parties.[7]
* **Elite Limosuine & Coach** offers sedans, limousines, vans, limo-buses, and motor coaches.[8]
* **J&J Luxury Transportation** offers limousine service as well as sedans, vans, SUVs, stretched SUVs, luxury coaches and small and large motor coaches.[9]
* **Limousines 4 Less** [10]
* **Pocono Limousine** caters to casino trips to Mount Airy Casino Resort as well as all special events.[11]
* **Racing Limos** serves the Lehigh Valley and the Poconos and offers limousine service with an auto racing theme.[12]
* **Rhoads Limousine Service, Inc.**[13]

Horse & Carriage

* **Bethlehem Carriage Company** offers historical tours and weddings across the eastern Pennsylvania area.[14]
* **Ironton Livery & Coach** provides carriage rides for special events such as weddings.[15]

Bridges

The Lehigh Valley is filled with many bridges. The Albertus L. Meyers Bridge crosses Little Lehigh Creek in Allentown. The Hill to Hill Bridge, the Philip J. Fahy Memorial Bridge, and the Minsi Trail Bridge all cross the Lehigh River in Bethlehem. The Interstate 78 Toll Bridge, the Northampton Street Bridge, and the Easton-Phillipsburg Toll Bridge all cross the Delaware River.

Future

There is a possibility for passenger rail service to connect the Lehigh Valley area with New York City to eliminate some of the bus traffic. This is being investigated because rail lines already are in place in Phillipsburg, when the town once had rail service. The cost to run new tracks to Allentown is being evaluated to find if train service is worth the money.

See also

- Lehigh Valley
- Allentown, Pennsylvania

Lehigh Valley International Airport

Lehigh Valley International Airport	
IATA: ABE – ICAO: KABE – FAA LID: ABE	
Summary	
Airport type	Public
Owner	Lehigh-Northampton Airport Authority
Serves	Lehigh Valley
Location	Allentown, Pennsylvania
Elevation AMSL	393 ft / 120 m
Coordinates	40°39′07″N 075°26′26″W
Website	www.lvia.org [1]

Runways			
Direction	**Length**		**Surface**
	ft	**m**	
6/24	7,600	2,316	Asphalt
13/31	5,797	1,767	Asphalt

Statistics (2006)	
Aircraft operations	122,012
Based aircraft	117

Sources: airport website and FAA

Lehigh Valley International Airport (IATA: **ABE**, ICAO: **KABE**, FAA LID: **ABE**), formerly **Allentown-Bethlehem-Easton International Airport**, is a public airport in Hanover Township, Lehigh County, Pennsylvania.

The airport is located three miles (5 km) northeast of Allentown, in the Lehigh Valley region of Pennsylvania, the third most populated metropolitan region in the state (after Philadelphia and Pittsburgh).

It is owned and operated by the Lehigh-Northampton Airport Authority. In 2007, 847,256 people used the airport.

In recent years, Lehigh Valley International Airport has encountered stiff competition from nearby airports such as Philadelphia International Airport (75 miles away) and Newark Liberty International

Airport (80 miles away). These airports often offer a greater selection of flights and sometimes lower fares. This was exacerbated by the completion of the Pennsylvania extension of Interstate 78 in 1990, which allowed for a faster drive to Newark; and the opening of Interstate 476 in 1991 that made it easier to connect to Interstate 95 near Philadelphia.

History

Allentown Airport opened in 1929 and is one of the very few in the nation that still serves its community from its original location. Scheduled airline service began on September 16, 1935 by United Airlines with Boeing 247 service. At the time, the airport hangar served as the passenger terminal. The first terminal building at the airport was built in 1938 as a Works Projects Administration (WPA) project.

During World War II the U. S. Navy V-5 flight training program was conducted at the airport in conjunction with ground training held at Muhlenberg College. In addition, Headquarters of Group 312 of the Civil Air Patrol was at **Allentown-Bethlehem Airport**. One of its activities was to provide a courier service for cargo defense plants. Allentown CAP pilots also patrolled the Atlantic coastline, and was active in recruiting young men for the air cadet program of the Army Air Force.

By January 1944, work on a new runway was completed and a Class A United States Weather Bureau station had been installed. About 1,000 Naval Aviation Cadets had been trained during 1943, and a large increase in the amount of civilian and military air traffic had occurred. In late July, the War Production Board approved the construction of a second story addition to the administration building. The building housed the Lehigh Aircraft Company, the weather bureau station, the Civil Aeronautic communications station, and the office and waiting room of United Air Lines. In August, the V-5 flight training program ended when the Navy decided to move all flight training to naval air bases under Navy pilots.

In the immediate postwar years, in April 1946, the **Lehigh Airport Authority** was created to own and manage the airport. This made the airport a public enterprise. 1948 saw the beginning of construction for a new passenger terminal, being finished in 1950. **Allentown-Bethlehem-Easton (ABE)** airport, as it was now called, also expanded passenger service by offering flights with United, Trans World Airlines (TWA), and Colonial airlines. DC-4 and DC-6 service was offered with the addition of 5,000 ft of runway.

Throughout the 1950s, both passenger service as well as air cargo service expanded at ABE. Eastern and Allegheny Airlines began service. In 1960, both Vice President Richard Nixon and Senator John F. Kennedy made campaign stops at ABE. Construction began in late 1972 for the new terminal, which was opened on December 14, 1975.

Today **Lehigh Valley International Airport** continues to serve the Lehigh Valley.

Allentown PA Airport in the early 1930s before the addition of hard-surfaced runways.

Naval pilot training graduation ceremony at the Allentown PA Airport - 1943

Lehigh Valley International Airport before terminal expansion.

Facilities and aircraft

Lehigh Valley International Airport covers an area of 2,629 acres (1,064 ha) at an elevation of 393 feet (120 m) above mean sea level. It has two asphalt paved runways: 6/24 measuring 7,600 by 150 feet (2,316 x 46 m) and 13/31 measuring 5,797 by 150 feet (1,767 x 46 m).

For the 12-month period ending December 31, 2006, the airport had 122,012 aircraft operations, an average of 334 per day: 69% general aviation, 15% air taxi (18,365), 14% scheduled commercial and 2% military. At that time there were 117 aircraft based at this airport: 59% single-engine, 11% multi-engine, 24% jet and 6% helicopter.

The airport also is one of several dozen designated landing facilities for the Space Shuttle.[citation needed]

Dining and Shopping

Lehigh Valley International Airport contains a number of restaurants: two Subway restaurants, one on the landside terminal and one on the airside terminal, a restaurant called the L.A. Cafe on the landside terminal, and a snack bar restaurant on the airside terminal. It has 2 Hudson News gift shops, one on the landside and one on the airside terminals, respectively.

Airlines and destinations

Airlines	Destinations
Air Canada Jazz operated by Air Georgian	Toronto-Pearson
AirTran Airways	Fort Lauderdale **Seasonal**: Atlanta, Orlando
Allegiant Air	Myrtle Beach, Orlando, St. Petersburg/Clearwater
American Eagle	Chicago-O'Hare
Continental Airlines	Newark [bus service]
Delta Air Lines	Atlanta
Delta Connection operated by Atlantic Southeast Airlines	Atlanta
Delta Connection operated by Comair	Detroit
Delta Connection operated by Mesaba Airlines	Detroit
Delta Connection operated by Pinnacle Airlines	Detroit
Direct Air operated by Falcon Air Express	**Seasonal**: Fort Myers/Punta Gorda
United Express operated by Colgan Air	Washington-Dulles
United Express operated by Expressjet Airlines	Chicago-O'Hare
United Express operated by Mesa Airlines	Chicago-O'Hare
United Express operated by SkyWest Airlines	Chicago-O'Hare
US Airways	Charlotte
US Airways Express operated by Piedmont Airlines	Philadelphia
US Airways Express operated by PSA Airlines	Charlotte

Cargo Operations

- FedEx Express (Indianapolis, Memphis, Newark)

Incidents

On Sunday, November 16, 2008, US Airways Flight 4551, a US Airways Express deHavilland Dash-8 turboprop operated by Piedmont Airlines, took off from Lehigh Valley International Airport at 8:20am heading to Philadelphia International Airport, had to make an emergency landing. The flight crew indicated that the front nose gear had not come down, and the plane had to make a flyover the runway for confirmation. Of 35 passengers and 3 crew, there were no injuries.

On Saturday, June 27, 2009, Allegiant Air Flight 746, a McDonnell Douglas MD-80 aircraft made an emergency landing after flames were observed coming from the aircraft's left engine. The flight was bound for Orlando Sanford International Airport. During takeoff, one of the aircraft's tires had shredded and a piece of that tire was sucked into the engine, causing it to fail and momentarily catch on fire. The airliner landed safely minutes later with no injuries reported.

References

- Allentown 1762-1987 A 225-Year History, Volume Two, 1921-1987. Mahlon H. Hellerich, editor, Lehigh County Historical Society, 1987.

External links

- Lehigh Valley International Airport [1]
- Pennsylvania Bureau of Aviation: Lehigh Valley International Airport [2]
- FAA Airport Diagram [1] (PDF), effective 23 Sep 2010
- FAA Terminal Procedures for ABE [2], effective 23 Sep 2010
- Resources for this airport:
  - AirNav airport information for KABE [3]
  - ASN accident history for ABE [4]
  - FlightAware airport information [5] and live flight tracker [6]
  - NOAA/NWS latest weather observations [7]
  - SkyVector aeronautical chart for KABE [8]
  - FAA current ABE delay information [9]

Trans-Bridge Lines

Trans-Bridge #8560 lays over in Manhattan.

Slogan	*Take the Bridge*
Parent	Trans-Bridge Lines
Founded	1941
Headquarters	2012 Industrial Drive Bethlehem, PA 18017
Locale	Lehigh Valley
Service area	Lehigh Valley, PA Skylands Region, NJ
Service type	Line-run, contract, charter
Alliance	International Motor Coach Group
Routes	3 directly controlled 2 under contract
Fleet	58 (route service) 83 (total)
Daily ridership	3,802 (weekday)
Operator	Trans-Bridge Lines
Chief executive	Thomas JeBran
Web site	Trans-Bridge Lines [1]

Trans-Bridge Lines is a line-run operator servicing the Lehigh Valley region of Pennsylvania and the southwestern Skylands Region of New Jersey with line run service between New York City and the Lehigh Valley, via the I-78 corridor daily, and charter and casino service in the same region. Casino routes run to both Atlantic City and the Sands Casino Resort Bethlehem.

Routes

Directly controlled

Route	Terminal A	Terminal B
Via I-78, US 22, PA 33, and PA 412	**Port Authority Bus Terminal** (full-time) **Lower Manhattan-Wall St.** or **Jersey City-Newport Centre** (rush hours only)	**Allentown** (full route)
Via I-78, US 202, NJ 12, NJ 29, PA 313, PA 309, and PA 378	**Port Authority Bus Terminal**	**Bethlehem** via **Doylestown train station**
Via I-78 express	**Port Authority Bus Terminal**	**Sands Bethlehem**

Connections are also available on certain Trans-Bridge schedules to John F. Kennedy International Airport, with service running to and from Terminal 4 at the Q10 bus stop, twice daily.

Under contract

Under contract to New Jersey Transit, Trans-Bridge Lines operates the 890 and 891 lines running between Pohatcong Township, New Jersey and Easton, Pennsylvania, with connections available to LANTA routes in downtown Easton at Center Square, as well as Trans-Bridge's line run via Route 22.

External links

- Trans-Bridge Lines [1]

Interstate 78

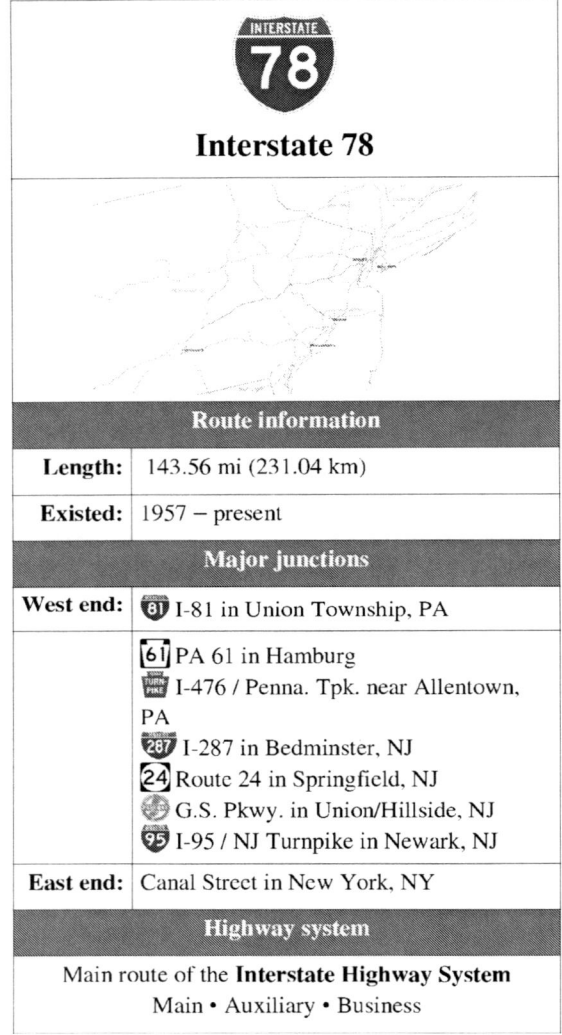

Interstate 78	
Route information	
Length:	143.56 mi (231.04 km)
Existed:	1957 – present
Major junctions	
West end:	I-81 in Union Township, PA
	PA 61 in Hamburg I-476 / Penna. Tpk. near Allentown, PA I-287 in Bedminster, NJ Route 24 in Springfield, NJ G.S. Pkwy. in Union/Hillside, NJ I-95 / NJ Turnpike in Newark, NJ
East end:	Canal Street in New York, NY
Highway system	
Main route of the **Interstate Highway System** Main • Auxiliary • Business	

Interstate 78 (abbreviated **I-78**) is an Interstate Highway in the Northeast United States, running 144 miles (231 km) from Interstate 81 northeast of Harrisburg, Pennsylvania, through Allentown, Pennsylvania, and western and northern New Jersey to the Holland Tunnel and Lower Manhattan in New York City.

I-78 is a major road linking ports in the New York City and New Jersey area to points west, and sees over 4 million trucks annually, with trucks representing 24% of all traffic. Truck traffic on the road is projected to rise once the widening of the Panama Canal is completed in 2015, when more Asian ships are expected to use East Coast ports.

Route description

Pennsylvania

Main article: Interstate 78 in Pennsylvania

Approaching the Interstate 78 interchange on Interstate 81 north in Union Township, Lebanon County, Pennsylvania.

I-78 begins at a directional-T interchange with Interstate 81 in Union Township, Lebanon County, Pennsylvania, about 25 miles (40 km) northeast of Harrisburg. Near the east end of the county, at exit 8, U.S. Route 22 merges with I-78, running concurrently for the next 43 miles (69 km).

At exit 51, in Upper Macungie Township, US 22 leaves the highway. Passengers traveling on I-78 eastbound must use this exit to access I-476 (Northeast Extension of the Pennsylvania Turnpike) and westbound travelers must use exit 53. From exits 53 to 60, I-78 runs concurrently with Pennsylvania Route 309. The six lane overlap bypasses the City of Allentown to the south and crosses South Mountain.

At exit 60 (A-B going westbound), PA 309 south leaves for Quakertown. Six miles later, there is an interchange between Pennsylvania Route 412 and I-78 in Hellertown. Highway 412 also goes to Bethlehem and Lehigh University. At mile marker 71, Pennsylvania Route 33 intersects at Exit 71. Route 33 traverses the Pocono Mountains and goes to Bangor and Interstate 80. The final exit on Interstate 78 in Pennsylvania is for Morgan Hill Road, which goes to Pennsylvania Route 611 and Easton. Interstate 78 then crosses the Interstate 78 Toll Bridge and enters New Jersey.

New Jersey

Main article: Interstate 78 in New Jersey

After the Interstate 78 Toll Bridge, I-78 enters New Jersey as the *Phillipsburg-Newark Expressway*. The road begins by running parallel with County Route 642 in the town of Alpha. At 3.94 miles (6.34 km), Exit 3, a partial cloverleaf interchange brings together U.S. Route 22, New Jersey Route 122 and New Jersey Route 173 with Interstate 78 in Phillipsburg. U.S. Route 22 now runs concurrently with I-78 for the next 15 miles (24 km). Going westbound, exit 4 leaves to the right for County Route 637 and Warren Glen. The next exit, Exit 6, is for County Route 632 in Bloomsbury. However the route number is not signed on Interstate 78. Exit 7 is the first of several eastbound exits for NJ 173. This one is located in Bloomsbury as 173 begins to parallel the interstate. Four miles later, Exit 11 leaves to the right as another Exit for NJ 173. Warren County 614 also is located off the exit. Exit 12, westbound is for NJ 173 again. However, Exit 12 eastbound is for a frontage road parallelling Interstate 78.

I-78, US 1-9, US 22, and NJ 21 junction.

Exit 13 is only westbound and is another exit for NJ 173. Nearby the exit, going eastbound, the frontage road merges in. Exit 15 is for NJ 173 and County Route 513 in Franklin Township. Exit 17 is for NJ 31 in Clinton. In the town of Annandale, US 22 leaves Interstate 78 at exit 18. Route 22 continues towards Bound Brook and Union County. At exit 20, Hunterdon CR 639 intersects. Hunterdon 639 heads towards the Round Valley Recreational Area. Exit 24 is for County Route 523 towards Oldwick. At exit 29, Interstate 287, U.S. Route 202 and U.S. Route 206 interchange with I-78 in Bedminster. At this point, in Somerset County, Exits 33, 36 and 40 are for county routes in Warren Township. At exit 41, I-78 enters Union County. At exit 45, County Route 527 intersects after paralleling for some time. West of exit 48, I-78 splits into express and local highways. Exit 48 is for New Jersey Route 24 in Springfield. Exit 49A is for one of Route 24's spur routes, New Jersey Route 124. Going westbound, Exit 52 is for the Garden State Parkway in Union. At Exits 57 and 58, New Jersey Route 21, U.S. Route 1, U.S. Route 9 and U.S. Route 22 intersect Interstate 78. The exit provides access to Newark Airport.

East of exit 58 at the eastern tip of Newark, I-78 becomes the **Newark Bay Extension** of the New Jersey Turnpike. Past the first toll plaza, I-78 has an interchange with Interstate 95 (The New Jersey Turnpike) and crosses Newark Bay via the Newark Bay Bridge. The first exit, 14A, is for New Jersey Route 440 in Bayonne. Liberty State Park and the Liberty Science Center can be reached by taking Exit 14B. Exit 14C is the final numbered exit, providing access to the New Jersey Turnpike. New Jersey Route 139 runs concurrently with I-78 as it approaches the Holland Tunnel and enters New York State.

I-78 eastbound at the Newark Bay Bridge.

New York City

Main article: Interstate 78 in New York

See also: Holland Tunnel

I-78's length in New York is only 1/2 mile (1 km) - half of the Holland Tunnel and the egress-only roundabout immediately beyond the end of the tunnel. The route was planned to run east and north through New York City to end at Interstate 95 in the Bronx, but sections of the planned route, including the Lower Manhattan Expressway, were cancelled.

I-78 at the Holland Tunnel.

In New York City, I-78 continues through the limited access egress-only roundabout known as the Saint John's Rotary. The five separate exits from the Rotary are assigned numbers — exits 1 to 5 - in counterclockwise order. The last one — and the logical continuation east — is Exit 5, Canal Street. Under the original plans, I-78 was to continue across Manhattan as the Lower Manhattan Expressway onto the Williamsburg Bridge, and then beyond I-278 on the never-built Bushwick Expressway through Brooklyn into Queens near the John F. Kennedy Airport. A section of I-78 at the airport was built as the Nassau Expressway, later Interstate 878 and now NY 878, though most of the westbound side was never built. East of the airport, I-78 would have turned north on the Clearview Expressway (built north of Hillside Avenue in Queens and now I-295), run across the Throgs Neck Bridge, and forked into two spurs, ending at Interstate 95 via the Throgs Neck Expressway (now I-695) and the Bruckner Interchange via the Cross Bronx Expressway (now part of I-295).

Major intersections

- Interstate 81 in Union Township, Pennsylvania
- U.S. Route 22 in Union Township and Upper Macungie Township
- Interstate 476 via U.S. Route 22 near Allentown
- Interstate 287 in Bedminster, New Jersey
- U.S. Route 1-9 in Newark
- Interstate 95 (New Jersey Turnpike) in Newark

Auxiliary routes

All of I-78's auxiliary routes serve New York City; however, none of these routes actually intersects I-78, following the route's truncation at the eastern end of the Holland Tunnel.

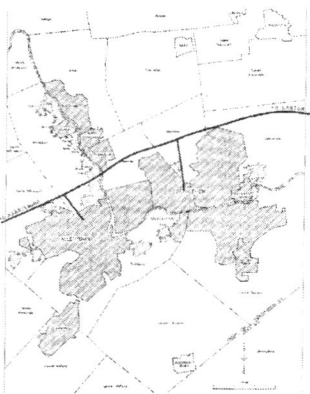

1955 map of I-178 and I-378

- Interstate 278 runs from U.S. Route 1/9 near Elizabeth, New Jersey over the Goethals Bridge, through Staten Island, over the Verrazano Narrows Bridge and through Brooklyn and Queens, and across the Triborough Bridge into the Bronx to end at Interstate 95 at the Bruckner Interchange. Interstate 278 was planned to extend west from Elizabeth to Interstate 78 in Springfield, Union County, New Jersey, and was to intersect I-78 at the east end of the Williamsburg Bridge in Brooklyn. Until 1972, I-278 ran along Interstate 895 and a proposed extension to Interstate 95, while Interstate 278 east of I-895 was I-878.

- Interstate 478 is an unsigned designation for the Brooklyn-Battery Tunnel, a spur from Interstate 278 into lower Manhattan. Plans were made to continue it north along the West Side Highway (Route 9A) to Interstate 78 at the Holland Tunnel, but have been canceled. Older plans would have given it the same purpose — connecting I-78 with I-278 - but along the Manhattan Bridge.

- Interstate 678 runs from I-278 at the Bruckner Interchange south over the Bronx-Whitestone Bridge to John F. Kennedy International Airport. It was to intersect Interstate 78 at its south end. Original plans took I-678 west on the Grand Central Parkway to I-278.

- Interstate 878 is an unsigned designation for part of New York State Route 878, a short east–west freeway on the north edge of Kennedy Airport. It was once planned as part of I-78, and now intersects I-678. The number was assigned in 1989.

- A former Interstate 878 existed from 1959 to 1972 along present I-278 east of Interstate 895. (I-895 was part of I-278.)

In eastern Pennsylvania, Route 378 into downtown Bethlehem was once Interstate 378, but was redesignated as a state route after I-78 was rerouted to a new southerly alignment. An Interstate 178 was initially planned as an extension into downtown Allentown, but was canceled due to local opposition.

References

Main US Interstate Highways (major interstates highlighted)																	
4	5	8	10	12	15	16	17	19	20	22	24	25	26	27	29	30	
35	37	39	40	43	44	45	49	55	57	59	64	65	66	68	69		
70	71	72	73	74	75	76 (W)		76 (E)		77	78	79	80	81	82		
83	84 (W)		84 (E)		85	86 (W)		86 (E)		87	88 (W)		88 (E)		89	90	
91	93	94	95	96	97	99	(238)		H-1		H-2		H-3				
Unsigned			Λ-1		Λ-2		Λ-3		Λ-4		PRI-1		PRI-2		PRI-3		
Lists		**Primary**		Main - Intrastate - Suffixed - Future - Gaps													
		Auxiliary		Main - Future - Unsigned													
		Other		Standards - Business - Bypassed													

Allentown Queen City Municipal Airport

Allentown Queen City Municipal Airport Queen City Airport	
USGS aerial image, 13 April 1999	
IATA: *none* – **ICAO: KXLL** – **FAA LID: XLL**	
Summary	
Airport type	Public
Owner	Lehigh-Northampton Airport Authority
Serves	Allentown, Pennsylvania
Hub for	{{{hub}}}
Elevation AMSL	399 ft / 122 m
Coordinates	40°34′13″N 075°29′18″W

Direction	Length		Surface
	ft	**m**	
7/25	3,949	1,204	Asphalt
15/33	3,159	963	Asphalt

Statistics (2008)

Aircraft operations	54,220
Based aircraft	95

Source: Federal Aviation Administration

Allentown Queen City Municipal Airport (ICAO: **KXLL**, FAA LID: **XLL**) is a public use airport located in Lehigh County, Pennsylvania, United States. The airport is two nautical miles (3.7 km) southwest of the central business district of Allentown, Pennsylvania. It is owned by the

Lehigh-Northampton Airport Authority. Also known as **Queen City Airport**, it is home to the Civil Air Patrol Squadron 805 and Lehigh Valley Aviation Services, a fixed base operator (FBO).

On July 31, 2008, the FAA airport identifier was briefly changed from **1N9** to **JVU**. However, after seeking approval for an identifier associated with the area, the FAA approved the change to **XLL** (Little Lehigh Executive, in honor of the local Little Lehigh Creek) effective November 20, 2008.

Although most U.S. airports use the same three-letter location identifier for the FAA and IATA, this airport currently has no designation from the IATA.

History

In mid-December 1942, it was announced that Allentown was the site of a new aircraft production plant. Vultee Aircraft and Consolidated Aircraft announced that Consolidated Vultee (later known as Convair) would lease Mack Truck's Plant 5C for production of the Consolidated Vultee TBY-2 Sea Wolf Torpedo Plane for the United States Navy. In addition to 5C, Consolidated Vultee would build an office building, a hangar, an airport and a highway linking 5C with the new airport complex.

Mack officials were initially reluctant to give up Plant 5C because they considered it essential for Truck war production, however the War Production Board and the Navy overruled them.

Convair Field, as the airfield was originally named, was dedicated on October 10, 1943. When the plant reached full production, it employed several thousand people, over half of which were women. Consolidated Vultee became Allentown's second largest industry, handling over $100,000,000 in war contracts. By the end of 1943, the facility was producing TBY-2 Sea Wolves as well as components for the BT-13 Valiant Trainer and B-24 Liberator Bomber.

Along with the airfield and manufacturing facilities, an entire new neighborhood of homes was built for the aircraft workers and their families. In December 1943, the National Housing Center approved the construction of 250 units for Vultee workers on a tract bounded by Twelfth, Fourteenth, Harrison and Wyoming streets by the Allentown Housing Authority. This neighborhood, containing streets named "Liberator Avenue", "Catalina Avenue", and "Vultee Street", still exists.

With the end of the war in 1945, aircraft production was shut down. Plant 5C was returned to Mack Trucks and the remainder of the facility was declared surplus by the War Assets Administration. The property was obtained by General Electric to manufacture small appliances, particularly toasters. In 1962 the facility again was closed and the property was obtained by the city.

It is currently owned and operated by the Lehigh-Northampton Airport Authority. LNAA also manages the Lehigh Valley International Airport and Braden Airpark. In 2006, the airport received an award for the General Aviation Airport of the Year by the Eastern Region of the Federal Aviation Administration.

Facilities and aircraft

Allentown Queen City Municipal Airport covers an area of 201 acres (81 ha) at an elevation of 399 feet (122 m) above mean sea level. It has two asphalt paved runways: 7/25 is 3,949 by 75 feet (1,204 x 23 m) and 15/33 is 3,159 by 75 feet (963 x 23 m).

For the 12-month period ending June 10, 2008, the airport had 54,220 aircraft operations, an average of 148 per day: 97% general aviation, 2% air taxi and 1% military. At that time there were 95 aircraft based at this airport: 78% single-engine, 16% multi-engine and 6% helicopter.

External links

- Queen City Municipal Airport [28] at PennDOT Bureau of Aviation
- Civil Air Patrol Squadron 805 [1]
- FAA Terminal Procedures for XLL [2], effective 23 Sep 2010
- Resources for this airport:
  - AirNav airport information for KXLL [3]
  - FlightAware airport information [4] and live flight tracker [5]
  - NOAA/NWS latest weather observations [6]
  - SkyVector aeronautical chart [7], Terminal Procedures [8] for KXLL

Lehigh and Northampton Transportation Authority

LANTA #0354 works the E line in downtown Easton.

Founded	1972
Headquarters	1060 Lehigh Steet Allentown, PA 18103
Locale	Allentown, Pennsylvania
Service area	Lehigh Valley
Service type	Local Transit bus Service
Routes	24 local 7 evening and Sunday 4 Special services (35 total)
Destinations	Allentown Bethlehem Easton
Hubs	Allentown Transportation Center (ATC)
Fleet	82 Buses
Daily ridership	15,000 (weekday)
Operator	LANTA
Chief executive	Armando Greco
Web site	www.lantabus.com [1]

The **Lehigh and Northampton Transportation Authority** (known as **LANTA**), is a transit agency that provides public, fixed-route bus service throughout Lehigh County and Northampton County, in Pennsylvania, United States. The primary area that LANTA serves is the Lehigh Valley region of Pennsylvania, serving the cities of Allentown, Bethlehem, and Easton.

History

The Lehigh and Northampton Transportation Authority (LANTA) has ten voting and two non-voting members appointed by the County Executives.

The agency was created in March 1972 in response to the transportation crisis that was occurring in Lehigh, and Northampton. The solution was to create a bi-county, municipal Authority that would operate all public transit services in the two counties. Lehigh Valley Transit Company, a private for-profit entity, formally operated transit services in the Valley.

The Authority's main service is in the urbanized area of Allentown, Bethlehem and Easton and surrounding boroughs and townships. About 380,000 people live within 3/4 mile of a fixed-route bus line.

About 15,000 trips are taken daily on the Metro city transit system.

In 1973, the Authority replaced the entire 65-vehicle fleet with modern air-conditioned city transit coaches. In 1974, LANTA added 30% more service hours and established a peak/off-peak fare structure offering discounts in the off-peak hours and Saturdays to encourage ridership. Seniors, through a state lottery funded program, were offered free fare access during off-peak hours and weekends in 1975.

In the mid-1980s, as the community transformed from a manufacturing based economy to a service and retail based economy, was completely revamped and a new "Metro" system was introduced in 1985. A color-coded route information system was introduced at the same time to make riding transit more 'user-friendly.' The following year, 'deep-discount' fares were introduced as LANTA raised the case fares but kept ticket and pass prices the same and providing frequent riders with a 25% discount.

In 1988 Metro Plus services for the elderly and people with disabilities were introduced. Fully accessible vans are available through contracts with private operators to take people to destinations door-to-door for a higher, zoned fare.

About 2,000 trips are taken each weekday on the Metro Plus paratransit system.

A transportation center was established in Bethlehem and centers in Allentown and Easton are on the drawing board.

As the years went on, the agency grew adding more and more bus routes around the Lehigh Valley. Ridership has grown 75% since LANTA's inception. On October 21, 2001 that LANTA started offering Sunday bus service to further increase access to public transit. The Authority is funded through revenues from the farebox; a grant from the Pennsylvania Lottery program with revenue generated by rides taken on the system by seniors 65 and older, grants from Lehigh and Northampton counties, the Pennsylvania Department of Transportation and the Federal Transit Administration. Combined these grants pay approximately 60% of the cost of operation; the remaining funds come through the lottery program and passenger fares.

Eighty buses are in the Metro city transit fleet; 118 vans are used to provide the Metro Plus door-to-door van services. The Authority owns all vehicles. LANTA has two operating facilities: the main office, garage and maintenance building is at 1060 Lehigh Street Allentown Lehigh County and there is a satellite facility located at 3610 Nicholas Street in Easton, Northampton County.

LANTA has three operating divisions:

- Metro: The main transit service that is made up of 28 core, fixed bus routes in the Lehigh Valley. Special service routes add another 17 routes to the total.
- Metro Plus: A special door-to-door transportation service for people with disabilities and the elderly.
- CCCT (Carbon County Community Transit): A service the Authority agreed to manage in 1996 for the County of Carbon. Shared ride van services and a fixed-route bus line comprise the Carbon County Community Transportation service.

LANTA is also involved with these services:

- Starlight Evening Service
- Night Owl Service
- The Slater Express Van
- The 400 Routes
- The Lynx
- Silverline Express
- The Bethlehem Loop

Routes

LANTA currently operates 35 fixed bus routes in its Metro service. Seventeen lettered routes serve the inner city areas of the Lehigh Valley, while five numbered routes serve the surrounding areas. Two shuttles named "The Rover" and "The Whirlybird", that operate from the Lehigh Valley Mall and Palmer Park Malls to various neighboring shopping strips and centers, serve as the final daily fixed routes. In the evening, LANTA operates the Starlight service made of seven fixed routes which service center city Allentown, the Lehigh Valley Mall and Palmer Park Mall, Whitehall, and Emmaus. There is also the Night Owl service that runs late-night from center city Allentown to the Lehigh Valley Hospital. Metro also operates the Silverline Express which is an express bus that serves the Allentown, Bethlehem, and Easton areas via Route 22, as well as The Bethelem Loop, which serves as a shuttle for that city's downtown core.

List of Metro Lettered Routes

Route	Terminals		Major streets
A	Village West Shopping Center	Broad & Guetter Streets (Bethlehem)	Cedar Crest Blvd., Tilghman St., Hanover Ave.
B	East Hills/Fountain Hill	Freemansburg Ave.	Stefko Blvd., Freemansburg Ave.
C	Broad & Guetter (Bethlehem)	Center Square (Easton)	Freemansburg Ave.
D	Northampton	Emmaus	Lehigh St., MacArthur Rd.
E	Easton	Allentown	Hanover Ave., William Penn Highway
F	Westgate Mall	Creekside Shopping Center (Hellertown)	Schoenersville Rd, W. Broad St.
G	Union Blvd.	Susquehanna St.	Broadway, E. 4th St.
H	Dorney Park & Wildwater Kingdom	Fullerton Ave.	Hamilton Blvd., Fullerton Ave.
J	Boroline	Crest Plaza	E. Emmaus Ave., N. 19th St., Walbert Ave.
K	Lehigh Valley Hospital	Presidential Village	S. 24th St., Hamilton St., MacArthur Rd.
L	Lehigh Valley Mall	Parkway Shopping Center	MacArthur Rd., Allen St., 15th St.
N	Palmer Park Mall	Berwick St./Line St.	Northampton St., S. 3rd St.
P	Stones Crossing	Berwick St./Line St.	Freemansburg Ave.
R	West Easton	Harlen House	Northampton St., Freemansburg Ave.
S	Slate Belt	Broad & Guetter Streets (Bethlehem)	Route 512, Route 115, Route 248
V	Riverside Road	Broad & Guetter Streets (Bethlehem)	Riverside Rd., New St.
W	Allentown	Slatington	Route 309, Route 873, Main St.

List of Metro Suburban Routes

Route	Terminals		Major streets
1	East Catasauqua	Egypt	MacArthur Rd., Race St.
2	Fogelsville	Allentown	Route 100, Tilghman St.
3	Trexlertown	Allentown	Route 100, Hamilton St.
4	Stabler Center	Lehigh Valley College	S. 8th St., Mack Blvd., Interstate 78
5	Forks Industrial Park	Palmer Industrial Park	Main St., Sullivan Trail, Cattel St.

Route	Route Name	Service Area	Fare
6	The Rover	West Easton, Palmer Park Mall	US$0.50
7	The Whirlybird	Lehigh Valley Mall, Whitehall Mall	US$0.50
8	The Bethlehem Loop	Downtown Bethlehem, Historic District, Sands Casino	US$2.50

List of Metro Rapid Transit Routes

Route	Terminals		Major streets
Silverline Express	Lehigh Valley Mall	Easton	MacArthur Rd., Route 22, N. 3rd St.

List of Metro Starlight Evening Routes

- **Starlight 1** - Lehigh Valley Mall/Allentown Loop
- **Starlight 2** - Lehigh Valley Mall/Susquehanna St.
- **Starlight 3** - Allentown/Easton
- **Starlight 4** - Whitehall/Northampton Loop
- **Starlight 5** - Allentown/Emmaus
- **Starlight 6** - Palmer Park Mall/South Easton
- **Starlight 7** - Dorney Park/Allentown

List of Other Metro Services

- **The Slater Express Van** - weekend mall shuttle
- **The Lynx** - Carbon County transit routes, which alternate depending on the day of the week
- **The 400 Routes** - school bus services

Fares

Metro

Fare category	Description	Cash
One Ride Fare	One Ride Fare	US$2.00
Day Pass	Unlimited rides all day	US$3.00
Whirlybird Express	One Ride Fare	US$0.50
The Rover	One Ride Fare	US$0.50
Transfers	Valid 2 hours after purchase	US$0.25
Senior Citizens (65+)	Free all day with ID	
People with disabilities	US$1.00 all day pass with ID	
Children (5 and under)	Free with paying adult	

FareSaver Tickets

Fare category	Description	Cash
10 Ride Ticket	FareSaver Ticket	US$14.00
31 Day Pass	Good for 31 days after purchase or activation	US$50.00

Metro Plus

Full Fare	General fare to access Metro Plus paratransit services - each way	US$22.50
Subsidized Fare	Seniors (65+) and others subsidized by agencies - each way	US$3.40
Ticket Books	6 Tickets, good for 6 one-way trips or 3 round trips	US$18.20

External links

- LANTA Official Web Site [2]

Article Sources and Contributors

Pennsylvania *Source*: http://en.wikipedia.org/?oldid=390415276 *Contributors*: Diannaa

Harrisburg, Pennsylvania *Source*: http://en.wikipedia.org/?oldid=388466635 *Contributors*: 1 anonymous edits

Geography of Pennsylvania *Source*: http://en.wikipedia.org/?oldid=387066890 *Contributors*:

List of counties in Pennsylvania *Source*: http://en.wikipedia.org/?oldid=387006251 *Contributors*: GrahamHardy

Climate of Pennsylvania *Source*: http://en.wikipedia.org/?oldid=389975196 *Contributors*: 1 anonymous edits

History of Pennsylvania *Source*: http://en.wikipedia.org/?oldid=388745222 *Contributors*: Marek69

List of towns and boroughs in Pennsylvania *Source*: http://en.wikipedia.org/?oldid=389860836 *Contributors*: Xiong

List of cities in Pennsylvania *Source*: http://en.wikipedia.org/?oldid=390108887 *Contributors*: RadioFan

Education in Pennsylvania *Source*: http://en.wikipedia.org/?oldid=370936852 *Contributors*:

Philadelphia Zoo *Source*: http://en.wikipedia.org/?oldid=387612977 *Contributors*:

List of airports in Pennsylvania *Source*: http://en.wikipedia.org/?oldid=382797542 *Contributors*: Derekbridges

Sports in Pennsylvania *Source*: http://en.wikipedia.org/?oldid=388490229 *Contributors*: 1 anonymous edits

Bethlehem, Pennsylvania *Source*: http://en.wikipedia.org/?oldid=390301343 *Contributors*: 1 anonymous edits

Lehigh County, Pennsylvania *Source*: http://en.wikipedia.org/?oldid=387181854 *Contributors*:

Northampton County, Pennsylvania *Source*: http://en.wikipedia.org/?oldid=384600018 *Contributors*: TRBP

Center Valley, Pennsylvania *Source*: http://en.wikipedia.org/?oldid=380782037 *Contributors*: 1 anonymous edits

Hanover Township, Pennsylvania *Source*: http://en.wikipedia.org/?oldid=250393666 *Contributors*: Auntof6

Musikfest *Source*: http://en.wikipedia.org/?oldid=388469284 *Contributors*:

Zoellner Arts Center *Source*: http://en.wikipedia.org/?oldid=350081362 *Contributors*: JLaTondre

Sands Casino Resort Bethlehem *Source*: http://en.wikipedia.org/?oldid=387514875 *Contributors*: 1 anonymous edits

NEARfest *Source*: http://en.wikipedia.org/?oldid=351481922 *Contributors*: Chutch15

SouthSide Film Festival *Source*: http://en.wikipedia.org/?oldid=292802185 *Contributors*: 1 anonymous edits

Lehigh Canal *Source*: http://en.wikipedia.org/?oldid=359185413 *Contributors*: Bearcat

Lehigh River *Source*: http://en.wikipedia.org/?oldid=389869613 *Contributors*: Rich Farmbrough

Bethlehem Steel F.C. *Source*: http://en.wikipedia.org/?oldid=389989797 *Contributors*:

John Andretti *Source*: http://en.wikipedia.org/?oldid=388652250 *Contributors*: VanBurns

Michael Andretti *Source*: http://en.wikipedia.org/?oldid=387799936 *Contributors*:

Dwayne Johnson *Source*: http://en.wikipedia.org/?oldid=390604286 *Contributors*: Looie496

Transportation in the Lehigh Valley *Source*: http://en.wikipedia.org/?oldid=359183171 *Contributors*: Bearcat

Lehigh Valley International Airport *Source*: http://en.wikipedia.org/?oldid=390640779 *Contributors*: Snoozlepet

Trans-Bridge Lines *Source*: http://en.wikipedia.org/?oldid=359184428 *Contributors*: Bearcat

Interstate 78 *Source*: http://en.wikipedia.org/?oldid=380400644 *Contributors*: PAWiki

Allentown Queen City Municipal Airport *Source*: http://en.wikipedia.org/?oldid=359183429 *Contributors*: Bearcat

Lehigh and Northampton Transportation Authority *Source*: http://en.wikipedia.org/?oldid=388005009 *Contributors*: 1 anonymous edits

Image Sources, Licenses and Contributors

CPSIA information can be obtained at www.ICGtesting.com
Printed in the USA
BVOW062119151012

303046BV00003BA/9/P